DEDICATIONS

Michael Bradley: *To my parents, Garr and Pat Bradley, my coaches and all of the athletes with whom I've been privileged to work.*

Matt Brzycki: *To my lovely wife, Alicia, and our darling son, Ryan. Thanks for being there.*

Luke Carlson: *To my family for all of their patience, love and support.*

Chip Harrison: *To my wife and children whose absolute love, support and immeasurable patience make the job possible. And to my parents who instilled the importance of perspective and the need for education and are always there unconditionally.*

Rachael Picone: *To my family and friends who continue to bless my life with their support, kindness and love. And to all of the wonderful, dedicated female athletes who give it their best and strive even farther each day.*

Tim "Red" Wakeham: *To my friends Brian, Nemo, Chris, Kim, Auge, the Monty's, Pasty, Ger, Dano, Corn, Porky, Monk and Sawa. Thanks!*

ACKNOWLEDGEMENTS

Jason Gallucci and Lisa Shall for providing several photographs for the book.

Tolu Onigbanjo who appeared in numerous photographs in the book.

Jim Reilly of Image Extreme (http://www.imageextreme.com) who provided many photographs in Chapters 9 and 10.

Pete Silletti who took numerous photographs for the book.

Tanda Tucker at The Wardlaw-Hartridge School in Edison, New Jersey (http://whschool.org/) who provided many photographs in Chapters 9 and 10.

Table of Contents

Foreword

Rene Portland, Women's Basketball Coach, Penn State University

Long gone are the days when people were unaware of women athletes. Participation is at an all time high and young girls and women have athletic visions. They understand the sacrifice and are doing the work with positive and undying attitudes.

There are those who see Title IX as a turning point. Certainly the change in family structure has also had its effect. Whatever initiated the change, the wheels are in motion and it is here to stay. Young girls and women involved in sports, whether on an individual or team basis, have felt and enjoyed Title IX being a part of their lives. When you play sports, you have fun. There are happy faces, infectious laughter and limitless energy. Prior to Title IX, approximately 300,000 girls played interscholastic sports across the nation. Now more than 25 years later, that figure has leapt to over 2.25 million participants. These young girls and women reap numerous benefits from an active life. Scientific research supports the thought that participation in sports leads to better physical health and increased resistance to the common cold and flu, while decreasing the risks for obesity, heart disease and osteoporosis. Better mental health is also a positive result by reducing anxiety and promoting confidence and self-esteem. Participation in sports promotes development of motor skills and provides a great place for social interaction with peers and adults.

Involvement at any level is a positive experience. Even the losing part comes with some good. The lessons learned are life lessons that some day will replay in your mind in a different situation. I sum it up by saying:

"Her body will be stronger. Her grades will be better. And as her confidence grows, so will her opportunities teach her how to dream!"

When I was asked to be a part of this book, I certainly wondered if it would be consistent with the progress I see being made in women's athletics. As a college athlete in the early '70s prior to Title IX to now as a college coach at a major Division I university with all its advantages, I do believe I have seen it go from "the outhouse to the penthouse." There is still room for growth and acceptance but we are seen, heard and enjoyed on many fronts.

In the recruiting process I am often asked what is the biggest difference between high school sports and college sports and what is required to make the adjustment from one level to the next. Without hesitation I answer, "The difference is strength training and conditioning." The number one priority in our summer training program has been and will continue to be strength training and conditioning.

Now you have a picture of a bodybuilder in your mind. Change it! It's not about what you look like in the team photo. It's about being explosive, improving flexibility and more importantly keeping healthy. That is imperative to your success as well as your team's especially during the post-season.

Just like everything else, there is a right way and a wrong way to do things. In the world of weight lifting and strength training, there is also a male way and now a female way. Even though there is a difference between the sexes, the goal remains the same, which is to give your body the best chance of being at the top of its performance level. I enjoyed this book because it recognizes that there is a difference to reach the same goal. This book introduces different ways, different aspects and different programs, but with the right attitude about dealing with the female body and its need for differences in weight training. It integrates teaching techniques and recovering strategies, while touching on specific training areas for different sports. The book also addresses areas that are usually neglected, such as nutrition and eating disorders, the high frequency of ACL tears, and the premature onset of osteoporosis.

Whether you are a multi-sport athlete, a weekend warrior, or sport specific athlete, you need to treat your body as a machine that performs better warmed up and stretched. Be ready to go the distance! Do it right! Establish a safe and disciplined way to weight training. Let this book teach you, motivate you and be your coach. Now, all you have to do is provide the effort.

You have more energy inside you than has ever been tapped, more talent than has ever been explored, more strength than has ever been tested and more to give than you can ever give. Anything can be achieved with the right attitude and focus. Good luck and enjoy the challenge.

The Role of Strength and Conditioning in Women's Athletics

Michael Bradley, M.A.

Over the years, the role of the strength and conditioning program in athletics has changed and, not surprisingly, followed a similar path for both women's and men's sports. In a few short decades, conventional wisdom about lifting weights has moved from one end of the spectrum to the other. Where in the past, athletes were often discouraged from lifting weights by their coaches because it was thought that it would be detrimental to their athletic performance; nowadays, strength and conditioning coaches are often fired when an athletic team has a poor win-loss record. This brief but revealing historical perspective — along with all of the various thoughts and opinions about what constitutes proper training and the various myths that still circulate regarding women and strength training — requires that the role of strength and conditioning in women's athletics be clearly understood.

Strength and conditioning in women's athletics is only of value if kept within the context of sports. It's not uncommon to see the same people both expect unrealistic results from some aspects of training while at the same time not appreciate the truly great and realistic benefits that can be obtained by participating in a program of strength and conditioning that's properly coached. Consequently, the *perspective* that a coach, parent or athlete takes in relation to the role of training in a person's life and athletic career will greatly dictate the choices that are made. This adopted viewpoint should enable an athlete or coach to make value judgments with regards to the huge flood of training information that she will be exposed to over her career. This will answer such questions as: How much time should be invested? What exercises should be performed? How much effort should be exerted? And the big question: What protocols should be used?

The ability to properly judge and assess information is critical because not every type of training is of equal value or carries the same cost and benefits — though the ubiquitous charlatans in the field of strength and conditioning may have you believe so. There's literally almost an infinite number of ways in which to train and one cannot do them all — nor are they all of the same worth in terms of effectiveness, safety, risk and reward. Today's athlete doesn't have an infinite amount of time, energy or — and this is a critically overlooked factor — recovery ability to perform every type of training under the sun. Choices will have to be made.

Despite all the debate about the best way to train in order to improve performance, one factor rarely discussed is that training can negatively affect perfor-

Without question, a stronger, well-conditioned athlete has the potential to be a better athlete. (Photo by Michael Bradley)

mance . . . and in a major way. The average athlete is usually on the verge of overtraining due to the practice, drills, supplemental conditioning, meetings, travel and games that she is required to do in order to compete. Compared to a rested athlete, a fatigued athlete is less skillful and explosive, has less endurance and mental sharpness and is more susceptible to injury. So before discussions of the "best way to improve jumping," the bigger context of rest and recovery must be considered. Coaches and athletes must make decisions based upon the relative value of each activity. As absurd as it may seem, at least one coach has placed the juggling of beanbags on the same value level as practicing and doing progressive-resistance exercise. Coaches and athletes can sometimes panic and feel as if they must try everything when sometimes, the best choice is to do nothing in order to allow the body time to heal and rest.

THE MAIN COMPONENTS

A discussion of the role of strength and conditioning in women's athletics can be divided into physical and mental components. Specifically, what can someone expect in terms of results? What's possible? What's impossible? How should time and energy be directed? How does a coach evaluate the success — or failure — of a strength and conditioning program? And, finally, what's the proper perspective to have with regards to the role that this activity will play in an athletic career and in a lifetime?

The Physical Component

Without question, a stronger, well-conditioned athlete has the *potential* to be a better athlete. Trained athletes can typically run faster, jump higher and play more explosively. They'll have more endurance, pushing back the onset of fatigue allowing for a higher level of effort for a greater duration. Stronger muscles require less effort to perform any skill, allowing that task to be performed with greater precision and expertise. Anything that can be done well can be done as good or better with stronger muscles.

These are obvious points. What's less obvious is that while athletes will improve their physical capacities, they'll do so within their genetic limitations. While no one would expect that every woman who picks up a tennis racket will play at Wimbledon one day, many people do expect that everyone who trains will either look like the models and bodybuilders in magazines or run like the track stars in the Olympics. The truth is that how well athletes respond to training is largely determined by their inherited or genetic traits.

The Role of Genetics

Training is really a type of stress adaptation. While everyone will improve, they will not do so to the same degree. An example will help illustrate this point. The skin responds to the stress of sunlight — or, more specifically, to ultraviolet radiation — by becoming darker. The production of melanin protects the skin against further stress from sunlight. Similarly, the muscles respond to the stress of exercise — or, more specifically, to muscular loading and metabolic stress — by becoming stronger (and, in some cases, larger). In this case, the production of muscle and strength protects the body against further muscular loading and metabolic stress. And just as people have different abilities to develop their tans, they have different abilities to develop their physiques. Consequently, comparing athletes in their ability to respond to exercise is a poor method of motivating and teaching a proper strength and conditioning program. Motivational techniques that rely on demeaning or glorifying athletes based upon their training weights or running times in comparison to their teammates makes as much sense as saying to an athlete, "Look at her tan. Why can't you tan like that? You aren't tanning hard enough. You need to tan the way that she does." Never mind that the glorified "tanning athlete" may have the skin and genetic heritage of someone from South America and the demeaned athlete may have the skin and genetic heritage of someone from Scandinavia. If the coach isn't getting the "tanning results" that she thinks should be obtained, she may bring in a "tanning consultant" or a "tanning coach" who writes articles in the "tanning magazines." And what do you know? This "tanning expert" is from Venezuela, not Denmark. And by the way, she's selling a special "anabolic tanning lotion" that will make you look like her. Absurd? You bet. But change the word "tan" to "muscle" or "speed" and this same exchange is played out every day on teams and in athletic departments around the world. Most athletes can see this for what it is and don't find it helpful or inspiring. The next chapter will detail the correct way for coaches to supervise and motivate a proper strength and conditioning program but, in brief, coaches should reward behavior, not genetically controlled results.

And just as it's easy to expose oneself to too much sunlight stress, it's easy to expose oneself to too much exercise stress. What happens when the skin is overexposed to ultraviolet radiation? It burns. It blisters. It peels. In short, the skin breaks down. Systemically, heat stroke, heat exhaustion, skin cancer and even death can result. And what happens when muscles are overexposed to exercise stress? They atrophy. They weaken. They become less explosive and less resilient to fatigue. They get injured. In short, muscle breaks down. Systemically, fatigue, colds, infections and lethargy can result.

So the proper perspective of the coach and athlete should be that while everyone can improve, they will not develop to the same degree. Also, each athlete has an individual tolerance as to how much exercise she can endure. Therefore, instead of seeing how much exercise an athlete *tolerates*, try determining how little exercise an athlete *needs* in order to stimulate her body to make favorable changes.

Realistic Expectations

Here's another question that's a large point of confusion: "What exactly can physical training do for an athlete?" While the strength and conditioning program will prescribe exercises from "the neck down," it's from "the neck up" that controls what happens from "the neck down." Misunderstanding this concept can set up unrealistic expectations by coaches and athletes and instill frustration and resentment in teams.

Imagine the body as a modern personal computer system. Physical training can do the equivalent of producing a bigger monitor, a slightly faster printer, a stronger outer case and a better warranty. But the computer is still driven by the CPU. Most of the physical qualities that are needed in competition are under the control of the body's CPU: the brain and nervous system. Such things as balance, hand-to-eye coordination, reflexes and response time — while outwardly appearing physical — are largely dominated by how quickly the brain and nervous system process and relay information. More basic traits — such as speed and jumping ability — have a large neural component that's primarily inherited. Just as a Pentium 1 chip doesn't run at the same speed as a Pentium 4 chip, not all athletes' nervous systems are created equally. And just as it's impossible to change a Pentium 1 chip into a Pentium 4 chip, most of the "hardwiring" of an athlete's nervous system is genetically determined or "programmed" at an early age. While to some this may seem limiting and defeatist, it's actually quite liberating. Knowing that many of the qualities for which they're looking are controlled by the nervous system and have a genetic component to them, coaches who must select athletes through a recruiting process can narrow their list of prospects. If an athlete is found to be lacking in a particular quality before getting recruited, it'll be much easier to predict and project how much improvement can be made. Once an athlete is under a coach's direction, the coach must identify how well the athlete can process coaching and tactical information as well as response and reflexive information such as visual and auditory cues. Software programmers will not write a software code for a computer running a Pentium 1 chip in the same way that they'll write it for a Pentium 4 chip. If they do, the computer will not run. In fact, it'll slow down and crash. The programmers must write to the level of the processing power of the computer. Likewise, coaches must teach to the processing power of the athlete. They must only present that information which can be acted upon in an efficient way that doesn't require long thought and confusion. Each athlete has a different capacity for this. In addition, a software manufacturer writes specific code in order to make the machine perform exactly as it should. A coach is the software writer for the athlete. They must teach with precision and have the athlete "encode" the program through drills and practice which "writes" precisely the task needed in competition. Realizing this, a coach can structure practice in such a way as to get maximum benefit in minimum time. This is why coaching is so important. Athletes will know to practice competition-level skills and avoid poor practice habits and "junk" drills, as these are the ones that the brain will need to retain and exhibit in the heat of battle.

What does this have to do with the strength and conditioning program? In today's athletic environment, understanding the answer to this question can be everything. An athlete may double her strength but that doesn't mean she'll play twice as well. An athlete may add eight pounds of muscle but if she doesn't also improve her skills, there will be little improvement in her playing ability. Is it logical for a basketball player to spend eight hours a week in the weight room and one hour a week shooting free throws? Should she spend one hour a day riding a stationary bike and five minutes a day dribbling a ball? The proper *perspective* of the role of the strength and conditioning program will prevent these very common misappropriations of time and energy. A strength and conditioning program can develop an athlete's *potential* to develop force but how that force is *applied* is a function of the neural traits that an athlete has inherited and the "programming" of those skills in practice. The highly sought-after *power* for which coaches and athletes are searching lies in the skillful application of force.

To illustrate the confusion that can exist, a sport coach once asked a strength coach about what his athletes can do in the weight room to keep them from slipping on the athletic field. The fact of the matter is that with complex motor skills that involve responding to rapidly changing conditions, there's *no* skill learned in the weight room that can transfer to the athletic arena. Trying to do so is a terrible waste of time and potentially dangerous. Which brings up the most important point: the prevention of injuries.

Injury Prevention

Knowing what strength and conditioning can and cannot do should make it obvious that the biggest role of the strength and conditioning program must be the prevention of injuries. A proper strength and conditioning program should increase the strength of the tendons, ligaments and bones. This will help reduce the incidence and severity of injuries and help expedite recovery time if an injury does occur. Stronger muscles will act as shock absorbers around the joints, taking stress off the connective tissues and helping to decrease both sudden injuries and overuse type injuries.

When one considers the amount of time, money and resources spent at the collegiate level identifying, evaluating and recruiting talented athletes, it makes sense that the strength and conditioning program should act as an insurance policy on the health of those athletes. At younger ages, the risk of injury to the growth plates of an immature skeleton — along with the risk that's inherent in sports — requires an athlete to be physically prepared before competing. A coach's best chance of winning is when her best athletes are playing as much as possible. In addition, an athlete can only improve by practice. Lost practice time due to injuries severely limit an athlete from becoming better. Doesn't it make sense, then, that injury prevention should lead the list of reasons to train? If so, this *perspective* on the role of the strength and conditioning program will greatly influence the type of exercises performed and the protocols used. Exercises should be chosen that train the entire body, with specific attention paid to the prevalence and severity of injury in each particular sport. Protocols should be chosen that leave no doubt as to their safety and effectiveness. After all, if one of the main purposes of the strength and conditioning program is to reduce injuries, what sense does it make to get injured in the weight room or on the running track? Coaches are charged with the well being of their athletes. An athlete takes a risk every time she steps into the competitive arena. Morally, it's wrong for a coach to take a risk with athletes in preparation for their events — especially when that preparation is to help prevent injury. Athletes aren't science projects to be experimented on by coaches.

The Mental Component

The psychological advantage that an athlete can receive from participating in a properly supervised strength and conditioning program can be enormous. Physical improvement should happen but it's difficult to know just how much good the training will do for an athlete. Reduced injuries should be a benefit of training but some injuries are just a function of being in the wrong place at the wrong time. The mental benefits of training, though, should be a guarantee. A program that's physically and mentally tough, disciplined, accountable, supervised and motivated will change the psychology of any athlete and team. What follows can be for the coaches and parents but it's written directly to the competitive athlete.

Privileges

Being able to train hard at this point in your life is a privilege. To be a competitive athlete places you in a select group of people. Think of all the people who are less fortunate: Those with little talent, those with debilitating conditions and those in hospitals. To be able to lift, condition and play hard is a gift that's easily taken for granted. At some point in your life you won't be able to push your body as you can now. You'll then look back with fond memories and wish you could still do what you can now.

Training hard is a privilege. Remind yourself of this when conditioning. Remind yourself of this on the last repetitions of a set. Tell yourself this as you go through the workout trying to catch your breath. You won't be able to do this forever. Some people will never be able to do this at all. Enjoy the experience while you can

Discipline and Self Esteem

Contrary to what you might expect, discipline isn't the most significant component of individual or team success. Talent and skill are the most important attributes of successful athletes. But without discipline, absolutely nothing of value can be accomplished. How you prepare yourself physically and mentally are indications of your commitment. The same players who commit to training are the same players who study more film, take better notes, practice harder and play harder. They're the players on whom the team can rely. Discipline isn't something that can be turned on and off. Successful teams cannot have athletes decide when they will or will not have discipline.

The nature of the human mind demands that you embrace discipline in order to be happy. The happiest people in the world are the most disciplined. They can see beyond the immediate. They can delay gratification until another time. *The process alone* gives them satisfaction and reaffirms their place in the world. Lazy and undisciplined people are invariably miserable, unsatisfied and unhappy. They never attempt anything difficult and they never accomplish anything worthwhile.

Sooner or later you'll cross paths with friends and acquaintances from your scholastic days. Eventually, you'll meet someone who, in school, was shy, introverted and unsure of herself. But upon graduation, she went on to do something difficult such as joining the military. The change in this person will no doubt be dramatic. She radiates confidence, has a bounce in her step, looks you in the eye and tells great stories of all the things that she has done. You'll also meet people who have done nothing since they left high school. They complain constantly, believe "society" is out to get them, have a victim's mentality and sit around reliving their days in high school.

The biggest role of the strength and conditioning program must be the prevention of injuries. (Photo by Michael Bradley)

Coaches, teachers and parents who don't set expectations, provide structure and expect self-control are doing young people an enormous — and sometimes irreparable — disservice. They're robbing those individuals of the only way that they can truly be happy. Self-esteem and self-confidence are earned by working hard and accomplishing goals. They don't just *happen* to you.

Athletes are required to compete at a much higher level when they enter college. Athletes who were successful on pure talent may become easily frustrated if they haven't been required to have a consistent work ethic. These emotionally fragile and "high-maintenance" personalities will take an unfair share of their teammates' and coaches' attention, patience and energy. A person cannot have self-confidence without struggle and accomplishment. Self-esteem cannot be taught. Rather, it's earned.

Effective training is based on effort. High-intensity effort is expected in everything that's done. Whether lifting or running, practicing or playing, less than all-out effort is unacceptable. This effort — combined with talent — is why athletes are successful. It's your *effort* that will provide the happiness and satisfaction of your athletic career.

Concentration

The ability to focus your attention for the purpose of attaining a goal is one of the characteristics of being human. It defines your actions and separates you from animals. Observe a dog for a few moments. All it can do is react to its environment. Every sight, sound and smell draws its attention equally. Its actions are limited to responding. It cannot focus its mind to achieve a goal. You, being different from an animal, can decide where you'll focus your mental energy. The things on which you choose to concentrate will dictate what you do and, ultimately, what you become.

Concentration is the consolidation, collection and application of what's important at the moment. Noted psychologist Dr. Mihaly Csikszentimihalyi has stated that the human mind is only capable of consciously evaluating about 126 bits per second. And even this processing rate can be limited. For instance, it's very difficult to hear two conversations at the same time and it's impossible to hear and understand three or more conversations taking place at once. This limitation on how much information your mind can process dictates that you cannot be passive, unconscious and oblivious to the world around you and accomplish anything of value. You *must choose* the elements on which you'll focus your mind.

A high level of mental focus doesn't come naturally but it can improve with practice. Concentration is only developed through the *choice* and *effort* to improve your ability to focus your mental labor. Your ability to concentrate will ultimately decide your success in any endeavor. The world is full of talented yet unsuccessful people who let their minds wander or fixate their attention on unproductive and unimportant things. The ability to consolidate your mental effort on a task can make up for a lack of talent simply because so few people are willing to exert the required energy *over the long run*.

Training for athletics is serious business. There's no way that you can be successful at training if your attention is divided. The high-intensity effort and attention to detail that are necessary in order to attain maximum results demand a singleness of purpose while training. Athletes who look for excuses and distractions will easily find them. They can complain about the music, the weather or the early morning hours. They can talk about their schoolwork or about last night's party. Ultimately, each athlete must *choose* whether or not *this* workout will be important and successful *before* she walks through the door.

The phrase "she has potential" is loaded with unfulfilled promise. It implies that an athlete isn't realizing her complete talent. Why? What's stopping her? What's her rate-limiting factor? Your ability to reach your potential during your athletic career will be a function of your willingness to focus your mind on the immediate task at hand. Over the course of your life, you'll become the product of the *choices* of where you put your *mental effort* and concentration.

Leadership and Coachability

All successful teams have effective leaders who provide encouragement and discipline. They demonstrate how to behave and establish the team work ethic.

They're the confidence and reinsurance in adverse times. They pass to the younger players the team traditions of work ethic, personal accountability, practice pace, training hard and playing hard. They serve as extensions of the coaching staff.

A leader must want the responsibility that comes with that place on the team. A leader must want to shape the team in her image. To become a leader, you must first learn to follow instructions. You won't know how to give instructions or enforce team rules until you've followed them yourself. Your credibility as a leader will only be as good as your ability to follow. Your work ethic and practice habits will determine whether or not your teammates listen when you speak. A person who is only a vocal leader is ineffective and can actually produce effects that are the opposite of what everyone desires. Teammates will resent her and tune out her and, consequently, not listen to others who have something valuable to say. So before you "talk the talk," be sure that you can "walk the walk." Effective leaders have a *command presence*. Everyone knows who is in charge without anyone saying it. Everyone knows that this person "walks the walk."

Here's an interesting question for an athlete to ask herself: "Am I coachable?" Read that question again. If you're uncoachable, why? For the most part, coaches, teachers and parents want only the best for you. They want to see you improve. They want to see you win. Certainly, a coach with 20 years of experience has information that can help you. If you want to lead the team, you'll also have to be able to follow directions. Leadership and coachability are inseparable.

The Training Mentality

The highest compliment that a coach can give one of her athletes is to say of her "she has a training mentality." This person has an enthusiasm for effort. She expects and forces improvement in every workout. Her *personal accountability* is at a higher standard than anyone else could hold. She *takes an interest and responsibility in her teammate's training and progress.*

When they begin with a coach, few athletes have a "training mentality." But it can be developed. Athletes will go through three distinct mental phases (or stages) during their training career. They are:

1. *Fear and Apprehension.* This phase is marked by a genuine terror and potential attempts at avoiding the upcoming workout and ensuing discomfort that's associated with it. For a minority of these athletes, the psychological stress is very real and can be related to any number of things, including a low tolerance for pain. The majority of athletes who stay for very long in this phase are typically talented and extremely successful at lower levels without ever having discipline, accountability or a work ethic demanded of them. Because of their overwhelming talent, they've had coaches, parents and administrators hold their hands, coddle them and make excuses for them for most of their lives. Athletes who stay in this phase of training usually have character flaws and very fundamental problems with personal responsibility (as long as it doesn't affect their playing time). They don't register for class on time. They miss appointments with doctors and tutors. They

forget to be at events. People who hold them accountable for their responsibilities are always viewed as "wrong" and "out to get them." They hold a victim's mentality. In the Fear and Apprehension Phase, athletes respond best to a coaching style that can be described as "animated." The coach will have to scream, turn up the music and run around like a maniac. The coach will lie and cajole and shout "one more!" seven times in row in order to get six more repetitions out of the person. At this stage, the coach is the only one who is capable of generating any intensity or energy. Most responsible people don't stay in this phase for very long.

2. *Acceptance and Duty.* Virtually all athletes should reach this mental phase of training provided that their programs encourage accountability, attendance, consistency and effort. The majority of athletes will settle at this level, if allowed. They'll start their workouts on time, rarely miss a workout, train hard and accept training as something that they must do. Athletes in this mental phase of training are good soldiers. Unfortunately, unless they have unbelievable talent or a very strong personality, they won't be good leaders. They cannot be leaders in strength training or in conditioning . . . at least not consistently. Like most people, they're inherently self-centered. They're concerned with their own development but they'll only occasionally show concern for a teammate's training. They cannot *sustain* interest in other people, their activities, their development or their accountability to the team. They'll "talk the talk" of a leader, though, because it's what they think is expected of them. *Sustained effort* outside of their own interests is their rate-limiting factor in team dynamics and leadership roles.

3. *The Training Mentality.* This is the highest mental phase that an athlete can reach. Almost all athletes can achieve this *if they choose.* This mindset is neither a magical, mystical place nor does an individual need to have talent for athletics or training in order to achieve this level. Athletes who have this mindset have *chosen* it. Working at the absolute highest levels of effort is no longer really that big of a deal for them. They no longer view training as a requirement but as something that they "just do." They don't need to psych out themselves beforehand. They don't panic while the levels of intensity and pain increase. *They can separate physical discomfort from their emotional response to the discomfort.* This doesn't mean that they're emotionally apathetic to the pain. Instead, they can identify the discomfort and their response for what it is. They realize that the source of their discomfort and their responses to it are separable entities. At the highest level of effort and concentration, these athletes will *draw into themselves.* Rather than project their pain and discomfort for the whole room to view, they internalize that energy and place it into the repetition that they're trying to complete. Coaches and athletes who observe this for the first time are usually stunned. While there isn't the usual "dog-and-pony show" that passes for "hard training" at most schools, there's a quiet confidence and building of physical and mental energy with each repetition. First-time observers will think to them-

selves "surely that's her last repetition. She'll set down the weight now." And they'll think this for up to six repetitions in row. These athletes have the potential to be the best leaders because they're the most *credible*. Regardless of talent, their teammates respect them because of their courage and consistency. These athletes can lead by action, even if they're not the most vocal or most skilled. When they speak, their teammates know that what's stated is coming from someone who can truly "walk the walk." An athlete with a high level of talent, a strong personality and a "training mentality" can become a phenomenal leader. These individuals can shape the complete personality of the team. They can literally change the course of season. A handful of athletes such as this can turn good soldiers into champions.

Athletes who have this level of mental ability respond to a style of coaching that can best be described as "subtle." As the exercise becomes more intense, the athlete has learned to draw deeper and deeper into her mental reserves. She's involved in an internal dialogue that doesn't use words. Yelling and screaming are distractions. Other people are distractions. A coach who is training such an athlete should make the most of her points before the set starts. Once the exercise begins, the coach should pick her words and moments appropriately. If the coach doesn't have the years of experience supervising and teaching athletes such as this or if she doesn't know this particular athlete's psychological make up as good as her own, the coach should just be silent. Unfortunately, most coaches who fall in this category won't recognize the situation. Or, they will not be able to identify the athletes who have a "training mentality." This is part of the "art of coaching." It cannot be taught. The coach will have to make some sincere, honest mistakes along the way and then figure it out for herself.

SUSTAINED EFFORT

> *"Never give in, never give in, never, never, never, never — in nothing."*
> — Winston Churchill

Most people can get excited for a short burst of time. Everybody can give maximum effort sporadically. Most everyone can concentrate on a task for a few minutes. But the true measure of character is the ability of a person to *sustain that effort over the long run.*

None of this is easy. If it were easy, everyone would do this. *Never allow yourself the luxury of having a bad day.* Create intensity for yourself. Create energy for your teammates. Always be "on." Be the bright spot. Never allow self-pity and self-doubt to creep in. Never quit on a repetition. Never quit on a set. Never yield to fatigue. Never concede a possession. Never quit playing to win. Never quit. Never quit. Never quit. Never.

Truly, the greatest role of strength and conditioning in women's athletics is the development of the mind.

2

Coaching and Motivating the Female Athlete in the Weight Room

Michael Bradley, M.A.

Proper strength training requires teaching. It must be instructed and supervised, just as an individual or team sport must be. And just as coaching can make a difference on the athletic field, supervision and motivation will determine the results of the strength and conditioning program. The abilities of the coach will play a major determining factor of whether or not an athlete progresses up to her genetic potential for physical development.

Coaching and teaching are synonymous. The field of teaching and the means by which people learn has been studied for decades. Many of the techniques that work well in the classroom work well in the weight room and in the athletic arena. These techniques can include whole-part-whole presentation, use of analogies from other subjects, modeling, concrete and abstract examples and peer-to-peer instruction.

The words and actions of the leadership can have dramatic and far-reaching impact, sometimes in ways not even anticipated. The great coaches and teachers convey their love of the subject to their athletes and students but the essence of coaching can be boiled down to instruction and programming. By continually telling individuals something about themselves, they'll start to believe it to be true.

An example from a past behavioral study will illustrate this point. In 1939, Dr. Wendell Johnson performed a secret research project on orphans in order to examine stuttering. The experiment used psychological pressure to make children stutter. At the time, the leading theory was that stuttering was genetic in cause. Dr. Johnson was a stutter himself while as a boy and also in college. He participated in just about every known treatment that was in vogue and eventually came to question the genetic theory of stuttering. He made a breakthrough in his research when he conducted interviews with the parents of stuttering children. Dr. Johnson discovered that virtually all children had been labeled a stutterer at a very early age. He came to the following conclusion: "Stuttering begins in the ear of the listener, not in the mouth of the child." By criticizing the normal speech difficulties that all young children have, well meaning but misguided parents drew attention to their children's speech and made them self-conscious of every mistake. Eventually, the children would become so overly attuned to their own speech that they would be unable to talk without stuttering. This was quite a difference in the thinking of the time. Essentially, diagnosing and labeling a young child as a stutterer while correcting each stammer would turn them into stutterers.

Dr. Johnson decided to perform an experiment in which he would try to induce stuttering in normal-speaking children. He took a group of orphans, half of whom stuttered and half of whom were normal speakers. He then randomly assigned half the children to an experimental group and half to a control group. The children in the experimental group were labeled "stutterers" and received negative therapy to fix the "problem"; the children in the control group were labeled "normal speakers" and received positive therapy. In the experimental group, children read passages aloud and were systematically sensitized to their speech. They were warned and lectured every time they repeated a word. The researchers also lied to the teachers and caretakers at the orphanage: They were told that the children in the experimental group were stutterers and to correct their speech whenever they repeated a word. By the end of the experiment, speech had deteriorated for five of the six normal speakers and three of the five stutterers in the experimental group. Sixty years later, the living subjects of that experiment still had speech and social problems.

Obviously, to a large degree, behavior can be positively and negatively programmed. It's possible for a strength coach to create an environment in which very high-intensity training can be a positive experience to which athletes look forward. Does this mean that everything the coach says and does has to be all sweetness and light? Absolutely not. But it does mean that coaches need to be aware of how their words and actions will affect athletes. The evaluation of the success or failure of the strength and conditioning program should be based upon the athletes' attitudes toward training and their work ethic. Every person has a different genetic potential for strength and conditioning results. Wins and losses can be attributed to a whole host of unrelated variables. But the leadership of the coach must create an environment of positive attitudes toward training and a culture of hard work. The purpose of this chapter is to explore in detail the coaching and motivational methods that work in the real world of the daily training and supervision of hundreds of athletes from diverse backgrounds.

COACHING

A great coach can teach anything once the material is known and understood. Unfortunately, much of what's taught regarding strength and conditioning is "hand-me-down" information that's passed from coach to coach and is never critically evaluated. Coaches must actively seek out information and determine if it makes sense and if can it be applied practically in their setting.

The best teacher is experience. In order to be understood, proper training must be experienced. Even in today's high-tech world, much of what passes for training information are anecdotal aphorisms that are tossed around like shiny magical coins that are used by people to convince themselves that they actually understand what's happening when they train. In reality, for coaches to truly be able to teach a strength-training system, they need to experience it under the watchful eye of an expert in that system.

It would be pointless for one person to explain to another what "hot" feels like. Another person can only understand by actually touching and experiencing "hot." The main goal of the person who supervises the learning of "hot" is to make sure that no one gets destroyed in the process. After touching heat several times, the "student" should be able to comprehend what's meant by heat. At this point, meaningful discussions can begin of "hot." Theoretical discussions can take place regarding how heat relates to the body, how much heat is "too hot," how long in the heat is too long, how best to manage heat and how frequently a person should be exposed to heat. But until both people understand "hot," these theoretical and practical considerations will be worse than worthless because the ideas that will come from them will have nothing to do with reality.

The abilities of the coach will play a major determining factor of whether or not an athlete progresses up to her genetic potential for physical development. (Photo by Mary Ciolek)

Regardless of the activity, no amount of discussion, theory or even careful observation will allow for clear understanding unless that activity is actually experienced. This is especially true for strength and sport coaches who may be far removed from their competitive and training days and have lost perspective or, more likely, never developed the perspective necessary for the training being performed today. There are many coaches who spout opinions about training in which they have absolutely no experience. This chapter and this book are about the real world of strength coaching and the methods that are used effectively "in the trenches" every day with hundreds of athletes.

Coaching is more of an art than a science. It's also hard work. Strength coaching, above all else, requires a "blue collar" work ethic. It requires physical, mental and emotional effort that must be sustained for long hours. The same tasks need to be taught and coached with fresh enthusiasm day after day, year after year. The athletes need to see their strength coach working. There's room for positive, enthusiastic people in strength coaching. Negative people who don't enjoy young people or view the weight room as a laboratory in which the athletes under their supervision train on the programs that they "designed" (what's called "programarama") while walking around with a cup of coffee, going to meetings, writing papers and getting caught up in the professorial side of academia shouldn't be a strength coach. It's not for everyone and it's not for those who aren't willing to work harder than they ever have before. The intrinsic rewards are enormous but only the strength coach will know about them. The relationships that a strength coach will develop can impact athletes for a lifetime. Literally. For the people who are cut out for it, being a strength coach can be the greatest job in the world.

Coaching women is no different than coaching men. In each case, the coach must deal with people as individuals. Each person responds to different teaching and motivational styles in their own way. It's up to the coach to discover how to best motivate and get teaching points across regardless if the athlete is a man or a woman.

Personally, my experience has been that female athletes will train just as hard or harder than most men. They can be extremely tough minded. If the activity is presented in the correct way, there will be a great "buy in." They'll get great results and be some of the biggest proponents of a program. The following are some recommended guidelines of which several are specifically for women:

1. *Coach women as equals.* Even in this day and age, there's a perception by some people that women are second-class athletes. A coach who works in a mixed-gender setting — as is true of most athletic departments — will obtain the best coaching results from dealing with teams, genders and individuals on an equal basis. For most people, the greatest motivator is in knowing that what they do really matters and is truly appreciated. Therefore, there must be no hint whatsoever of a "star system" in terms of who gets attention and coaching and who doesn't. Most people will be very appreciative of the coaching that they receive. And they'll notice when they're being treated less importantly than someone else.

2. *Address the myths.* There are many myths surrounding strength training and even more with women and strength training. This isn't nearly the problem that it once was but it still exists. At one time, the prevailing thought was that if a woman trained, she would get "bulky," look like a man and lose her femininity. Today, with most female athletes doing some form of strength training and very few of them looking "huge" by any stretch of the imagination, those worries aren't as prevalent. Some of the current myths and misconceptions pertain to such issues as food fetishes and nutrition quacks, "muscle building" versus "toning" exercises and the general fads that come and go every six months in strength training. There's probably at least one woman in every program who is dealing with one or more of these issues. Clearly, proper education can go a long way toward women accepting the importance of strength training.

3. *Be credible.* Related to addressing the myths and misconceptions, strength coaches must be credible sources of information. The world doesn't need anyone else spreading misinformation about training. The information that's taught should be based upon facts and the system of training that's implemented shouldn't be contradictory. Athletes should observe consistency in the message being presented. If each person or each exercise has a different standard of performance, the athletes will note the contradiction. An athlete

who is told to perform three sets of one exercise and five sets of another while a teammate is being told the opposite will rightfully question the inconsistent information that's being presented. If a set-and-rep scheme is offered as "being the best" then it should be used for all exercises, not just a select few. If strength coaches use gimmicks or they change their system every time the wind blows, it will undermine their credentials. Along the same lines, athletic departments tend to turn over a large percentage of their staffs each year. New people will come in with ideas of their own, some of which will be very good and should be implemented. At the same time, strength coaches have the need and obligation to be consistent with their athletes. If every athletic-department official is allowed to greatly alter the underlying philosophical coaching base of the strength and conditioning program, the strength coach will lose the athletes.

Strength coaches will be asked many questions; strength coaches don't have to have the answer to all of them. Stating, "I don't know but I'll find out" will go a long way toward developing trust with the athletes. Avoid grasping at straws and changing the program radically every week or every time that a new article is read. Avoid the need to be seen as a "guru" as this will eventually come off as insincere. Avoid gimmicks at all cost. Develop a reputation for providing good, solid information and being a source of consistency.

4. *Provide a non-intimidating atmosphere.* Coaches must be aware of the environment in which they're putting the athletes. Grouping 15 female freshmen who run cross country in the same weight room with 30 male seniors who play football isn't the best idea. There may come a time when they're very comfortable in that situation but to place them there initially is a mistake. At the same time, it's the responsibility of the strength coach to ensure that only respectful behavior is tolerated. Make the weight room a place where athletes feel great about being in. An excellent motto is: "The weight room is the most comfortable place to become uncomfortable."

5. *Don't try to be someone else.* Strength coaches should teach within their personalities. A coach who is loud and boisterous should teach with that same personality; a coach who is precise and analytical should teach with that same personality. Athletes are very perceptive and cannot be fooled. If there's something about an approach that's even 1% fake, they'll detect it and the strength coach will be less effective.

Keep an even personality and avoid being moody. The athletes should know what coaching personality to expect each day. If they're asking, "Is the strength coach going to be happy or grouchy today?" the coach is in trouble. Athletes should look forward to being around their strength coach.

6. *Make no excuses.* Strength coaches should create opportunities in their programs, not excuses. If coaches complain about something in which their program is lacking, it will come back to haunt them. Coaches whose facilities

are limited shouldn't point out what's missing. Rather, they should emphasize how great it is that proper training can be performed without elaborate equipment.

Here's a real-life example of creating excuses: One major college program provides food supplements for some of its athletes and not others. When one of the athletes was struggling in his development, his response was, "Well, I'm not getting the products everyone else is getting." And when the supplements ran out, the athletes who were taking them felt as if they were now being cheated. By providing what was perceived — however innocently — as a short cut, excuses were brought into the program. The athletes should only hear about opportunities, not excuses. They should never be given or shown a short cut. Even if the short cut did work, a strength coach would be giving away the greatest transfer of the strength and conditioning program — the mental edge that it should be developing.

7. *Never miss a teachable moment*. It's too easy for strength coaches to get into a comfort zone when it seems as if they've taught everything repeatedly and the weight room is running smoothly. Strength coaches have to guard themselves against complacency. Actively search to call attention to the things that are good and bad in the training environment. The athletes must feel the presence of their strength coach in the weight room. They must feel that their strength coach is watching them at all times. A strength coach must be unrelenting in presenting the same consistent message each day. If a strength coach has slipped into complacency, it's a safe bet that the athletes aren't far behind. This isn't something that must be guarded against every day; it must be guarded against every *second*. Ultimately, only strength coaches know if they're coaching with 100% effort or if they're on cruise control. In an activity like strength training in which the same fundamentals must be reinforced repeatedly every minute of the day while motivating athletes to do something that's far beyond the realm of physical and mental comfort, the strength coach has to be the most self-critical person in the room with regards as to their mental state.

Strength coaches don't have to teach everything they know during the first meeting with their athletes. At this point, pummeling athletes with every theory and fact about training will only turn them off. Opportunities for deeper explanations will present themselves and at that moment, the athletes will be much more receptive to what the strength coach has to say.

In the first one or two sessions in the weight room, the strength coach should instruct athletes using the following progression:

- Give them a very detailed explanation about the level of effort that they must use in their training and the exact reasons for it.
- Allow them to watch the required level of effort in action as an experienced teammate is taken through a set or a workout.

- Have them experience first hand what it feels like to work as hard as is expected and learn just how much mental effort and concentration is involved.
- After a desirable level of effort level is ingrained in them, give them a detailed explanation of how each repetition should be performed in the weight room and why it must be done this way.
- Let them see a demonstration of the aforementioned coaching points.
- Have them perform an exercise using these techniques with the level of effort that was first drilled into them.

So, establishing the level of effort and technique should comprise the first one or two coaching sessions with the athletes. At this point, they'll know how to perform four or five exercises. Then, during each workout over the next two or three months, one or two new exercises are introduced and taught in detail. During this period, the athletes are gradually taught the mental components of training, the attitude that's expected of them and the different protocols for different workouts. In addition, they're taught how to record information, determine and adjust seat heights for each machine, load weights and spot and coach teammates. The athletes should also be losing their fears of discomfort and learning the joy and privilege of performing high-intensity exercise. This period should take about 15 - 20 workouts to complete since scientific research of the learning process has shown that it's a mistake to present too much information at one time.

MOTIVATION

Leaders are always trying to motivate people. And motivating people has become a big industry. "Team building" and motivational speakers command huge fees to speak to corporations and other groups. Many theories exist about motivation. Psychologists have studied motivation extensively. Most teachers have heard or read about intrinsic and extrinsic motivational factors. Coaches should read, study and listen to anyone who has anything to say about motivating people.

It's well beyond the scope and intent of this chapter to provide a detailed discussion of motivational theory. Instead, practical information concerning the three best "triggers" for internal and external motivation will be presented. These three triggers — which will work for virtually everyone in all cases — are: (1) the work ethic of the leadership; (2) recent past success; and (3) appreciation for the effort. Note that each of these is based on the *actions* of the people involved, not slogans or sayings. Importantly, they've been tried and tested "in the trenches" virtually every day for years with thousands of athletes.

1. *The work ethic of the leadership.* Few things inspire people like seeing their bosses work. The best way for a coach to motivate athletes is for the coach to be motivated. The athletes need to see the coach working; the athletes need to see the coach hustling; the athletes need to see and feel a sense of urgency.

A strength coach tries to get athletes to do something that's initially counterintuitive, very uncomfortable and, for some, downright scary. The athletes will mirror the personality of their coaches. They're looking to the coaches to see how to act. If a coach is excited, they're excited; if a coach is tired, they're tired. Coaches — who may have been on the floor sustaining a high level of energy for 10 hours or more — must always be alert as to how they come across to their athletes. At the end of the day, a coach may have to "pray for strength" in order to continue presenting a fresh and enthusiastic personality. Keep in mind that it may be the hundredth athlete that the strength coach has seen that day but it's the first time that the athlete has seen the strength coach.

Don't underestimate the mental toughness that's needed to be a great motivator and strength coach. Few people have such close contact with athletes and the opportunity to impact their lives as the strength coach. A strength coach will need a moment to mentally prepare for each day and each session. Most athletes can get themselves excited for one workout, one day or one week. But strength coaches must separate themselves from the masses by their ability to *sustain effort over the course of months and years*. Strength coaches must be their own toughest critics. They must ask themselves: "Am I coasting?" "Am I missing teachable moments?"

The majority of athletes will have a great attitude toward recreational-type training. However, their attitude toward brutally hard training is another story and is a direct reflection of their strength coach. The development of a "training mentality" takes effort, time and great coaching. A mentality in which every repetition of every set is productive; in which every set is truly attacked and driven to the point of going all-out; in which no excuses are made or allowed; in which joy is found in the hardest of efforts; in which the athlete looks forward to doing it again the next time. These are the measures of great coaching. Remember this: Attitudes are caught, not taught.

2. *Recent past success*. A very strong motivator for athletes is recent success. The more success that they have, the more motivated that they'll be to continue working toward a goal. Success makes athletes feel as if they're in control; it makes them feel as if they're mastering the task. Success is comforting; it removes doubt.

Consider this: What would be the motivation for students if they failed test after test while studying harder and longer each time? What would be the motivation for athletes if they lost game after game while practicing harder and longer each time?

The best way to motivate athletes is to let them *repeatedly* experience success. A strength coach needs to put athletes in situations in which they can see improvement on a regular basis.

An effective system of training is based upon effort and technique. Progression is the driving force of workouts with the goal to improve in each exercise every workout. Every repetition, set and workout should be meticulously recorded and documented. This holds strength coaches and their athletes accountable for improvements. Each repetition, set and workout, then, becomes a test. At the end of each repetition, each set and each workout, it can be determined whether or not an athlete passed the test. This provides *immediate*, daily feedback as to the success or failure of the training program. As athletes see their strength improving each and every workout, their motivation to train is either increased or sustained. This is one of the reasons why athletes are so motivated to train.

3. *Appreciation for the effort.* One of the strongest human desires is to be appreciated. Athletes want to feel that what they do matters. Athletes want to be noticed for their work. Athletes want their contributions to be valued.

It's truly a mystery as to what people in leadership positions can be thinking when they're stingy with complements in regards to the effort of the people whom they're leading. They act as if they only have a dollar and each compliment that they make will cost them a quarter so they better not say too many at once. Management in large corporations and organizations could greatly reduce employee turnover by showing appreciation to their workers. Indeed, most studies have shown that people leave jobs not so much for more money but, rather, because they feel that their work isn't valued.

It's amazing what a few words of appreciation can do to sustain others. Here's another real-life example: A famous coach of a major university entered a hotel with his team. By the time he was done talking to the employees of the hotel, every bellhop, desk attendant, concierge and cook thought they had the most important job in the world. They couldn't do enough for that team — and they were more than glad to do it. For an investment of five minutes of his time and some verbal "maintenance" — such as saying "thank you," "this is important" and "you're doing great" his team got the best treatment possible. The message is clear: Make people feel important.

THE BOTTOM LINE

The fundamental principles of leading, coaching, teaching and motivating are universal and can be applied to any coaching, teaching and business situation. Strength coaches never know when they're going to say something to an athlete at just the time when she is receptive to learning. Strength coaches never know when their encouraging words will be just what's needed to keep someone going. As John Wooden once said, "Not all coaches are the same."

Coaching makes a difference. You make a difference.

3

Strength Training 101:
The Principles of Strength Development

Chip Harrison, M.S.

Despite some very obvious physical differences between the genders, there are few discernable differences between men and women in the area of strength training. Research indicates that the creation of a stimulus and the body's response to that stimulus are relatively consistent across gender lines. Interestingly, this also appears to be consistent across age lines as well (particularly in dealing with post-pubescent individuals). So while some modifications may be appropriate in other areas of training, the best results from strength training are obtained the same way regardless of gender, age or training goals.

This is not to imply that men and women should use the same amount of weight or that they'll respond to the same motivational cues. What it does mean is that even between the genders, the weight room is a great equalizer. One small difference between men and women is the way in which muscular strength is improved. For men, due in large part to higher levels of circulating testosterone (the male sex hormone), long-term improvements in strength generally coincide with significant increases in muscular size (or hypertrophy); for women, while some small increases in muscular size commonly accompany a strength-training program, long-term improvements in strength appear to be much more associated with changes in neural efficiency than with increased muscular size.

When it comes to understanding the principles of strength development, while some might have you believe otherwise, it's really a pretty simple process of stress adaptation. The process is much more dependent on effort and consistency than it is on fancy tools, complicated programming or a special diet and supplementation. Fortunately for most of us, strength training is far less complicated than learning a sophisticated sports skill or refining a special "talent." In fact, there are few training protocols that can be delineated so clearly and yet are the source of so much discussion and confusion.

As the general interest in strength training has increased over the past several years, so has our exposure to information on the subject. It's nearly impossible to flip through the pages of a newspaper or magazine or surf the channels on the television without running into an article, advertisement or infomercial that espouses the virtues of strength training and recommends a special program or tool to speed the process. In many cases, these so-called resources are much more interested in opening your checkbook than in disseminating good training information. Even those magazines or workout shows that specifically target the fitness population all too often mix solid training information with endorsements of products or programming that are questionable at best. Therefore, it's important for you to seek good sources of information and recognize whether an individual is primarily interested in educating someone or selling something. As with anything else, the best consumer is one who is knowledgeable about their product.

This chapter will provide you with an overview of the principles used and the physiological processes behind the ability to impart changes on the body through strength training.

As just eluded, strength-training programs take advantage of the body's innate ability to adapt to the stresses imposed upon it. This stress-adaptation response is really the training response that facilitates the physiological changes for which we're looking. In order to create an environment from which a training response can be elicited, several parameters must be met. These criteria include selecting exercises that use the desired muscles/muscle groups, choosing an appropriate and progressive training load, targeting muscles around a joint, allowing enough recovery time and then repeating the process with just the right amount of frequency to make progressive adaptations.

A FOUNDATION FOR MOVEMENT

Movement is made by the combined efforts of several systems. A few underlying principles influence these efforts and, together, form a foundation for movement.

Connective Tissues

The skeleton is the framework around which skeletal muscles are "hung." Bones provide a rigid support system for the body and the underlying structure from which movement can occur. Interestingly, bone tissue is actually one of the body's more active tissues. It's in a constant state of change, remodeling to reflect the external stresses being placed upon it. This can be clearly illustrated by the body's ability to repair a broken bone in a relatively short period of time or lose significant amounts of bone tissue when subject to inactivity (such as bed rest or in the case of zero-gravity space flight). Bone tissue is also the body's primary pool of calcium and phosphorus, two elements that are essential to our existence.

In most cases, bones articulate (or end) in a cartilaginous pad. This pad forms a "shock absorber" between the bones and a tremendously smooth surface that facilitates bone movement. Ligaments are made up of a fibrous tissue that connect bones together and function as the "hardware" necessary to maintain proper joint alignment. Tendons are made up of a different fibrous tissue and function to connect muscles to bones. In a truly magnificent engineering feat, tendon tissue is actually integrated into both bone and muscle tissues to provide a seamless means of anchoring the muscle to the body's framework and facilitating movement around a joint. This framework of connective tissue provides the structure around which skeletal muscle does its job. Without all these ingredients, the skeleton would be unable to provide the solid framework and the muscles would be unable to function effectively. Damage or injury to any of these connective tissues could present a significant obstacle to proper joint function and compromise movements around the affected joints.

Muscle Tissue

Skeletal muscle tissue is very different in makeup than the connective tissues with which it functions. Though integrated with the tendon and bound together by connective tissues in various sheaths, muscle tissue is made up of unique contractile proteins that allow it to function as a force-generating "motor." And it's these motors that move and/or stabilize the skeleton around various joints and facilitate all the actions of the human body.

The structure of muscle is as much an engineering marvel as any other within the body. Thin protein strands (actin) integrate with thicker protein strands (myosin) in a series of structural bridges that allow for a contraction (or shortening) of the muscle fiber. As a contraction propagates across the entire muscle cell and combines with similar contractions in adjoining cells, the whole of the muscle can contract and thereby generate force and movement. Through systematic activation of specific muscle cells and working in series with other muscle cells (motor units), motor pathways are established and specific movements are possible.

Different movements require the activation of specific and different motor pathways. Therefore, all movements require a series of unique activation sequences and contractile patterns that make each movement possible. It's through training different movements at different angles that complete muscular activation is achieved and maximal strength training benefits may be obtained.

Muscular Innervation

The final component of the movement equation is that of activation (referred to previously). The activation of muscle tissue takes place via an electrochemical reaction that's facilitated by the motor nerves. In most cases, this process begins in the brain as a signal to perform a particular task. The signal is then sent from the brain by way of a motor neuron (or neurons) to the specific muscle cells (within the muscle) necessary to perform the specific task. The signal is then conducted through the muscle cells and contraction occurs. If an adequate stimulus is present, the appropriate motor units located throughout a muscle are activated and the muscle will contract and perform the desired movement.

This innervation is essential to our ability to execute the nearly limitless variety of possible movements. Without the specific sequences of muscular recruitment provided by the nervous system, contractions would occur in a jerky, random fashion and the smooth, directed movements necessary for sports performance and the completion of our daily activities wouldn't be possible.

The All-or-None Law

Both nerve and muscle tissues operate under a principle known as the "All-or-None Law." In simple terms, this means that a stimulus is either sufficient to cause depolarization (or activation) or it isn't. In essence, there are no real strong impulses or weak impulses. Either the stimulus is of sufficient magnitude to propagate throughout the cell or it's effectively ignored. How then is it possible to generate appropriate force to perform the task at hand? How are we capable of both picking up a pen and writing a letter in one instant and pulling a tire from the trunk and changing a flat in another? The answer lies in how our nervous system functions to activate greater or lesser numbers of motor units (muscle tissue) for a given situation.

In order to perform light or intricate movements, the nervous system activates smaller motor units and, effectively, less muscle tissue. At other times, in order to produce greater force, the nervous system activates large numbers of motor units and a greater amount of muscle tissue. In essence, the nervous system functions to activate these various motor units in an additive way in order to produce the greater amounts of force necessary to perform more strenuous tasks.

For most of us, the vast majority of our daily activities are accomplished by utilizing only a small fraction of the motor units we have available. There's a huge untapped reservoir of muscle tissue only called upon during extreme circumstances. When engaged in an appropriate strength-training program, this reservoir is utilized and the muscle is stressed beyond its normal requirements. In doing so, stress adaptation is required and a training response is elicited.

While extreme circumstances don't necessarily mean defending the family cave from a saber-toothed tiger, they do mean asking the muscles to perform beyond their typical duties. And while "typical" for a computer programmer and "typical" for a construction worker may mean two very different things, the presence of an "overload" is paramount to promoting a training response.

For women, long-term improvements in strength appear to be much more associated with changes in neural efficiency than with increased muscular size. (Photo by Pete Silletti)

The Size Principle

As mentioned previously, most of our daily activities require only sub-maximal contractions of the muscles involved. Because of this, the body's most frequently and easily activated motor units are small by design. It would make little sense metabolically/physiologically to activate large motor units and great quantities of muscle tissue in order to perform light duties. As such, most of these motor units are made up of fatigue-resistant, endurance-type muscle fibers (Type I, slow-twitch fibers). This only makes sense, as these fibers would be called upon to perform time and time again over the course of the day. Larger motor units that are made up of more powerful and more fatigable type muscle fibers (Type II, fast-twitch fibers) require a greater stimulus and are more difficult — and, therefore, less likely — to activate. Again this makes physiological and metabolic sense since a larger muscular activation would require more energy and deliver forces in excess of what's necessary to perform most jobs. Indeed, why use a fire hose to fill up the Kool-Aid container?

So, muscular activation occurs in a physiologically "logical" and economical way. By activating smaller fatigue-resistant motor units and moving towards larger, more powerful motor units as circumstances demand, the body is capable of performing its most "common" activities with great economy while maintaining a significant reserve for those times it's needed. Activation of these various motor units always occurs in this "orderly" fashion from smaller to larger. However, the body doesn't preferentially recruit small motor units for lighter jobs and larger motor units for heavier jobs. There's an additive effect in play. When greater demands for muscle involvement are introduced, both small and large motor units are affected. In short, larger, more powerful motor units are activated in addition to the smaller units as demand dictates. It's important to understand that motor recruitment always occurs in this order.

This also becomes important when engaged in an activity like strength training. In order to stimulate the musculature significantly enough to elicit a training response, a sizeable amount of the available musculature (and available motor units) must be activated. Therefore, a significant load must be placed on the muscle or muscle groups being utilized in order to derive any training benefit. As such, in order for the strength of a given muscle or muscle group to be improved, it must be placed under an appropriate and large enough load.

The Stimulus

As just discussed, there's an effective "threshold" stimulus required in order to produce a training effect. Since eliciting a training effect is the primary goal of any well-designed training program, it's important to make sure that the program is sufficiently challenging to the body's systems to produce that training effect.

When looking at aerobic conditioning, there's an accepted and reasonably well-known minimum training stimulus referred to as "target heart rate" (THR). An individual's THR is based on a percentage of her estimated (or measured) maximum heart rate and provides a guideline for what would constitute an appropriate training intensity. For most individuals, this ranges from 70 to 85% of their maximum heart rate. Typically, trainees become quite familiar with their individual THR and manipulate exercise intensity in order to maintain their heart rate in the appropriate training "zone" for the desired duration in order to improve their aerobic conditioning.

Like aerobic conditioning, strength training requires a minimum level of intensity in order to elicit progressive improvements in muscular strength. Unlike aerobic conditioning, however, this training intensity isn't dependant on heart rate but, rather, on the resistance used. The training load necessary to produce consistent improvements in strength is equivalent to approximately 70% of the maximum resistance that can be overcome one time (70% of a one-repetition maximum or 1-RM). In essence, a load must be equal to or greater than about 70% of what can be lifted one time in order to stimulate improvements in strength. For example, if it were possible to perform only one repetition of a particular exercise in good form with 100 pounds, a training load of roughly 70 pounds or more would be necessary in order to produce consistent strength gains.

While it would be possible to determine the 1-RM for every exercise and then use at least 70% of that load as a training weight, the process would be incredibly time consuming and would expose the trainee to the added risks associated with performing exercises with maximal weights. Additionally, the process would then need to be repeated every few weeks in order to maintain an appropriate maximum from which to base training levels. Fortunately, there's a much safer and easier way to determine an appropriate training load. Since there are a maximum number of proper repetitions that can be performed with any given load, training loads can be effectively determined by using repetition maximums. For most people, a training load of about 70% of their 1-RM will result in being able to complete 10 - 15 repetitions in proper form. Therefore, any resistance that's substantial enough to cause an inability to perform proper repetitions in excess of 15 is an appropriate training load to produce consistent improvements in strength.

It's important to remember that while a load that the trainee is capable of lifting more than 15 times is likely to be inadequate to create a consistent training stimulus, it doesn't mean that there's no value to using training loads that allow higher repetitions. In fact, such loads are appropriate during the initial phases of training when learning a new exercise or routine and when increases in strength aren't the primary goal and increased muscular endurance is desired. Variations in the training load are also important in order to provide variety in the training stimulus and avoid an accommodation to the training routine.

Overload Principle

The human body is a marvel of stress adaptation. When subject to different environmental stimuli, the body demonstrates a remarkable ability to adapt and thrive. Whether increasing sweat rate in warmer conditions, developing a tan when exposed to ultraviolet rays or recovering from an injury, the body shows an almost incredible ability to rise to a given challenge.

The process of strength training is really no different than any of those that were noted earlier. By exposing the body (the muscles) to an appropriately challenging load, an adaptation response is initiated that culminates in improved strength. While this may sound much too simple, that really is the process of a strength-training routine.

Initiating and maintaining the appropriate stimulus follows what's commonly referred to as the "Overload Principle." In practice, the principle boils down to exposing the musculature to loads in excess of "normal" activities and thereby creating a stimulus for adaptation. By consistently re-exposing those muscles to an overload over time, the adaptation response is facilitated and will continue. While consistent exposure to a stimulus is essential to long-term progress, so too is progressively increasing the stimulus (as adaptation occurs) so that the overload is maintained.

As one might expect, over time the muscles will adapt to a particular load — that is, after all, what we're trying to accomplish — and continued exposure to the same load will cease to stimulate further changes. For example, if you were to begin a strength-training program and find that 100 pounds was sufficient to allow you to complete only 10 proper repetitions in the leg press (approximately 70% of your 1-RM), an adaptation response would be initiated that would cause improvements in strength in the exercised muscles. If you continued to use that 100-pound load for a period of time, you would eventually reach a point where that stimulus was no longer sufficient to produce improvements in strength. This process is called "accommodation." In order for further adaptation to take place, a greater load must be placed on the muscles. This is, in effect, progressive resistance training. Simply speaking, this means that a strength-training program must subject the muscles to progressively greater loads in order to be effective.

There are a number of variables that influence the effectiveness of a training program that will be discussed further in Chapter 4. However, two main factors will always continue to be required: (1) creating a training stimulus from which the body must adapt and (2) making that stimulus progressive over time so that the adaptation process will continue.

The Training Response

There are a number of different physiological responses caused by strength training. The first and most obvious is improved strength in the exercised muscles. Other, less obvious responses include improvements in the strength of the bones and other connective tissues, more appropriate neural recruitment in the exercises done and increased metabolic activity through improvements in body composition (decreased body fat and increased muscle mass). Still other by-products of a well-designed training regimen include better joint integrity, improved posture, increases in joint flexibility and an overall improvement in self-esteem.

Most people initiate a program in order to promote at least one of these responses. Fortunately, a well-designed program will facilitate other changes simply through its execution. As mentioned previously, the body responds relatively indiscriminately to the stresses placed upon it. Therefore, the fact that certain physiological improvements are taking place isn't necessarily an indication that the program has been well designed. In fact, some changes may be taking place in spite of — rather than because of — the program. As a result, it's especially important to examine all the parameters of the program in order to make sure that the desired responses are being facilitated in a manner that's as efficient and appropriate as possible.

CONCLUSION

In summary, while there are many ways to promote desirable changes in strength, body composition and preparation for other activities, there are specific physiological principles that must be considered along the way. In order to make the most efficient use of your time and energy, it's essential that you understand and exploit these principles.

By exercising some care and taking a small amount of time in the initial design of your strength-training program, a myriad of pitfalls can be avoided and the desired results obtained.

4

Strength Training 102: Designing the Program

Chip Harrison, M.S.

As discussed in Chapter 3, engaging in some form of activity (training) that produces improvements in muscular strength is a pretty simple process. A stimulus that's sufficient to cause an adaptation response isn't hard to come by. Virtually any routine that combines an appropriately challenging resistance with adequate recovery time is likely to produce a training effect. Thus, even poorly designed programs are capable of producing responses given the right stimuli. That fact is probably the main source of confusion when it comes to program design.

Unfortunately, our propensity to adapt to either positive or negative stimuli indiscriminately can make it difficult for the trainee to evaluate the efficacy of a given program. In other words, a risky, unbalanced, poorly designed program could produce many of the same adaptations as that of a safe, balanced, comprehensive, well-designed program in certain body systems. Thus, while jumping up and down with a car chassis on your shoulders might elicit similar improvements in leg strength as a properly performed leg press, it's just as likely to facilitate a multitude of undesirable adaptations such as severe bruising, damaged ligaments and bulging discs as compared to the more appropriate movement. How then can one identify a solid, well-designed program from a nasty program just lucky enough to cause some desirable changes?

Fortunately, there are definitive characteristics that are common to all well-designed programs. These characteristics comprise a foundation for safe, efficient and, ultimately, effective training protocols.

CHARACTERISTICS

The first characteristic of well-designed programs is that of dynamic, full-range movement. While strength improvements do occur when the muscle is stimulated isometrically (without movement taking place), these types of contractions improve strength only at or near the angles where the contractions occur. Thus, if one were to contract the biceps isometrically with the elbow bent at 90 degrees, strength improvements would only occur at that 90-degree angle (plus or minus about 10 - 15 degrees). Since most individuals are interested in improving strength throughout the entire range of motion (ROM) of a joint, a series of isometric contractions would be required to train the 135-degree ROM of the elbow. Obviously, this would necessitate a somewhat complicated arrangement of contractions in order to produce the desired results. A

The best results are obtained when a resistance is both raised and lowered in a deliberate fashion. (Photo by Pete Silletti)

simpler process would be to select an appropriate resistance that can be lifted through a full ROM. This would allow for improvements in strength through the entire range of the contraction thereby eliminating the need for a series of separate contractions.

Another characteristic of an appropriate repetition is the inclusion of both a concentric (raising) and eccentric (lowering) phase. In essence, this means that the best results are obtained when a resistance is both raised and lowered in a deliberate fashion. When observing people training in the weight room, it's often the case that much more attention is paid to the raising of the weight. In fact, it sometimes appears as if the lowering of the resistance is merely a formality necessary to get the weight back into a position to be raised for the next repetition — supposedly the "important" part of the lift. But in reality, there's an expanding body of evidence to indicate that the lowering portion of the lift is actually more important for improving strength than is the raising portion. Therefore, it's both reasonable and appropriate that special attention be paid to the eccentric phase of the repetition.

The advantages of dynamic training are clear. Training through the full ROM of a joint allows for improvements in strength at all of the angles that are specific to each exercise. Since daily activities require a variety of movements, full-range training can positively impact many different activities. In addition to producing strength at a variety of angles, such a training protocol would allow for a maintenance or improvement in joint flexibility — thus eliminating the possibility of producing a "muscle-bound" trainee. Use of limited-ROM exercise can adversely affect joint flexibility and predispose a joint to orthopedic injury.

A third characteristic common to well-designed programs is that of balance. This means that muscles/muscle groups on "both sides" of a joint are trained equally. It's not uncommon for individuals to develop "lateral dominance" on one side of the body — that is, right or left arm/leg dominance — through long-term repetition of certain activities. Likewise, it's not uncommon for "one side" of the body to develop strength disproportionately to the "other side." In other words, the "pushing" movements become stronger than the "pulling" movements. Since joints are both moved and stabilized by opposing muscles/muscle groups, developing strength disproportionately on one side or the other could lead to decreased joint stability and potential injury.

Children engage in all sorts of different movements and activities. This develops strength and flexibility throughout their bodies to the point where older adults envy the "little ones" that they love. As children mature, their activities have a tendency to specialize and inevitably so do the joints and muscles that are involved in those activities. (Remember stress adaptation from Chapter 3?) Similarly, those muscles and joints that aren't utilized as frequently have a tendency to decrease in size (or atrophy) and lose some of their flexibility. This is a natural and highly predictable outcome of the specialization process. However, through engaging in an appropriate strength-training routine, this process can be mitigated or eliminated.

Therefore, a well-designed program can improve joint integrity by improving strength in opposing muscles/muscle groups, aid in maintaining and improving joint flexibility by utilizing full-ROM training and reduce — or reverse — many of the negative side-effects of the "specialization" process. In effect, a well-designed strength-training program can mitigate many of the physical changes associated with aging. Another byproduct of strength training is a lessening of the differences between dominant and non-dominant limbs. In many cases, it becomes difficult to determine dominance by simply looking at the strength of the left and right sides.

A final characteristic that's common to well-designed programs is a total-body approach. While it's widespread practice for the trainee to address specific areas of interest, overemphasis on one area or another should be avoided. Thus, exercises should be chosen to enhance strength in all the major areas of the body. This practice ensures that all the major muscles/muscle groups of the body derive some training benefit and helps minimize the possibility of developing or exacerbating muscular imbalances. Additionally, since the demands of daily activities are nearly impossible to predict, enhanced joint stability and improved muscular strength throughout the body offer a bit of insurance that new activities will be possible and well tolerated.

In theory, all well-designed programs — whether for general fitness or specific to sports preparation — are after the same thing: an overall improvement in the strength of all the muscles of the body combined with specific improvements in the areas of particular interest to the trainee. In practice, this means that there will be certain similarities in exercise selection and a relative resemblance in program organization regardless of personal goals. This is not to imply that every program will look exactly the same. On the contrary, the variety that's inherent in strength training is so vast that the likelihood of one program being exactly the same as another is quite low. Even between individuals with the same training goals, it's highly conceivable that the specifics of exercise choices or training modalities will make the individual routines very different. This allows each trainee a substantial leeway to "fine tune" the program to her particular goals and preferences. Nevertheless, when examining the basic movement patterns and overall design characteristics of the program, there will be many more similarities than differences.

It should be noted that there are a number of individual considerations that could affect some of the specific characteristics of a training program. Orthopedic or other medical concerns, equipment availability and personal preferences in exercise selection or modality could potentially influence the structure of specific routines. However, it's unlikely that any of these considerations would necessitate a complete departure from the recommendations outlined earlier. Even modified routines should consist of dynamic exercises chosen for balance and total-body exposure. With the plethora of possibilities available, it should be feasible to work around any preferential or medical contraindication.

EXERCISE AND MODALITY CHOICES

With these characteristics in mind, the process of developing an appropriate strength-training program comes down to applying them in a manner that addresses individual goals. By default (following the previously outlined parameters) this means that the majority of programming decisions will revolve around selection of specific exercises and modalities for training. Like most other things in life, each exercise and/or modality has inherent advantages and disadvantages associated with its use. The following section will outline some of the strengths and weaknesses of exercise and modality choices.

Once again, each different modality (or equipment choice) offers specific advantages and disadvantages with its use. The best programs incorporate a variety of training modalities in order to compliment the advantages and minimize the disadvantages of the particular modalities that are used. Any program that makes exclusive use of one particular modality or another will always be limited by the disadvantages associated with that choice.

Free Weights

One of the most common modality choices is free weights (barbells and dumbbells). Over the past several years, the use of free weights has become increasing popular in large part due to its prevalence in the media. Unfortunately, there's often the implication that if free weights aren't used, the strength-training program is left wanting. As has been discussed, however, an appropriate training load can be supplied by any number of modality choices and free weights aren't inherently superior to other choices.

One of the main advantages of free weights is their availability. Nearly every facility provides some opportunity to utilize this type of modality. Whether by way of Olympic bars and plates, various dumbbells or fixed-weight barbells, free weights are a mainstay of most modern facilities. Additionally, free weights offer a universal consistency in load — that is, a 10-pound dumbbell in one facility is the same weight as a 10-pound dumbbell in another. This characteristic isn't necessarily true of selectorized (or weight-stacked) machines that are made by different manufacturers. Another significant advantage is the ability to execute a wide variety of exercises. Nearly any movement desired can be done in some form with a barbell or dumbbell.

In terms of advantages, free weights also . . .

- Provide many possible angles of execution
- Allow varied grip widths
- Are well-suited for multi-joint exercises
- Utilize many muscles/muscle groups at once
- Involve a significant amount of stabilizing muscles/muscle groups
- Accommodate users of various sizes
- Are relatively inexpensive

The main drawback of free weights is the fact that exercises are more technical and, therefore, can be more dangerous than other modalities. Because the weight must be controlled in all three dimensions, movements are more complex and require practice to be done with proficiency. The increased technical nature of these movements also necessitates that a more conservative load be used in order to complete the exercise, thereby limiting the trainee in how "aggressively" the musculoskeletal system can be safely loaded. Another significant disadvantage of free weights is that the resistance is provided in a straight line. In simple terms, this means that regardless of whether the movement pattern is linear or rotational, the weight is always acting in a straight line with gravity. This dramatically affects rotational movements — such as the bicep curl — at the beginning and end of their arc. Since a large number of strength-training movements occur in an arcing motion, free weights could provide a sizeable limitation in the completion of specific exercises.

In terms of disadvantages, free weights also . . .

- Offer non-variable resistance throughout the range of motion
- Have a restricted range of motion
- Apply straight-line resistance
- Have a large space requirement
- Make it difficult to isolate individual muscles/muscle groups
- Require a usual weight adjustment of at least five pounds
- Are more difficult to change or "select" weights
- Aren't well-suited to single-limb exercises
- Require gripping of a bar or dumbbell (which isn't well-suited to hand injuries)

Machines

Another very common modality choice involves the use of machines. There are a wide variety of machine ranging from selectorized equipment to plate-loaded equipment to various pneumatic equipment. Over the years, the variety of machine equipment that's available has expanded dramatically. Consumers were once limited to two or three viable manufacturers. Today, there are literally dozens of manufacturers that offer different grades of equipment and variations on machine design. While each of these offer specific advantages and disadvantages as well, they also share certain characteristics in their movements.

The main difference between machines and free weights is that most machines are more restrictive in their movement patterns than are free weights — some more than others. While this *may* mean that there's less activation of "stabilizing" muscles, it most definitely *does* mean that the movements are easier and safer to execute. The less technical nature of these movements also means that a more substantial load can be safely used and, consequently, a greater training stimulus can be provided to the musculature. The other very notable advantage of machines is that resistance can be applied directly to the movement. As a result, movements aren't limited by the straight-line influence of gravity and resistance is possible throughout any number of joint arcs. This allows meaningful resistance to be applied throughout joint ROM, thereby producing more complete development of full-range strength.

One byproduct of this full-range resistance has been the development of variable-resistance machines — a common attribute of many machines that are now available. Simply speaking, this means that the resistance that's applied to a muscle/muscle group can be changed — often by use of an "offset" pulley called a "cam" — in order to provide increased resistance at stronger joint angles and reduced resistance at weaker ones. This variable resistance can facilitate strength development at joint angles that may not have been sufficiently stressed with a straight-line resistance.

In terms of advantages, machines also . . .

- Allow smaller increments of weight adjustment
- Require only enough space to accommodate various stations
- Are user "friendly" for novice trainees
- Can be safely modified to accommodate limited ranges of motion
- Allow easy weight changes
- Are well-suited to "no-hand" workouts
- Are available in most facilities

The primary disadvantage of machines is the limitation of the number of stations available. Since it's unusual to be able to use a machine for more than one exercise, the number of machines that are available determines the number of exercises that can be done. Additionally, most manufacturers offer only a limited number of machines. Therefore, angular variations can be somewhat limited. Another disadvantage is that machines don't fit all people. Extremes in height (tall or short), frame size and limb length aren't always well accommodated by particular machines. And let's face it: Many individuals have anthropometric measurements that fall outside the "norm." Therefore, some machines that are made by a number of manufacturers will simply not fit all users appropriately.

In terms of disadvantages, machines also . . .

- Are relatively expensive
- Are less adjustable to individual limb/torso dimensions
- Don't generally allow varying grip widths
- May not allow single-limb movements

There are many modality choices that fall outside of those previously outlined, ranging from manual-resistance (or partner-resisted) exercises to stretch-cord exercises to bodyweight exercises. If done properly, all of these modalities can provide an adequate training stimulus. In most programs, however, it's likely that free weights and machines will be utilized for the majority of exercises and provide the foundation of the program. The other modalities provide a wealth of opportunity for variety and for performing specific movements that aren't available elsewhere. As with other modality choices, some movements can be done with great effectiveness while others are less desirable. So, some care should be exercised when choosing these modality types.

Once a selection of exercises and modality choices has been identified, programming becomes a matter of putting the exercises into a routine that addresses the goals of the individual trainee. As noted previously, it's very likely that a number of exercises (or movements) will be common to all routines. These include compound (or multi-joint) movements for the legs, chest, shoulders and upper back. Examples might be a leg press, incline press, shoulder press and seated row. These exercises would often be complimented with iso-lation (or single-joint) movements for the same areas of the body. Exercise choices here might include a leg curl, chest fly, side lateral raise and pullover. In combination, the differing movement patterns allow for a greater stimulation of the muscle/muscle group and activation of a greater number of motor units than repetition of the same movement would. By varying the movement pattern, a more complete training stimulus can then be provided and strength developed over a wider range of movement angles. By then adding any number of other movements that are more specific — such as hip ab/adduction, rotator-cuff exercises and wrist curls — additional muscle groups can be trained

One properly performed set of an exercise is sufficient to elicit significant strength gains that are comparable to those seen in a multiple-set routine. (Photo by Michael Bradley)

and the routine can be personalized to the specific goals of the trainee.

In addition to adding specific supplemental movements to individualize the routine, greater emphasis may be placed on the "major" muscles/muscle groups of the body by incorporating more exercises for any of those body areas. The important point to remember is that an overemphasis shouldn't be placed on certain parts of the body so as not to create or exacerbate muscular imbalances across a joint. One guide to use is to make sure that a comparable number of exercises are done for both "sides" of the joint. For example, if three "pushing" movements are done around the shoulders, three "pulling" movements should be done as well. This will help make certain that comparable loading of the muscles occurs and joint stability is maintained.

A basic routine might consist of 10 to 12 exercises for the entire body. (Figure 4.1 details two samples of basic routines.) By taking advantage of different movement angles and modality choices, such a routine could be executed almost indefinitely. A more advanced (and more personalized) routine might consist of 15 to 18 exercises and target more specific areas of particular interest to the trainee. (Figure 4.2 details two samples of advanced routines.) Again, by varying the specific movement selections and modality choices, adequate variety can be maintained to promote long-term success.

Most trainees find that changing routines on a regular basis (such as every few months) provides added opportunity to try different exercises and explore the effectiveness of specific exercises or routines. This variation also offers a needed break in the regularity of the routine that can be psychologically appealing and physically invigorating. As discussed in Chapter 3, there's good reason to vary the stimulus that's applied to the muscles. While it's essential to increase the resistance in an exercise so that an appropriate training load is maintained, this progressive change alone may not be sufficient to avoid the accommodation process. Therefore, it's both reasonable and valuable to incorporate broader changes to the exercise routine as it's executed over time.

The next question that's most often raised when setting up a routine pertains to how many sets of each exercise should be performed in order to produce maximum benefit. It has long been common practice to recommend that three or more sets of each exercise be done in order to adequately train the musculature. Interestingly, that "standard" recommendation has been deemed appropriate regardless of the experience level or performance goals of the trainee. This is another area of strength training where tradition and science don't coincide. While there's still some debate as to how many sets are necessary to maximize results, suffice to say that performing three or more sets of any one exercise is likely to be unnecessary. In fact, one properly performed set of an exercise is sufficient to elicit significant strength gains — gains that are comparable to those seen in a multiple-set routine. In most cases, there's little need to do more than one or two sets of any one exercise. Such an approach would provide the opportunity to do more exercises at different movement angles and facilitate a greater range in muscular development. A multiple-set

BASIC ROUTINE	BASIC ROUTINE (VARIED)
Leg Extension (SM)	Leg Extension (PM)
Leg Curl (SM)	Leg Curl (PM)
Bench Press (BB)	Bench Press (DB)
Chest Flies (DB)	Chest Flies (SM)
Seated Row (PM)	Seated Row (CM)
Pullover (SM)	Pullover (DB)
Overhand Pulldown (SM)	Overhand Pulldown (CM)
Shoulder Press (DB)	Shoulder Press (BB)
Side Lateral Raise (DB)	Side Lateral Raise (SM)
Bicep Curl (SM)	Bicep Curl (DB)
Tricep Extension (SM)	Tricep Extension (PM)

FIGURE 4.1: TWO SAMPLE BASIC ROUTINES
Note: BB – barbell; CM – cable machine; DB – dumbbell; PM – plate-loaded machine; SM – selectorized machine

approach requires repetition of the same movement pattern over and over again, activating and eventually overtraining the exact same muscle fibers. By utilizing a variety of exercises and movement patterns, more muscle fibers are activated and stimulated and more complete development is possible.

Rather than concentrating on how many sets of each exercise should be done, a better question might relate to how many sets can be effectively done for any muscle/muscle group during a single training session. Again, a traditional approach might recommend a volume of 12, 15 or even 20 sets per body part. However, again, there's no scientific research to support this assertion. In order to support such an exorbitant expenditure of time and effort, such a routine would need to produce results far beyond those attained through more time-efficient means. This is simply not the case. (Imagine doing 20 sets per body part while exercising 4 body parts per day for a total of 80 sets of exercise. Who has an extra two hours to spend at the gym?) The truth is that there's no research to indicate that there's any increased benefit to doing more than six to eight sets for any body part. More likely, the benefit lies in performing fewer total sets executed with greater effort thereby allowing greater stimulation of the exercised muscles/muscle groups and a greater range of strength improvement (through the use of different movements). Essentially, this means that choosing two or three exercises and performing one or two intense sets each would provide all of the stimulation that's necessary to produce maximum improvements in strength without the risk of doing more work than which the body can recover.

Recovery Time

As alluded in the last paragraph, another factor that significantly contributes to the overall success of any training program lies in the recovery time allowed between sessions. Unlike skill acquisition — which takes place at the time of the practice — systemic improvements in strength (and other physi-ological variables) occur subsequent to the application of the stimulus thereby necessitating appropriate and adequate recovery from the stimulus. In essence, the adaptation response that facilitates improvements in strength is activated during training while the response itself occurs during the recovery period. This can be illustrated very effectively in the following two examples. One: Over the course of a practice session on the tennis court, the skills necessary to return a ball with a backhand can be dramatically improved and more balls kept in play. Therefore, specific skills are improved at the time of the practice. Two: When performing the bench press during a training session in the weight room, the muscles involved in the movement become fatigued and will even-tually reach a point of being incapable of overcoming the resistance applied. The muscles don't become stronger and more capable during the exercise. There-fore, the strength improvements that occur over time don't take place at the time of the "practice."

While there are a myriad of factors that influence the body's ability to recover — including age, training status, nutritional status and other lifestyle factors — the main contributor is the amount of rest that's provided between training sessions.

ADVANCED ROUTINE	ADVANCED ROUTINE (VARIED)
Leg Press (PM)	Squat (BB)
Leg Extension (SM)	Leg Extension (PM)
Leg Curl (SM)	Leg Curl (PM)
Lunge (DB)	Lunge (BB)
Hip Adduction (SM)	Hip Adduction (CM)
Hip Abduction (SM)	Hip Abduction (CM)
Bench Press (BB)	Chest Press (PM)
Chest Flies (DB)	Chest Flies (SM)
Dip (BW)	Dip (BW)
Seated Row (PM)	Seated Row (CM)
Pullover (SM)	Pullover (PM)
Overhand Pulldown (SM)	Overhand Pulldown (PM)
Chin-up (BW)	Chin-up (BW)
Shoulder Press (DB)	Shoulder Press (SM)
Side Lateral Raise (DB)	Side Lateral Raise (SM)
Wrist Curl (DB)	Gripper (PM)
Bicep Curl (SM)	Bicep Curl (PM)
Tricep Extension (SM)	Tricep Extension (CM)

FIGURE 4.2: TWO SAMPLE ADVANCED ROUTINES
Note: BB – barbell; BW – bodyweight; CM – cable machine; DB – dumbbell; PM – plate-loaded machine; SM – selectorized machine

5

The Repetition: The Foundation of Strength Training

Luke Carlson, B.S.

What's the most important aspect of a strength-training program? If you were to randomly ask this question to some coaches, athletes, sportsmedical practitioners and exercise scientists, there'd be no shortage of opinions and recommendations. Here's a sampling of what you might expect to find:

- A basketball coach prefers to use free weights rather than machines because she believes that it will be better for improving the muscular strength of her players.

- A distance runner does more than 20 repetitions per set because she believes that it will develop her muscular endurance.

- An athletic trainer prescribes 3 sets of 10 repetitions for all athletes, including those who are rehabilitating injuries.

- An author of a textbook on exercise physiology recommends the use of low repetitions with heavy weight for strength development and high repetitions with light weight for endurance development.

Based upon these opinions, you'd likely conclude that the most important aspect of a strength-training program revolves around set/rep schemes and equipment preferences. It's no wonder, then, that these opinions reflect the current practices of exercise prescription as it pertains to a variety of athletes who are attempting to prepare for a variety of athletic endeavors. Simply stated, this shows what most individuals think are important when planning and implementing a strength-training program.

Unfortunately and surprisingly, these recommendations don't represent — or even begin to address — what's actually important in a strength-training program. In fact, most recommendations fail to even mention the foundation of all strength-training programs: the repetition.

This chapter will (1) explain why the repetition is the foundation of strength-training programs; (2) discuss the traditional performance of repetitions and examine its potential limitations; and (3) describe guidelines for proper performance of repetitions and provide sample repetition protocols that may be implemented into any strength-training program.

THE FOUNDATION OF STRENGTH-TRAINING PROGRAMS

The repetition — which can be defined as the act of moving one time through a range of motion during a particular exercise — is truly the foundation of all strength-training programs. Prescriptions that call for set/rep schemes [sets x repetitions] of 3x10, 2x20 or 5x5 or stipulate the use of free weights are meaningless recommendations unless the style of repetition performance is understood. But rarely, if ever, will you hear individuals offer specific advice as to the style in which repetitions should be performed. Instead, discussions that take place across the country in clinics/seminars, lecture halls/classrooms for students in exercise science, athletic arenas, training rooms and weight rooms focus on the number of sets and repetitions to be performed, the preference of equipment, the order of exercises and other components of the strength-training program that are far less important than the actual performance of the repetition. And when inquiring about other strength-training programs, questions are asked that target the aforementioned components. But these are the wrong questions. In order to better understand how to implement any strength-training program, the pertinent question is this: How are repetitions performed?

THE STIMULUS FOR STRENGTH IMPROVEMENT

The importance of the repetition is based upon the actual stimulus for gains in strength and the actual goal of a strength-training program. The stimulus for strength improvement — or any physiological adaptation that results from strength training — is the intensity of effort. Thus, repetitions should be performed in such a manner that makes the exercise as intense — or as difficult — as possible.

The present recommendations and practices of the vast majority of those involved in strength training would lead one to conclude that myriad other workout factors — including the choice of equipment (bias toward either free weights or machines) and the training volume (the number of sets and repetitions to be performed) — are the factors that determine the success or failure of a strength-training program. However, the preponderance of scientific research related to these topics suggests that these factors pale in comparison with the importance of training intensity. For example, a recent review of the scientific literature that examined the effectiveness of multiple-set and single-set strength-training programs found that performing multiple sets aren't more effective for the development of muscular size (hypertrophy) and strength (Carpinelli and Otto 1998). In reality, muscular size and strength can be improved by different numbers of sets and repetitions. Research has also shown that free weights aren't more effective than machines for the development of muscular size and strength.

Based on these findings, the time has come for coaches, athletes, sportsmedical practitioners and exercise scientists to quit wasting time by sharing or searching for set/rep schemes that will elicit superior results and stop perpetuating the myth that free weights are superior to machines. Instead, the technical aspects of the strength-training program should focus on making strength training more intense.

GOAL OF STRENGTH TRAINING

The immediate goal of a strength-training exercise is to create tension within a muscle over a given period of time, which will eventually lead to muscular fatigue. (This is also known as "overload.") Therefore, repetitions must be performed in a manner that keeps a load on a muscle, eventually leading to fatigue.

Strength training — as it pertains to the development of athletic performance potential — is a means to an end, not an end in itself. In practice, this means that actually moving a given amount of weight up and down a certain number of times has nothing to do with actually developing strength. Creating tension within a muscle thereby caus-

Factors such as exercise volume, type of resistance and exercise selection aren't as important as exercise intensity. Repetitions should be performed in such a manner that they make the exercise as intense as possible. (Photo by Sandy Ryan)

ing it to fatigue should be the goal, not simply moving a given amount of weight from point A to point B.

When performing repetitions, you should search for ways to increase the load on a targeted muscular structure, not ways to decrease it. And the ways that you select should be efficient and safe.

DEVELOPING THE FOUNDATION

Knowing that intensity is the stimulus for gains in strength and that the immediate goal of strength training is to develop tension in order to produce muscular fatigue, it's shocking that so many coaches and strength "experts" rarely, if ever, discuss these points; but, rather, they emphasize exercise volume, equipment selection and so on. The style of repetition performance should be considered before all other factors in a strength-training program. When coaches and other practitioners implement strength-training programs, they should begin by instructing proper repetition performance. Whatever style of repetition performance is chosen, individuals who supervise the training must spend their time and energy coaching this particular style. Moreover, athletes should be evaluated and rewarded based upon their adherence to the prescribed style of repetition performance.

TRADITIONAL PERFORMANCE OF REPETITIONS

Often, the traditional performance of repetitions doesn't reflect the importance of this critical element of the strength-training program. Few coaches or other practitioners — if any — specify a recommended way of performing repetitions when they design and implement strength-training programs.

Two factors affect the traditional performance of repetitions. The lack of delineation as to how a repetition should be performed results in the first fac-

tor: a lack of understanding that how a repetition is performed is of any importance. Stated otherwise, because athletes rarely hear differently, they perform
repetitions however they choose . . . and they typically choose to perform repetitions haphazardly with little or no regard for efficiency and safety. Those
who do suggest a speed of movement for repetitions vary greatly in their recommendations, which result in confusion.

The second factor that affects the traditional performance of repetitions is
the well-intended but misconceived notion that lifting a weight quickly will
make an athlete faster or more explosive. This misconception, although widely
practiced, isn't supported by science. Many coaches and exercise practitioners
purport that moving a weight with fast speeds of movement recruits more fast-
twitch muscle fibers (the fibers that are responsible for explosive movements
in an athletic context). However, a muscle's force-velocity relationship illustrates that as the concentric contraction speed becomes slower, the tension produced by the muscle increases; and as the concentric speed becomes faster, the
tension produced by the muscle decreases.

The truth is that motor units and their accompanying muscle fibers are
recruited in a systematic fashion according to the size of the motor unit and
dictated by the force requirements of an activity. Therefore, fast-twitch muscle
fibers can be recruited at very slow speeds of movement. Here's how: To illustrate the process of fiber recruitment, consider an athlete who performs a set of
12 repetitions on an exercise with a repetition speed that involves a two-second
concentric contraction, a one-second mid-range pause and a four-second eccentric contraction. In this set, the athlete attempts a 13th repetition but she is
unable to complete it. During the first few repetitions, the force requirements
of the exercise are relatively low and, consequently, she can perform the repeti-

tions fairly easily (that is, with relatively low
effort). During these repetitions, smaller
motor units that innervate Type I (slow-
twitch) muscle fibers are recruited. As more
repetitions are performed and continuous
tension is produced in the muscle thus leading to fatigue, larger motor units that innervate Type II (fast-twitch) muscle fibers are
recruited. Because the result of more muscular tension is greater fiber recruitment, athletes must do everything possible to keep the
load on the targeted muscle. Fast movements, however, incorporate an excessive
amount of momentum and, therefore, minimize muscular tension and subsequent fiber
recruitment.

**Constantly coaching perfect
repetition performance is a
central role of the strength coach,
personal trainer or training
partner. (Photo by Sandy Ryan)**

GUIDELINES FOR REPETITION PERFORMANCE

As stated earlier, intensity is the stimulus for increasing strength. Further, the primary and immediate goal of strength training is to fatigue a targeted muscle by exposing it to a meaningful load over a period of time. All guidelines of repetition performance must contribute to the outcome of creating muscular tension and in doing so make an exercise more intense. The following are six guidelines for the performance of repetitions:

1. Raise the resistance (perform the concentric movement) in a controlled manner, thus minimizing momentum.

Performing a controlled concentric contraction keeps a constant load on a muscle which leads to fatigue and the recruitment of more glycolytic, fast-twitch muscle fibers (Kreighbaum and Barthels 1996). According to the force-velocity relationship for muscle, if the velocity of shortening is slow, the tension that can be developed is large; and if the velocity of shortening is fast, the tension that can be developed is small (Kreighbaum and Barthels 1996). Because the goal of strength training is to create tension within a muscle and eventually fatigue it, athletes should be coached to lift the resistance slowly. In a study comparing slow-speed and standard-speed concentric-phase repetitions, subjects who trained with slow speeds had 50% greater gains in strength than subjects who trained with standard speeds (Westcott and Ramsden 2001). When a weight is raised quickly, a greater amount of momentum is incorporated which decreases the load on the targeted muscle. In some instances, the resistance may actually be moving by itself. In order to efficiently recruit and fatigue muscle fibers, tension must be continuous. This guideline is particularly important at the beginning of the set when the targeted musculature is fresh and repetitions are more easily performed. Because fatigue hasn't set in, a trainee is capable of moving the weight very quickly or "throwing" it. Throwing the weight greatly reduces the efficiency of the set (as described previously) and is dangerous due to excessive force encountered by the muscles and connective tissues during the acceleration phase. As the set nears momentary muscular fatigue, the lifter should be coached to attempt to lift the weight as quickly as possible. But because the exercising muscles are fatigued, the trainee is unable to lift the weight quickly. Although the trainee may *attempt* to lift the weight quickly, the actual outward display of movement of the resistance is quite slow. However, it's the *intent* to move the weight quickly or "explosively" that develops explosiveness, not the actual outward display of fast movement (Young and Bilby 1993).

2. Pause momentarily in the contracted (mid-range) position.

A pause in the contracted position demonstrates that the repetition speed is controlled and keeps the load on the targeted muscle. In addition, a distinct pause in the contracted position ensures that momentum didn't play a significant role in raising the resistance. Keep in mind that this guideline doesn't apply to multi-joint "pushing" movements such as the bench press and leg press. In these exercises, a pause would serve as a rest or a period in which the muscle is unloaded.

3. Change directions in a slow, smooth manner without incorporating an excessive amount of momentum.

Specific attention must be paid to changes of direction, from concentric to eccentric and eccentric to concentric; it's during these directional changes that excessive momentum is frequently incorporated, thereby minimizing muscle tension and muscle-fiber recruitment. The rapid unloading and loading of the joints and musculature is an inefficient means of fiber recruitment and may also lead to injury as a result of increased force.

4. Lower the resistance (perform the eccentric movement) in a slow and controlled fashion.

The same muscles that are used to raise a weight are also used to lower it. In order to keep a load on these muscles, this phase of the repetition mustn't be performed rapidly so that the weight drops or falls. Because eccentric (or negative) strength is estimated to be roughly 40% greater than concentric (or positive) strength, the lowering portion of a repetition should be approximately twice as slow as the raising portion. Research indicates that eccentric contractions produce greater tension than concentric or isometric contractions (Kreighbaum and Barthels 1996). For this reason, special attention should be paid to lower the resistance in a slow manner.

5. Move through the greatest possible range of motion that safety allows.

Performing repetitions through a full range of motion ensures that the entire muscle is worked. Generally, the greater the range of motion, the greater potential for gains in strength and protection from injury. Strength training that involves a full range of motion may also improve a joint's functional range of motion.

6. Avoid improving leverage by altering body position.

The human body will instinctively take the path of least resistance. Naturally, then, trainees will do anything possible to make a repetition easier, oftentimes while completely unaware that they're doing so. This usually includes shifting or changing body position in order to produce an improvement in leverage. Examples of this are arching the back on the bench press and raising the buttocks off the seat on the leg press.

REPETITION REPLICATION/REPRODUCTION

Essentially, every repetition should look identical to the first repetition. The only difference may be a slower concentric speed of movement toward the latter portion of the set because fatigue has set in and fast movement is momentarily impossible. Besides concentric speed of movement, other factors such as posture, eccentric speed of movement and range of motion should be the same on every single repetition. The effort to perform repetitions that are identical to the first repetition that's done has been coined "repetition replication" or "repetition reproduction." As soon as this repetition replication fails to exist, the repetition should no longer be "counted" as an acceptable or recordable repetition. One of the most challenging aspects of performing strength-training exercises is putting forth the high level of effort and concentration that's necessary to keep repetition performance perfect as momentary strength levels decrease and fatigue and physical discomfort increase. Herein lies a fundamental challenge to the strength coach or practitioner.

REPETITION PROTOCOLS

As long as all of the previous repetition guidelines are followed, tension will be created, a sufficient level of muscular fatigue will develop and, as a result, a high level of intensity and concurrent maximal muscular benefits will be achieved. To date, the perfect or ideal repetition speed is unknown. Instead, implementation of a variety of repetition performance protocols — all of which adhere to the six guidelines for repetition-performance — creates variety in the strength-training program while ensuring safe, efficient and effective training. Table 5.1 gives examples of repetition protocols that can be implemented into the strength-training program designed for the female athlete.

Maximal results can be achieved using any form of resistance. (Photo by Sandy Ryan)

PROTOCOL	CONCENTRIC SPEED	MID-RANGE PAUSE	ECCENTRIC SPEED	REP RANGE
Standard	2	1	4	8 - 20
Ten-Ten	10	1	10	3 - 5
Fab 5	5	5	5	4 - 7
Crazy 8	2	8	4	4 - 7
Negative-Accentuated	2	1	10	6 - 8

TABLE 5.1: REPETITION PROTOCOLS
Note: The numbers listed under concentric speed, mid-range pause and eccentric speed are seconds.

REFERENCES

Bradley, M. 1999. The repetition. In *Maximize your training: insights from leading strength and fitness professionals*, ed. M. Brzycki, 181-188. New York, NY: McGraw-Hill/Contemporary.

Carpinelli, R. N., and R. M. Otto. 1998. Strength training. Single versus multiple sets. *Sports Medicine* 6 (2): 73-84.

Kreighbaum, E., and K. M. Barthels. 1996. *Biomechanics: a qualitative approach for studying human movement. 4th ed.* Boston, MA: Allyn and Bacon, Inc.

McGuff, M. D. 1999. The dose-response relationship of exercise. In *Maximize your training: insights from leading strength and fitness professionals*, ed. M. Brzycki, 151-159. New York, NY: McGraw-Hill/Contemporary.

Young, W. B., and G. E. Bilby. 1993. The effect of voluntary effort to influence speed of contraction on strength, muscular power, and hypertrophy development. *Journal of Strength and Conditioning Research* 7 (3): 172-178.

Westcott, W. L., and S. F. Ramsden. 2001. *Specialized strength training.* Monterey, CA: Exercise Science Publishers.

6

Strength Training for the Multi-Sport Athlete

Luke Carlson, B.S.

The trend toward sport specialization in middle school and high school athletics has propelled coaches and athletes to search for specialized or sport - specific strength-training programs. Most coaches at the middle school, high school and collegiate levels, however, train teams that are comprised largely of multi-sport athletes — athletes who choose not to specialize in one sport but, instead, compete and "specialize" in more than one sport. Thus, the strength coach's responsibility is to design and implement a strength-training program that will enhance an athlete's ability to perform optimally in numerous sports. The strength coach or any individual interested in enhancing the performance of the female athlete should consider the following two basic questions:

1. Do individual sports require "sport-specific" strength-training programs?

2. What type of strength-training program should a multi-sport athlete perform?

In an attempt to answer these two questions, this chapter will (1) state the three primary goals of a strength-training program that are designed to meet the demands of the multi-sport athlete and subdivisions of these goals; (2) describe the three basic guidelines of a strength-training prescription; and (3) delineate a proper approach to strength training for the multi-sport athlete.

GOALS OF THE STRENGTH-TRAINING PROGRAM

Before a successful strength-training program can be designed, the goals of the strength-training program — which are a reflection of the demands placed on the multi-sport athlete — must first be identified.

In an attempt to meet the demands of particular sports, many coaches and athletes initially conclude that whatever movements which are performed most frequently in a particular sport must also be trained in the weight room with the greatest emphasis. This practice is usually termed "sport-specific" strength training. Myriad examples of this approach exist including the shot putter who emphasizes the incline bench press; the track and cross-country runners who move their arms as if running while holding dumbbells; and the high jumpers and basketball and volleyball players who stress calf training. The reasoning that underlies this approach assumes that if a particular group of muscles is required to perform the athletic skill, a strength-training exercise that's intended to enhance that skill must use the same muscles and "look" the same in terms of limb motion. But not only does this reasoning fail to comprehensively address the athlete's needs, it has also been proven to be faulty.

When designing and implementing a comprehensive strength-training program, there are three general and primary goals. These goals are applicable to strength-training programs that have been dubbed "sport-specific" as well as those designed to meet the needs of multi-sport athletes. Furthermore, these goals should be achieved regardless of the sport performance that the strength-training program is designed to enhance. A strength-training program that fulfills only one or two of these goals will not be as beneficial to the athlete as a program that fulfills all three goals. Many specific goals can be categorized under these general goals. The three primary goals are:

1. Reduce the likelihood and severity of injury.

Keeping athletes healthy and on the field of play is imperative to the success of a team throughout the competitive season and, particularly, during the post-season. Thus, the primary goal of all strength-training programs designed for athletes — regardless of the sport for which the strength-training program is designed — should be injury prevention. The application of this goal is two-fold: one, prevent/decrease the severity of injuries that occur in athletic practices and competitions; and two, eliminate injuries that occur in the weight room.

With respect to the first part of this goal, it follows that the first demand of the multi-sport athlete that must be considered is the potential sites for injury. A strength-training program must emphasize areas or muscular structures that are prone to injury as a result of competing in any number of athletic endeavors. Exercises should be selected to *prehabilitate* these injury-susceptible areas. If coaches — with the aide of sportsmedical professionals — investigated all of the potential and most frequently injured areas of the multi-sport athlete that would require strength training, they'd conclude that all areas of the body are subject to injury and therefore, all parts of the body must be strengthened with great importance placed on each and every area. Understanding this concept dictates the necessity of a total-body training prescription.

An injury occurs when a force imposed on a body part exceeds the tensile limits or "breaking strength" of the body part (such as muscle, connective tissues and bone). If the breaking strength of the body part is greater than the encountered forces, the injury will not occur (Peterson 1982). Although it's impossible to eliminate or avoid the forces that are encountered during athletic competition, strength training will increase the maximum tensile strength of these body parts, thereby reducing the likelihood of strains, sprains and other injuries that are associated with physical activity. Proper strength training will also improve the ability of the muscle to recover more quickly from the physical stresses that result from practices and games, enhance bone mineral density and increase the strength of connective tissues (Peterson and Bryant 1995).

The second part of the injury-prevention goal consists of eliminating injuries that occur in the weight room. Many coaches and athletes assume that in order to prepare for violent and potentially dangerous sports, it's necessary to perform violent and potentially dangerous exercises — even if the result is an occasional injury. Performing potentially dangerous exercises in the weight room in order to prepare for potentially dangerous activities in sports is like banging your head against the wall to prepare for a concussion (Mannie 1994). Any injury that happens in the weight room is unacceptable and shouldn't be tolerated by administrators, coaches or athletes. The intent of a strength-training program is to prevent injury and stimulate physiological changes that will lead to enhanced performance potential. Exposing an athlete to potential risk for injury in the weight room is contrary to these intentions. Certain exercises that are frequently implemented have a high degree of risk and needn't be performed in order to produce maximum results. These exercises — which usually involve relatively fast speeds of movement — include the power clean, hang clean, snatch and other so-called "quick lifts."

Understanding the etiology of injury that's associated with these exercises requires a brief examination of physics. The equation to determine force is as follows: Force = Mass x Acceleration. As stated earlier, an injury occurs when an external or internal force exceeds the tensile strength of a body part. In this equation, "mass" refers to the weight that's lifted. The acceleration component is increased when that mass — the weight that's lifted — is moved at a faster speed. This results in an increased force placed on the joints, connective tissues and muscles. The faster the weight is lifted (the greater the acceleration), the greater the force. In order to minimize these forces and lessen the potential for injury, slower speeds of movement — consisting of a smaller acceleration component — should be performed. Recommending that an athlete move at a fast or explosive speed of movement while strength training is suggesting musculoskeletal trauma (Brzycki 1995).

2. Stimulate positive physiological adaptations.

A properly designed strength-training program should stimulate copious physiological adaptations, all of which will enhance an athlete's performance potential. This goal is an all-encompassing one that includes the many benefits expected from a strength-training program. Physiological changes that result from a proper strength-training regimen include an improvement in strength and the ability of the musculoskeletal system to produce force; improved power/explosion capacity; achievement and maintenance of a functional range of joint motion; and an improvement in body composition. Exercises and the manner, order and frequency that these exercises are performed should be intended specifically to stimulate positive physiological adaptations. This goal may seem so obvious that it could be omitted and simply assumed. However, an evaluation of current strength-training practices that are implemented at all levels of athletics would reveal that many coaches and athletes are interested primarily in matters of little or no importance such as how much weight an athlete can lift for a one-repetition maximum or how many times a specific weight can be moved up and down. The focus isn't usually on stimulating the *development* of strength (a physiological adaptation) but, instead, the outward *demonstration* of strength.

This chapter questions the assertion of many coaches, athletes and fitness professionals who allege that the aforementioned qualities — namely, muscular strength/endurance, power, flexibility and body composition — must be developed separately by utilizing separate strength-training programs that purportedly specialize in a particular physiological enhancement. Regardless of the method that's used, the enhancement of these physiological characteristics should be the result of strength training.

3. Improve confidence and mental toughness.

A somewhat less tangible yet extremely valuable byproduct of proper strength training is the improved confidence and mental toughness of the athletes as well as the team. An aggressive approach to strength training will expand an athlete's tolerance for physical discomfort. Theoretically, an athlete

will compete harder because she has "invested" more in her training. The pain and conflict experienced during game-time situations should be bearable since the athlete has already endured tough times and stressful situations — both physiological and psychological. Furthermore, activities and exercises should be performed so that they expand the tolerance for physical discomfort and, in doing so, increase an athlete's confidence and mental toughness.

Intense strength training will not only result in physical improvements but can also enhance confidence and mental toughness. (Photo by Sandy Ryan)

By understanding these three general goals, a coach or an exercise specialist can design the strength-training program for the multi-sport athlete.

GUIDELINES FOR THE STRENGTH-TRAINING PRESCRIPTION

A survey of strength-training programs that are implemented by strength coaches at the high school, college and professional levels as well as those implemented by exercise specialists in health clubs and private-training facilities would produce a tremendously wide array of strength-training philosophies, routines, set/rep schemes and strength-training jargon. The enormity of current strength-training practices can leave coaches and athletes baffled as they attempt to adopt or design a strength-training program that will fit individual and team needs.

When it comes to evaluating the plethora of strength-training information available, where does one start? The guidelines for safety, efficiency and effectiveness comprise a simple but completely comprehensive framework for understanding and designing strength-training programs. When evaluating a component of a strength-training program — whether it's an exercise, a type of equipment or a set/rep scheme — these three guidelines can be used as a measuring stick or as "strainers" (Ritz 2002) through which all components of the strength-training program must pass.

1. Safety

All activities in the strength-training program must be performed in the safest manner possible. This concept is detailed in the previous discussion of injury prevention. If a coach considered every possible strength-training exercise, repetition-performance style, set/rep scheme, intensity level, type of equipment and other variables in the strength-training program and put them into the safety "strainer," only a portion would pass through. Other exercises, repetition-performance styles and so on wouldn't pass through the "strainer" due to the inherent potential risk for acute or chronic injury. A coach or exercise specialist must treat the safety "strainer" as the first guideline that should be considered when designing the strength-training program for the multi-sport athlete.

2. Efficiency

The second guideline or "strainer" that all strength-training program variables must pass through is the efficiency "strainer." Efficiency, in this instance, can be defined as "the ability of the strength-training program variable to stimulate a desired response in the shortest amount of time possible while adhering to the biomechanics of the human body." A massive number of exercises, set/rep schemes and so on pass through the safety "strainer." Therefore, the efficiency of an exercise is the next major factor that determines whether or not a component should be included in the strength-training program.

3. Effectiveness

If the strength-training program variable passes through the safety and efficiency "strainers," it can be deemed effective provided that the level of intensity is high and a system of progressive overload is implemented. It's really that simple.

SAFE, EFFICENT AND EFFECTIVE GUIDELINES: AN EXAMPLE

Having to select a multi-joint exercise to train the buttocks and legs illustrates the decision-making process using the safe, efficient and effective guidelines. First, the anatomical functions of these muscles must be understood. The buttocks and legs produce extension at the hips and knees. Thus, any exercise that involves both of these functions should be considered. A list of these exercises would include the power clean, barbell squat and leg press. Next, the safest of all these exercises should be selected. This safety "strainer" eliminates the power clean and barbell squat. Although both of these exercises require hip and knee extension, they carry an inherently high risk for acute and chronic injury due to the excessive forces that occur during the acceleration phase in the power clean and the vertical compression of the spinal column in the barbell squat. So the safest option that includes hip and knee extension should be selected: the leg press.

The merit of exercises that are intended to strengthen the buttocks and legs can also be evaluated using the efficiency "strainer." If the primary function of the muscles of the buttocks and legs is extension, an exercise must be chosen that requires an athlete to perform these movements in an efficient manner. Remember that intensity is the stimulus for gains in strength. Exercises should be selected that allow the targeted muscles — in this case, the buttocks and legs — to be trained with a very high level of intensity. The barbell squat, in this instance, isn't an efficient exercise for the target muscles because the low-back muscles fatigue before the muscles that cause hip and knee extension fatigue. For this reason, the barbell squat is an inefficient exercise to strengthen the buttocks and legs. The power clean suffers similar efficiency limitations due to the "weak link" of the musculature of the hands and arms and the inherent inefficiency of the performance speed that's required for this exercise.

The effective "strainer" is a byproduct of the safe and efficient "strainers." If an exercise is safe and efficient, it will be effective provided that the level of intensity is high and a system of progressive overload is implemented.

THE PROPER APPROACH TO STRENGTH TRAINING

Coaches and athletes from all sports must understand that there's truly no such thing as "sport-specific" strength training. Muscles are responsible for particular functions. When contracted, for example, some muscles cause extension while others cause flexion; some muscles cause abduction while others cause adduction. Regardless of the sport, a given muscle performs the same function. For instance, the gluteus maximus causes extension at the hip in a basketball player as well as a gymnast. Strengthening muscles allows for greater force to be produced during athletic movements. Combined with skill training, this increased potential to produce force will result in improved power. Because virtually all sports require the activation of all muscles and all body structures are subject to injury, all muscles must be trained with great emphasis.

The ultimate strength-training program for a basketball player is, for the most part, the same as the ultimate strength-training program for a gymnast. Professionals and organizations that claim otherwise usually do so in order to market a product to coaches and athletes of a particular sport. Needless to say, they're often motivated by financial reasons.

FOUNDATIONS OF THE STRENGTH WORKOUT

The following components comprise a researched, systematic and comprehensive approach to strength training for the multi-sport athlete. Adherence to the following 10 principles will result in productive strength training for athletes who participate in any of a multitude of sports. Each of the 10 components is outlined in detail.

1. Unify the program.

A unified strength-training program is one that has the support and total participation of all sport coaches and athletes. Confusion and doubt exists in the minds of athletes if coaches from different sports recommend different styles of strength training. For example, one coach may recommend fast speeds of movement while another may recommend slow speeds of movement. The athlete is torn between the two suggestions and is confused as to what approach will produce superior results. The athlete also questions the competency of both coaches and, as a result, may be less motivated to make a commitment to the strength-training program and sport participation in general.

2. Use appropriate intensity.

Besides genetics, an athlete's level of intensity is the most important factor that influences her response to strength training. The concept of intensity is synonymous with overload and the Overload Principle, which states that a system must be stressed beyond its present capacity in order to stimulate an adaptive response. The preponderance of scientific research indicates that a high level of intensity — not set/rep schemes — is the stimulus for maximal gains in strength (Carpinelli and Otto 1998). A high level of intensity will stimulate positive morphological improvements including muscular hypertrophy and concurrent improvements in the ability to generate force.

Intensity is the most important controllable factor in an athlete's response to a strength-training program. (Photo by Sandy Ryan)

The entire strength-training program must revolve around putting forth a high level of intensity. This level of intensity is necessary in order to recruit as many muscle fibers as possible. To ensure a high level of intensity and corresponding maximal recruitment of muscle fibers, athletes should train to the point of momentary muscular fatigue. This is the point where an athlete can no longer perform a repetition with perfect form. Essentially, athletes should be coached to perform as many repetitions as possible, which means that an athlete should never terminate a set when the prescribed number of repetitions is achieved or when an exercise becomes uncomfortable. When an athlete can no longer perform another repetition, she must attempt a partial repetition (such as a half or a quarter). When even an inch of movement is no longer possible, the athlete has reached momentary muscular fatigue. This is the type of effort that recruits a maximal number of muscle fibers and elicits optimal physical and mental adaptations. Additional sets or workout volume will not make up for a lack of intensity.

3. Apply progressive overload.

Strength training must not only be intense but must also be progressive. Every workout, on every exercise, the lifter must try to either increase the amount of resistance lifted or the number of repetitions performed. The attempt to improve either resistance or repetitions is known as a system of double progression. The following example illustrates the impact of progression: Suppose that a freshman athlete does 12 repetitions with 45 pounds in the barbell bench press. If she adds only one pound to the bar each week — an amount that appears minuscule — by her senior year, she would be performing 12 repetitions with an astonishing 201 pounds! Although this amount of improvement is unlikely, the example illustrates the power of progression and the continual attempt to add more weight to an exercise.

4. Do perfect repetitions.

Repetitions are truly the foundation of any strength-training program. The goal of performing proper repetitions is to create tension within a muscle. Perfect repetitions can be achieved through adherence to the following guidelines (which are explained in greater detail in Chapter 5):

- Raise the resistance in a controlled manner, thus minimizing momentum.
- Pause momentarily in the contracted position.
- Change directions in a slow, smooth manner without incorporating an excessive amount of momentum.
- Lower the resistance in a slow and controlled fashion.
- Move through the greatest possible range of motion that safety allows.
- Avoid improving leverage by altering body position.

Coaches would be wise to exert time and energy to teaching and reinforcing the performance of proper repetitions.

5. Perform brief and infrequent training.

The time/intensity continuum dictates that there's probably no such thing as truly hard *and* long work (Peterson 1982). As the level of intensity increases, the length of the activity must decrease. Because a high level of intensity is the stimulus for strength/power gains, brevity is a necessity.

Since high-intensity exercise is so demanding on the physiological systems of the body, only small amounts can be tolerated. Only a limited amount of exercises can be performed in a workout and only a limited amount of workouts can be performed in a week. An excessive amount of volume will cause overtraining which will lead to little or no results. Because of these facts, training sessions should last 20 - 30 minutes and should be performed only two or three times per week.

All strength-training workouts designed for the multi-sport athlete (or any athlete) should operate according to the dose-response relationship of exercise

(McGuff 1999). An athlete should perform the minimum amount of exercise that will stimulate the desired response (namely, gains in strength/power). Contrary to popular belief, more isn't better when it comes to exercise. Conveniently, a strength-training approach that yields optimal results also fits into the busy schedules — especially the in-season schedules — of multi-sport athlete.

6. Do total-body training.

Every athlete should train her entire body with equal emphasis placed on all exercises and muscular structures. In sharp contrast to current thinking, there's really no such thing as specific "core" and "auxiliary" exercises. Likewise, specific exercises aren't more important for specific athletes in specific sports. Athletic performance in all sports requires the muscular system to work synergistically. Thus, all muscular structures must be developed maximally.

In order to illustrate this point, an example that was used earlier will be revisited. Coaches who work with throwing athletes — including baseball players, quarterbacks and throwers in field events — often perform exercises that emphasize the chest and anterior portion of the shoulder, muscles that certainly contribute to the throwing motion. What's frequently overlooked, however, is that posterior muscles — such as the posterior deltoid and external rotators — act to decelerate the arm during the throwing motion. If an athlete fails to train these muscles — which is often the case — the deceleration phase will have to be initiated earlier which means that less time will be spent in the acceleration phase, resulting in a decrease in velocity. This example illustrates the importance of strengthening all muscular structures.

Also remember that the primary purpose of strength training is to decrease the potential for injury. Because all muscular structures and the joints upon which they act are subject to injury, all muscular structures must be strengthened in order to reduce the risk.

7. Incorporate variety.

Variety allows athletes to avoid mental and physical boredom and will often make their training experience more challenging and enjoyable. Variety can be achieved by using the following methods:

- Implementing all forms of resistance. This includes free weights, machines and manual resistance — all of which are effective if used properly.
- Modifying the repetition speed. A standard repetition speed of a two-second concentric contraction, a one-second mid-range pause and a four-second eccentric contraction is often recommended. However, there are many different protocols for repetition speed. An example of this is the 10/1/10 protocol in which the weight is raised in 10 seconds, held in a mid-range pause for one second and lowered in 10 seconds. Slowing down the speed in which a repetition is performed is an effective method for increasing muscular tension and the subsequent recruitment of muscle fibers.

- Changing the number of repetitions. Varying the ranges from 3 - 20 (which is often determined by the repetition speed) exposes athletes to a variety of metabolic challenges while still fatiguing and overloading the targeted musculature.
- Altering the order of exercises. This is a simple option yet highly effective.
- Changing the exercise movement plane. Multi-joint and single-joint "pushing" and "pulling" exercises can be performed in all planes including incline (above the shoulders), supine and decline (below the shoulders).
- Modifying the actual workouts performed. Athletes can "cycle" through a number of different workouts that are revised on a periodic basis such as weekly or every other week.

8. Perform productive exercises.

Exercises or activities that increase the potential for injury — either acute or chronic — needn't be performed. There's no reason to perform any potentially dangerous exercise if there's a safer alternative. A list of exercises and activities that shouldn't be performed due to their inherently high risk of injury or lack of effectiveness includes those that incorporate a great deal of momentum to help raise the weight; doing any form of clean or snatch; trying to mimic or imitate a skill with added resistance; and performing plyometrics.

9. Record data.

All pertinent workout information must be recorded in order to track the performance of all athletes. Every set of every exercise of every workout in the strength-training program should be viewed as a test. Thus, no other "traditional" testing — such as the determination of a one-repetition maximum (1-RM) — need be performed. Examining the workout card will provide all tracking of improvements in strength and power.

The workout card should allow for an athlete to record the following information:

- Machine/exercise seat adjustments
- Number of perfect repetitions achieved
- Amount of resistance used
- Date that the workout is performed
- Injury status of the athlete

10. Use training partners.

The success of a strength-training program relies on the supervision and coaching that each athlete receives. Athletes should always do their strength training with a partner or a coach who essentially acts as an athlete's personal trainer. The training partner shouldn't be viewed merely as a spotter but, instead, as a coach who makes demands and provides specific feedback on repetition speed, exercise form and posture. Performance-related feedback and motivation are essential in order for an athlete to provide all-out efforts.

PROGRAM ORGANIZATION

Nearly all coaches and athletes now appreciate the importance and impact that a strength-training program can have on the performance of not only an individual but also a team. Many athletes train extensively in the summer or seasons leading up to their particular competitive sport season. Unfortunately, many coaches and athletes make the mistake of discontinuing strength training when they begin practicing and competing. The reasons for this are widespread and are founded in a misunderstanding about the purpose and enormous potential benefits of intense in-season strength training. Dan Riley

Athletes and coaches should never merely supervise a strength-training exercise but, instead, should coach an athlete through every repetition, set and workout. (Photo by Sandy Ryan)

— a legendary strength and conditioning coach who has more than 25 years of experience at the professional and collegiate levels — notes that only doing strength training in the off-season but not during the season is analogous to only studying in June, July and August for an exam that will be taken in December. Although the student may learn the information, it will be lost with the passing of time and the performance on the exam will be poor (Riley 2003). The same is true with strength training: Because strength is lost rapidly, any physiological benefits that are stimulated by off-season training are rapidly lost when training is discontinued. Any improvements made in the off-season would be completely lost by the beginning to middle of the competitive season. When deciding whether or not to continue strength training during the season, coaches and athletes must remind themselves that the most important time to be strong is during the season. Oftentimes, the schedule of the multi-sport athlete provides little or no off-season. In-season strength training is especially imperative for these athletes.

Many coaches and athletes choose to do strength training when in-season. Many coaches and athletes, however, attempt to "maintain" strength levels during the season. "Maintaining" strength levels that are achieved during the off-season rather than trying to improve them throughout the season makes as much sense as "maintaining" skill levels that are achieved during the off-season rather than trying to improve them throughout the season (by adding more plays to the offense or defense, refining the execution of strategies and so on). The goal of every athlete should be to continually improve her levels of strength throughout the entire season — just as she would aim to improve all other components in her athletic portfolio). To achieve optimal levels of performance, in-season strength training is absolutely crucial for athletes in all sports.

STRENGTH-TRAINING WORKOUTS FOR THE MULTI-SPORT ATHLETE

The sample strength-training workouts that are given at the end of this chapter are safe, efficient and highly effective; they're designed to prevent injury, stimulate physiological adaptations and improve mental toughness in the multi-sport female athlete. Exercises can be performed using any equipment modality including machines, free weights and manual resistance. The first three workouts that are provided can be done three times per week on non-consecutive days; the fourth workout is an extremely time-efficient one that shouldn't take much more than about 15 – 20 minutes to complete. It can be used as a substitute for one of the other three workouts — particularly when time is an important factor. One final point: The commonality between these four sample workouts is that every set of every exercise should be performed to the point of momentary muscular fatigue.

Notes:

EXERCISE	# OF SETS	# OF REPS	CONCENTRIC SPEED	MID-RANGE PAUSE	ECCENTRIC SPEED
Neck Flexion	1	8-12	2	1	4
Neck Extension	1	8-12	2	1	4
Leg Press	1	8-12	2	0	4
Leg Extension	1	3-5	10	1	10
Hip Adduction	1	8-12	2	1	4
Dorsi Flexion	1	8-12	2	1	4
Front Raise	1	8-12	2	1	4
Rear Deltoid	1	4-7	2	8	4
Shoulder Press	1	8-12	2	0	4
Chin-up	1	8-12	2	1	4
Dip	1	8-12	2	0	4
Bicep Curl	1	8-12	2	1	4
Abdominal	1	8-12	2	1	4
Low-Back Extension	1	8-12	2	1	4

WORKOUT #1

EXERCISE	# OF SETS	# OF REPS	CONCENTRIC SPEED	MID-RANGE PAUSE	ECCENTRIC SPEED
Neck Lateral Flexion Left	1	8-12	2	1	4
Neck Lateral Flexion Right	1	8-12	2	1	4
Leg Press	1	8-12	2	0	4
Lunge	1	8-12	2	0	4
Leg Curl	1	4-7	2	8	4
Hip Abduction	1	8-12	2	1	4
Lateral Raise	1	8-12	2	1	4
Shrug	1	4-7	5	5	5
Pullover	1	8-12	2	1	4
Pulldown	1	8-12	2	1	4
Chest Press	1	8-12	2	0	4
Wrist Roll	1	1-2	*	*	*
Abdominal	1	8-12	2	1	4
Low-Back Extension	1	8-12	2	1	4

WORKOUT #2

EXERCISE	# OF SETS	# OF REPS	CONCENTRIC SPEED	MID-RANGE PAUSE	ECCENTRIC SPEED
Neck Flexion	1	8-12	2	1	4
Neck Extension	1	8-12	2	1	4
Calf Raise	1	4-7	2	8	4
Hip Extension	1	8-12	2	1	4
Leg Press	1	6-8	2	0	10
Leg Extension	1	4-7	2	5	5
Diagonal Shoulder Raise	1	8-12	2	1	4
Shoulder Press	1	8-12	2	0	4
Pulldown	1	8-12	2	1	4
Chest Fly	1	6-8	2	1	10
Chest Press	1	8-12	2	0	4
Tricep Extension	1	8-12	2	1	4
Hip Flexion	1	8-12	2	1	4
Low-Back Extension	1	8-12	2	1	4

WORKOUT #3

EXERCISE	# OF SETS	# OF REPS	CONCENTRIC SPEED	MID-RANGE PAUSE	ECCENTRIC SPEED
Leg Press	1	15-20	2	0	4
Pulldown	1	15-20	2	1	4
Chest Press	1	15-20	2	0	4
Leg Press	1	10-15	2	0	4
Pulldown	1	10-15	2	1	4
Chest Press	1	10-15	2	0	4
Leg Press	1	5-10	2	0	4
Pulldown	1	5-10	5	1	4
Chest Press	1	5-10	2	0	4

WORKOUT #4 (The 3x3)

Notes:

1. In all four workouts, the units for the numbers that are listed under concentric speed, mid-range pause and eccentric speed are seconds.
2. In Workout #2, the asterisks (*) noted under the wrist roll indicate that there's no specified repetition speed.
3. In Workout #4 (the 3x3 Workout), athletes should take as little rest as possible between sets. They should walk briskly or jog to the next exercise.

REFERENCES:

Brzycki, M. 1995. *A practical approach to strength training. 3rd ed*. New York, NY: McGraw-Hill/Contemporary.

_____., ed. 1999. *Maximize your training: insights from leading strength and fitness professionals*. New York, NY: McGraw-Hill/Contemporary.

Carpinelli, R. N., and R. M. Otto. 1998. Strength training. Single versus multiple sets. *Sports Medicine* 6 (2) 73-84.

Graves, J. E., and M. L. Pollock. 1995. Understanding the physiological basis of muscular fitness. In *The StairMaster fitness handbook. 2nd ed.*, ed. J. A. Peterson and C. X. Bryant, 67-80. Champaign. IL: Sagamore Publishing Inc.

Jones, A. 1982. Preventing injuries in sports. In *Total fitness: the Nautilus way. 2nd ed.*, ed. J. A. Peterson, 77-81. West Point, NY: Leisure Press.

Mannie, K. 1994. Some thoughts on explosive weight training. *High Intensity Training Newsletter* 5 (1 & 2): 13-18.

McGuff, M. D. 1999. The dose-response relationship of exercise. In *Maximize your training: insights from leading strength and fitness professionals*, ed. M. Brzycki, 151-159. New York, NY: McGraw-Hill/Contemporary.

Riley, D. 2003. Personal conversation with the author (March 14).

Ritz, S. J. 2002. Presentation at the 2002 National Strength & Science Seminar (March 16).

7

Enhancing Speed and Explosiveness

Tim "Red" Wakeham, M.S., S.C.C.C., C.S.C.C.

Movement speed and explosive power are two of the most talked about topics in strength and conditioning. Year after year, countless numbers of athletes ask for the "magic" recipe to increase sport-specific speed. Additionally, large numbers of coaches search for the latest pieces of equipment that are being marketed to enhance explosive power.

It's easy to understand the fascination with speed and power. In most sports, the players who demonstrate the greatest amount of explosive power dominate their opponents. In track and field, for example, the shot putter or javelin thrower who overcomes her implement's resistance with the greatest possible speed of movement should, in theory, produce the longest throw (all other variables being equal); in basketball, the players who are the most explosive will win (again, all other variables being equal).

There are many general and sport-specific methods that can be prescribed to enhance speed and power in sport. The purpose of this chapter is to review both general and sport-specific methods that can be used to improve the expression of speed and explosiveness.

GENERAL IMPROVEMENT METHODS

There are several ways to improve speed and explosiveness in a general manner. The methods include warm-up, body composition, biomechanical factors, weight training and rate of force development.

Warm-Up

McArdle, Katch and Katch (1991) state that raising body temperature can significantly increase the speed of contraction. This can be accomplished by a general warm-up. Activities in a general warm-up should incorporate the large muscle groups of the body, moving them in a rhythmic and repetitive manner for about 7 - 15 minutes. Warm-up activities that are specific to the training exercise should also be performed but with a lower level of effort.

Body Composition

Modifications of body composition may lead to the enhancement of movement speed and power through reductions in drag. For instance, in explosive jumping events (that is, the high jump, long jump and triple jump), a loss in body mass results in a reduction in the drag of gravity (a limiting factor to success in jumping events/movements). However, if the body mass that's lost is muscle tissue, reductions in the ability to produce force and explosiveness can be expected. Strategies for altering body composition should be carefully considered before being implemented so that explosive performances are enhanced rather than impaired.

To increase explosiveness through improved body composition, athletes should do the following:

- Consult with a registered dietician who can provide a body-composition analysis, evaluation of the current diet, determination of optimal and realistic body-composition expectations and strategies for modifying the diet.

- Perform a weight-training program that provides progressive overload to the large muscle groups of the body.

- Acknowledge and accept that there doesn't currently appear to be a safe and effective nutritional supplement that provides consistent body-composition enhancements in athletes.

Biomechanical Factors

Identifying biomechanical errors and teaching efficient movement mechanics may be the most significant method to improve quickness, acceleration, speed and agility. Specifically, the changing of body posture and joint positions may decrease air drag and maximize force-producing potential. The teaching of efficient running mechanics should be done while athletes are in a non-fatigued state. Even though most practitioners share a general consensus regarding what constitutes efficient movement mechanics, technique may be different from athlete to athlete in small but significant ways depending on their physiological characteristics. This being said, all technical refinements should be instituted on a trial-and-error basis to see how the athlete responds.

Quickness is commonly described as the first 2 - 3 steps from a starting position. Acceleration is usually described as the first 8 - 10 steps from a starting position. The speed phase of running is commonly described as the steps taken after the first 10 steps of acceleration. Agility includes the last two steps of deceleration and the first step in the new direction. Figures 7.1, 7.2 and 7.3 list coaching cues (body position and mechanics) and common mistakes for quickness and acceleration, straight-line speed and agility.

Perform a weight-training program that provides progressive overload to the large muscle groups of the body. (Photo by Tim "Red" Wakeham)

Weight Training

In theory, weight training that results in increased strength will improve explosive-

---

BODY POSITION

- Demonstrate a body lean of about a 45-degree angle in relation to the ground (created at the ankle joint) with the rest of the body forming a straight line. (To find the optimal/comfortable body lean for each individual, have the athletes stand up straight and lean forward until their heels leave the ground.)

MECHANICS

- Position the plant foot so that it lands slightly behind the hips to prevent a braking effect.
- Drive off the balls of the feet and extend completely at the hips, knees and ankles.
- Demonstrate a vigorous knee drive.
- Move the arms explosively!
- Maintain an appropriate stride length and rate. (With increasing stride length and rate, forward body lean decreases and the feet contact the ground more and more under the center of gravity.)

COMMON MISTAKES

- Taking a false step.
- Popping straight up.
- Stepping out too far causing a braking effect.
- Rotating the upper body.
- Performing anything but straight-line movements.

FIGURE 7.1: COACHING CUES AND COMMON MISTAKES FOR QUICKNESS AND ACCELERATION

ness. Whenever the force-producing capabilities of the muscles are increased, the potential to improve speed and power for skill execution is enhanced. Some studies have shown that a progressive weight-training program can increase sprint speed and throwing velocity (Napier 1991; Wooden et al. 1992). Some of this increase is due to greater amounts of myofibril proteins (actin and myosin) which means an increase in the ability to generate force. Adhering to the guidelines that follow may achieve enhancements in speed and power through weight training.

- Train the entire body. Current research suggests that strengthening opposing muscle groups (agonists and antagonists) enhances movement speed (Jaric et al. 1995). According to these data, strengthening a major muscle group such as the hamstrings may result in faster leg deceleration during high-speed activities (sprinting). Less time needed by the hamstrings to decelerate the leg (while running) leaves a longer period of time available for the quadriceps to increase leg acceleration, resulting in faster lower-limb speeds. Maximal strengthening of all the major muscle groups of the body may in-

BODY POSITION

- Keep the head in a neutral position.
- Relax the face, neck, shoulders and hands.
- Run tall (with an erect torso).
- Bend the elbow (approximately 90 degrees).

MECHANICS

- Maintain the elbows close to the body.
- Perform straight-line movements.
- Keep the hands level with the hip pocket during the back swing of the arms.
- Bring the hands to the height of the mouth during the forward swing of arms.
- Drive the knees forward.
- Keep the toes and ankles "cocked."
- Snap the feet down and back.
- Position the plant foot so that it lands under the hips to prevent a braking effect.
- Push off through the balls of the feet.
- Extend fully at the hips, knees and ankles.
- Step quickly and explosively — be "light" off the ground.

COMMON MISTAKES

- Maintaining a tense or tight upper body.
- Moving the head.
- Flexing at the waist.
- Elevating the shoulders.
- Having too much vertical lift.
- Overstriding.
- Rotating the torso.
- Bringing the knees too low or too high.
- Swinging the feet wildly.
- Pushing off the toes.
- Bringing the arms and/or legs across the mid-line of the body.

FIGURE 7.2: COACHING CUES AND COMMON MISTAKES FOR STRAIGHT-LINE SPEED

crease the time available for movement acceleration. The end result should be faster movement speeds and explosiveness in potentially all sport skills. While it's important to address all muscle groups, it may be especially important to emphasize the strengthening of certain muscle groups for specific running (sprint) distances. Young and his associates (2001) suggest that quadricep and gluteal strengthening is most important for very short-dis-

---

BODY POSITION

- Maintain the head in a neutral position.
- Flex at the hips, knees and ankles.
- Keep about 75% of the bodyweight on the forefoot and about 25% on the heel (if starting from a stationary position).

MECHANICS

- Keep the feet slightly in front of the hips (but as close as possible to directly under the hips during the last two steps of deceleration).
- Bend at the hips, knees and ankles.
- Throw the hands in the direction that you want to go.
- Create a forward body lean at the ankles.
- Position the plant foot so that it lands slightly behind the hips to prevent a braking effect.
- Drive off the balls of the feet and extend completely at the hips, knees and ankles.
- Demonstrate a vigorous knee drive.
- Move the arms explosively!

COMMON MISTAKES

- Placing too much weight on the heels.
- Running too erect.
- Having excessive head movement.
- Keeping the eyes and head down.
- Not using the arms.

FIGURE 7.3: COACHING CUES AND COMMON MISTAKES FOR AGILITY

tance/duration sprints (such as 10 meters) while hamstring strengthening is most important for maximum-speed sprints.

- Make the muscles work progressively harder over time. To increase muscle strength, make the muscles encounter progressively greater demands. The four most common methods to make the muscles work harder are to systematically (1) increase the repetitions; (2) increase the sets; (3) increase the load; and/or (4) decrease the rest time between sets/exercises.

Rate of Force Development

Increasing the size of one's engine (muscles) should allow the mass of the body (during jumping or sprinting) or an external object (such as an opponent in martial arts) to be accelerated more explosively. To be optimally successful in many speed and power sports, it's also important to be able to develop the engine's (muscle's) force rapidly. Having a big engine but not being able to get it to top speed quickly is like racing a Cadillac in the quarter mile. All that

Strengthening of all the major muscle groups of the body may increase the time available for movement acceleration. (Photo by Tim "Red" Wakeham)

power may still result in an unsuccessful performance if the driver cannot get to maximum speed until the half-mile mark. For optimal sport success, speed and power athletes should have large engines (muscles) that reach top speed quickly.

The rate of force development is the ability of the neuromuscular system to develop as much force as possible in a short period of time (Newton and Kraemer 1994). Enhancing the rate of force development improves explosiveness by decreasing the time that it takes to move over a given distance (provided other power variables are constant). Researchers suggest that the key stimulus for enhancing the rate of force development is maximum voluntary effort (the intent) to develop force as fast as possible, not the external speed of movement while training (Young and Bilby 1993).

SPECIFICITY

Coaches and athletes have the option of enhancing force-producing capabilities, the rate of force development and, ultimately, explosiveness by performing non-specific exercises in the weight room; using similar-to-sport, hybrid methods (such as plyometrics); or using exact sport-specific activities and situations. The amount of transferable affect from training to sport performance appears to be on a continuum, meaning that some methods may transfer or "carry over" greater benefits than others. Currently, there's research suggesting that general weight-room exercises — along with hybrid methods (plyometrics) — may improve some explosive sport performances (Wilson et al. 1993). However, "best" results appear to come from training in a sport-specific manner (Timm 1987; Rushall and Pyke 1991).

Sport-specific training is based on the theory of specificity. This principle states that maximum benefits of a training stimulus are only obtained when it replicates the movements and energy systems involved in the sport (Rushall and Pyke 1991). Adaptations in trained, healthy athletes are very specific. Sport scientists and motor-learning researchers indicate that the training and surrounding environment must be the same or virtually identical to actual sport situations for meaningful transfer to take place (Sage 1971; Caiozzo, Perrine and Edgerton 1981).

Dr. Richard Schmidt (1988), an authority in motor learning, states, "A common misconception is that fundamental abilities [like explosive strength] can be trained through various drills or other activities. The thinking is that, with some stronger ability, the athlete will see gains in performances with this underlying ability. For example, athletes are often given quickening exercises, with

1. Force of contraction.

2. Speed of contraction.

3. Type of contraction.

4. Joint angles trained.

5. Range of motion.

6. Postural positions.

7. Neuromuscular patterning (path of movements).

8. Energy system (or systems).

9. Environmental predictability (open versus closed).

10. Context of the situation.

11. Type of equipment (apparatus).

12. The amount of irrelevant elements surrounding the relevant elements. (The more non-specific "noise," the less transfer.)

13. Athlete's recognition of shared similarities between training and competitive settings.

14. Cognitive processing of stimuli.

15. Type of motor-response classification (discrete, continuous or serial).

16. Purpose or goal of the task.

FIGURE 7.4: VARIABLES TO CONSIDER WHEN COMPARING TRAINING TO PERFORMANCE

the hope that these exercises would train some fundamental ability to be quick, allowing quicker responses in their particular sport. Such attempts to train fundamental abilities may sound fine, but usually they simply do not work. Time, and often money, would be better spent practicing the eventual goal [sport skills]." Dr. George Sage (1971), another authority in motor learning, adds, "In regards to exercises that involve many rapid skillful movements, transfer is highly specific and occurs only when the practiced movements are identical."

Rushall and Pyke (1991), authorities in human performance, note, "Training for power and speed would seem to be relatively simple. The activity itself should form the basis of the movement, the technique should be as economical as possible and the action as intense as possible. Anything less than a maximum effort will train different neuromuscular patterns and should be considered counterproductive." Many authors concur with these experts stating that a significant drop in carryover is seen when the training modality and environment are different from the performance modality.

Kraemer and Newton (1994) add, "Weight training has little benefit for explosive strength performances for individuals with previous training or above average levels of strength." They suggest prescriptions be designed using specific-action training (the actual sport activity). Costill, Sharp and Troup (1980) agree, stating that sport-specific swimming strength is best achieved by repeated maximum exercises that duplicate as closely as possible the skill of swimming. Their suggestion: a series of maximum sprint swims.

As you can see, achieving measurable and/or meaningful transfer from training to performance may be difficult because there are many factors that influence the amount of motor quality enhancement seen in sport performance by trained athletes. Figure 7.4 lists 16 variables to consider when comparing training to performance. If any one of these variables differs, transfer from training to performance appears to drop significantly.

SPORT-SPECIFIC IMPROVEMENT METHODS

To maximize explosive carryover from training to performance, game film should be studied and drills should be designed that incorporate *identical* sport-performance movement patterns. Whenever possible, try to individualize sport prescriptions based on player and position needs along with their physical and training status.

If the primary goal is to improve absolute speed and power endurance, practice sport movements (starts, sprints, jumps) at maximum speed and with precise technique with total recovery between work intervals. To see optimal gains in movement efficiency and absolute explosiveness, athletes need to train in a non-fatigued state. This teaches the athletes to consistently demonstrate maximal efforts and coordinate their movements efficiently at high speeds.

If the primary goal is sport-specific speed endurance, the practice of repeated sport movements with maximal effort is still recommended. However, the specific energy system (or systems) used in the sport should be progressively overloaded by increasing the number of work intervals or decreasing rest times.

As examples, basketball and volleyball players should perform jumps; defensive-position lateral slides; diagonal, forward and backward cuts; twists; turns; and sprints. Use training movements that bring the athletes through the three cardinal planes and mimic the proprioceptive demands seen during sport performance. Start sport-specific training, emphasizing precise and coordinated acceleration, deceleration and stabilization in all movements. After athletes demonstrate competent movement efficiency, emphasize skillful explosiveness (game speeds). Eventually, expect the athletes to demonstrate the movement patterns as purposeful, conditioned, explosive reflexes rather than skills that must be thought about before execution. (An example of a sport-specific workout for volleyball is shown in Figure 7.5.)

Equally important to "neck-down" training is "neck-up" explosive training. In an effort to maximize explosive transfer from training to sport performance, try to design drills that have the same cerebral demands as the athlete's sport. Sport-specific drills should target an athlete's ability to focus attention (read) and react under pressure-filled competitive situations. Dr. Ted Lambrinides (1998), a sport physiologist, says, "Athletes may have a big, pow-

GOALS

1. Train the sport-specific energy system (or systems) to produce energy at a greater rate and for longer periods of time.
2. Train the neuromuscular system to produce more force in sport movements thereby enhancing sport-specific explosiveness.

MOVEMENTS/DRILLS

- Serves (or serving motions)
- Sets (or setting motions)
- Short-approach attack jumps
- Blocks
- Dives
- Passes (or passing motions)
- Block jumps
- Long-approach attack jumps
- Dashes

WORK TIMES

7 - 10 seconds (with 10% of drills lasting 20 - 40 seconds)

REST TIMES

12 - 14 seconds

NUMBER OF REPTITIONS

50 per workout

NOTES

1. The movements/drills, work and rest times and number of repetitions are virtually identical to what players encounter in games.
2. Players are subjectively evaluated on movement/drill efficiency (acceleration, deceleration, stabilization) along with "neck-up" and "neck-down" speed. They may be asked about appropriate foci for each movement/drill.
3. Work intervals consist of one or a combination of sport movement patterns. An example of a combination drill is a block jump followed by a back pedal and a short-approach attack jump.
4. Movements/drills are divided into sets of 10 with longer rest times in between each set.

FIGURE 7.5: SPORT-SPECIFIC EXPLOSIVE ENDURANCE TRAINING FOR VOLLEYBALL

erful gun [body] but some cannot pull the trigger [read and react appropriately] under competitive conditions, so the size of the gun and speed of the bullet [explosive movement speed] are irrelevant." Others cannot carry over strength, speed and power because of competitive anxiety and hesitation. Lambrinides (1998) adds, "Players who are fearful increase neural inhibitory input. In essence, they are trying to accelerate their car with one foot on the gas pedal and one foot on the brake." There's no doubt that athletes can learn to dominate fast-paced play by improving their sport-specific attentional focus and reaction time.

Every sport and event requires distinct attentional demands at specific times for proper reads. Attentional focus can be broad or narrow and internal or external. A broad-external focus is usually used to quickly assess situations. A soccer goalie, for example, should be able to keep this type of focus because relevant cues for success come from stimuli that are in the external environment (such as offensive player positions, defensive schemes, weather and so on). The broad-internal focus is customarily employed to analyze a game plan. A coach or athlete who is developing game strategies uses this type of attentional focus. A narrow-external concentration is practiced when minimal amounts of external cues need to be focused on for success. A golfer focusing attention on the ball that she's about to drive is using this type of concentration. The last type of attention is the narrow-internal. This focus is used to systematically rehearse a performance or to control arousal. A narrow-internal focus is used in competitive weightlifting where the primary focus is on effort. Knowing that there are distinctly different types of attentional focus makes it easier to understand how meaningful transfer between training and sport can be impacted.

To increase transfer from training to performance, operationally define the terms "focus" and "concentration" so that common language is used between coaches and athletes. Identify which type(s) of attentional focus are appropriate for each sport-specific drill or situation. Lastly, coach the athlete to mentally develop proper foci while physically performing the sport-specific drill.

Reaction time refers to the time that it takes to initiate a motor response to a presented stimulus (Grouios 1992). Reaction time can be improved by implementing several guidelines. Through film study, instruct athletes to identify a small number of relevant variables. The fewer situational and opponent cues to which an athlete needs to read and react, the shorter the response times (Nemish 1995). Watching a hockey goalie demonstrates this point. Most goalies have higher save success rates when they have to react to only one player on a breakaway as opposed to two or three.

Limit the amount of possible response choices that an athlete has to consider before reacting. For instance, a basketball player defending a three-on-one fast break who has been told to pressure the ball will read and respond faster than a player defending the break who has been told she has three defensive options to analyze before choosing a correct response.

It's important to scout adversaries. Doing so brings knowledge of opponent tendencies that may allow athletes to invest in early reads and responses. In softball, for example, a hitter may know that the pitcher has a tendency to throw the fastball for her "out" pitch. Knowing this, the hitter primes her concentration and physical readiness for the fastball on a 3-2 count, thereby improving response time and the probability of hitting the fastball (if it's thrown).

The combination of both physical and mental training using exact sport actions and speeds performed under competitive circumstances helps players to relax, focus, read, react and demonstrate sport movements as purposeful, conditioned, explosive reflexes.

CONCLUSIONS

Athletes have the capacity to improve speed and explosive power up to their genetic ceiling. At the present time, there doesn't appear to be one "best" method or recipe to improve speed and power for *all* athletes in *all* sport situations. Each sport, position and circumstance should be analyzed to decide how speed and power might best be improved to maximize performance. Realistic training and performance goals should then be set based on the speed and power improvement possible. As an example, Wilmore (1982) suggests that sprint speed may only be enhanced about 10% through training. Coaches and athletes need to understand that motor abilities — such as speed of limb movement and explosiveness — are, to a large degree, genetically determined.

When devising a speed- and power-training program, the goal is to assimilate as many of the required "neck-up," "neck-down" and environmental components as possible into a pattern that approximates competitive performance conditions.

In the big picture of specificity and transfer, traditional weight-room training and non-specific plyometric exercises are probably useful. However, because they usually aren't specific enough in "like" components when compared to sport performances, maximal improvements in explosiveness aren't produced in healthy, trained athletes. No matter what magic the marketers are trying to sell you, rest assured that a weight-training and/or plyometric program alone will not turn Norah Jones into Marion Jones. There are too many differences between these training exercises and actual sport performances.

An integrated approach that includes sport-specific physiological, biomechanical, psychological and environmental performance variables — while addressing individual needs — is the best way to maximize speed and power transfer and provide a meaningful affect on explosive sport performance.

Good luck!

REFERENCES

Beaulieu, J. E. 1981. Developing a stretching program. *Physician and Sportsmedicine* 9: 59-69.

Behm, D. G. 1988. Surgical tubing for sport and velocity specific training. *National Strength and Conditioning Journal* 10 (4): 66-70.

Brady, T. A., B. R. Cahill and L. M. Bodnar. 1982. Weight training-related injuries in the high school athlete. *The American Journal of Sports Medicine* 10 (1), 1-5.

Bryant, C. X. 1988. *How to develop muscular power*. Grand Rapids, MI: Masters Press.

Caiozzo, V. J., J. J. Perrine and V. R. Edgerton. 1981. Training-induced alterations of the in vivo force-velocity relationship of human muscle. *Journal of Applied Physiology* 51 (3): 750-754.

Carpinelli, R. N. 1997. More on multiple sets and muscular fatigue. *Master Trainer* 7 (1): 15-17.

Coleman, E. 2001. Burning 'round the basepaths. *Training & Conditioning* 11: 41-47.

Costill, D. L., R. Sharp and J. P. Troup. 1980. Muscle strength: contributions to sprint swimming. *Swimming World* 21: 29-34.

Fox, E., R. W. Bowers and M. L. Foss. 1993. *Physiological basis for exercise and sport. 5th ed.* Dubuque, IA: William C. Brown.

Grouios, G. 1992. On the reduction of reaction time with mental practice. *Journal of Sport Behavior* 15 (2): 141-157.

Hall, S. J. 1985. Effect of attempted lifting speed on forces and torque exerted on the lumbar spine. *Medicine and Science in Sports and Exercise* 17 (4): 440-444.

_____. 1991. *Basic biomechanics*. St. Louis, MO: Mosby Year Book, Inc.

Hay, J. G., and J. G. Reid. 1988. *Anatomy, mechanics, and human motion. 2nd ed.* Englewood Cliffs, NJ: Prentice-Hall, Inc.

Housh, D. J., and T. J. Housh. 1993. The effects of unilateral velocity specific concentric strength training. *Journal of Sports and Physical Therapy* 17 (5): 252-256.

Jaric, S., R. Ropret, M. Kukolj and D. B. Ilic. 1995. Role of agonist and antagonist muscle strength in performance of rapid movements. *European Journal of Applied Physiology* 71 (5): 464-468.

Knapik, J. J., C. L. Bauman, B. H. Jones, J. M. Harris and L. Vaughan. 1991. Preseason strength and flexibility imbalances associated with athletic injuries in female collegiate athletes. *The American Journal of Sports Medicine* 19 (1): 76-81.

Komarek, A. R. 1998. *A history of speed*. Unpublished essay. Tampa, FL: Tampa Bay Buccaneers.

Kraemer, W. J., and R. U. Newton. 1994. Training for improved vertical jump. *Sports Science Exchange* 7 (6): 1-5.

Lamb, D. R. 1995. Basic principles for improving sport performance. *Sports Science Exchange* 8 (2): 1-5.

Lambrinides, T. L. 1998. Personal communication with the author (April 3).

McArdle, W. D., F. I. Katch and V. L. Katch. 1991. *Exercise physiology: energy, nutrition, and human performance*. Philadelphia, PA: Lea & Febiger.

McCarroll, J. R., J. M. Miller and M. A. Ritter. 1986. Lumbar spondylolysis and spondylolisthesis in college football players: a prospective study. *The American Journal of Sports Medicine* 14 (5): 404-406.

Myers, B., and R. Munroe. 1981. Theory of training for explosive power. *Modern Athlete and Coach* 19 (4): 3-6.

Napier, M. E. 1991. *Effects of two different weight training regimens on twenty meter sprinting speed*. Unpublished master of science thesis. Starkville, MS: Mississippi State University.

Nemish, M. 1995. *Reaction time: implications for its reduction in an effort to enhance sport performance*. Unpublished essay. Grand Forks, ND: University of North Dakota.

Newton, R. U., and W. J. Kraemer. 1994. Developing explosive muscular power: implications for a mixed methods training strategy. *Strength and Conditioning* 16 (5): 20-31.

Nideffer, R. M. 1976. *The inner athlete: mind plus muscle for winning*. New York, NY: Ty Crowell Co.

Noakes, T. D., and S. Granger. 1990. *Running injuries: how to prevent and overcome them*. Cape Town, South Africa: Oxford University Press.

Posner, M. I. 1971. Components of attention. *Psychological Review* 78: 391-408.

Reid, C. M., R. A. Yeater and I. H. Ullrich. 1987. Weight training and strength, cardiorespiratory functioning and body composition of men. *British Journal of Sports Medicine* 21 (1): 40-44.

Riley, D. 1996. *Redskin conditioning*. Ashburn, VA: Washington Redskins.

Rushall, B. S., and F. S. Pyke. 1991. *Training for sports and fitness*. Melbourne, Australia: MacMillian Company of Australia.

Sage, G. H. 1971. *Introduction to motor behavior: a neuropsychological approach*. Reading, MA: Addison-Wesley Publishing Company.

_____. 1984. *Motor learning and control: a neuropsychological approach*. Dubuque, IA: William C. Brown.

Sale, D., and D. MacDougall. 1981. Specificity in strength training: a reiew for the coach and athlete. *Canadian Journal of Applied Sport Sciences* 6 (2): 87-92.

Schmidt, R. A. 1988. *Motor control and learning: a behavioral emphasis. 2nd ed.* Champaign, IL: Human Kinetics.

Smith, C. A. 1994. The warm-up procedure: to stretch or not to stretch. A brief review. *Journal of Orthopaedic & Sports Physical Therapy* 19 (1), 12-17.

Timm, K. E. 1987. Investigation of physiological overflow effect from speed-specific isokinetic activity. *Journal of Orthopaedic & Sports Physical Therapy* 9: 106-110.

Wakeham, T. 1994. *A cost vs. benefit analysis of ballistic training*. Unpublished essay. Grand Forks, ND: University of North Dakota.

Wilmore, J. H. 1982. *Training for sport and activity: the physiological basis of the conditioning process. 2nd ed.* Boston, MA: Allyn and Bacon, Inc.

Wilson, G. J., R. U. Newton, A. J. Murphy and B. J. Humphries. 1993. The optimal training load for the development of dynamic athletic performance. *Medicine and Science in Sports and Exercise* 25 (11): 1279-1286.

Wooden, M. J., B. Greenfield, M. Johanson, L. Litzelman, M. Mundrane and R. A. Donatelli. 1992. Effects of strength training on throwing velocity and shoulder muscle performance in teenage baseball players. *Journal of Orthopaedic & Sports Physical Therapy* 15 (5): 223-228.

Young, W. B., and G. E. Bilby. 1993. The effect of voluntary effort to influence speed of contraction on strength, muscular power, and hypertrophy development. *Journal of Strength and Conditioning Research* 7 (3): 172-178.

Young, W., D. Benton, G. Duthie and J.Pryor. 2001. Resistance training for short sprints and maximum-speed sprints. *Strength and Conditioning Journal* 23 (2): 7-13.

Ziemba, D. J. 1995. Teaching athletes how to move. *National Strength and Conditioning Journal* 17 (3): 64-65.

8

Non-Contact Anterior Cruciate Ligament (ACL) Injuries: Mechanisms to Prevention

Tim "Red" Wakeham, M.S., S.C.C.C., C.S.C.C.

During our conditioning drills, the teaching cues that you'll hear most often are, "Keep your feet under your hips," " Use several small steps when decelerating," "Land softly after a jump" and "Keep your knees in alignment between your first and second toes!" These cues are important to reduce the incidence of non-contact anterior cruciate ligament (ACL) injuries in females. As a female athlete, coach or administrator of female athletes, should you also be concerned about ACL injuries? Yes, and here's why:

Over the last 15 years, female athletes who compete in ground-based sports have endured an epidemic of ACL injuries (Schnirring 1997). Currently, it's estimated that one out of every 100 female athletes in high school and one out of every 10 in college will sustain an ACL rupture (Adams 2002). Studies show that females suffer 2 - 6 times more ACL injuries than males (Ireland and Wall 1990; Hutchinson and Ireland 1995). Variance in the incidence of the injuries is dependent upon the sport.

Talk with any injured athlete, her teammates, coaches, administrators and family and you hear about the physical challenges and emotional impact of an ACL injury. The athlete's season comes to an abrupt end, valuable learning time is lost and planned goals are left unaccomplished. Besides these tolls, ACL injuries also have a financial impact. For one thing, future scholarship and professional earnings are in jeopardy; for another, the surgical reconstruction and rehabilitation process for an ACL injury has been projected to be $17,000 - $25,000 (Boden, Griffin and Garrett 2000). Added to these challenges are the frustrations that the rehabilitation process takes 3 - 6 months and the surgery doesn't always achieve satisfactory knee stability.

There are over 80,000 ACL injuries in the United States each year (Silvers and Mandelbaum 2002). The purpose of this chapter is to review some of the most recognized mechanisms that influence non-contact ACL injuries in females and suggest injury-prevention strategies with the hope that this information will reduce the number of injuries.

PHYSIOLOGY OF THE ACL

Moore and Wade (1989) note that the anterior cruciate ligament stabilizes the knee and prevents side-to-side mobility, rotation and forward movement of the tibia (the shin bone) on the femur (the thigh bone). ACL injuries are divided into two categories: contact and non-contact. A blow to the lateral (outer) side of the leg or knee is the most common cause of contact ACL injuries (Cross 1998). A single common cause of non-contact ACL injuries hasn't been identified. This is a good-news, bad-news situation for female athletes: The bad news is that 70 - 75% of ACL ruptures are non-contact; the good news is that multiple reasons for the high incidence of non-contact ACL injuries in females have been identified, some of which may be controllable.

MECHANISMS OF NON-CONTACT ACL INJURIES

A number of mechanisms have been suggested as contributing to the risk of sustaining an ACL injury. These mechanisms may be grouped as either being non-controllable or controllable.

Practically Non-Controllable Factors

Various anatomical, physiological and environmental factors may affect the risk of an ACL injury. The factors include the "Q" angle, femoral notch, menstrual cycle, laxity, shoe/playing surface interaction and knee bracing.

"Q" Angle

A woman usually has a wider pelvis than a man. As a result, a woman has a wider "Q" angle (Silvers and Mandelbaum 2002). The "Q" angle is a measure of bone alignment between the hip and knee. Research performed by Haycock and Gillette (1976) suggested that a greater "Q" angle leaves the female knee vulnerable to inward torque when pivoting, stopping or landing from a jump.

Femoral Notch

Another difference between a man and a woman is the shape and width of the femoral notch. The femoral notch is the structure through which the ACL passes before attaching to the lower leg. There's evidence suggesting that notch width is less in individuals with bilateral ACL tears than in individuals with unilateral ACL tears; less in people who have had bilateral or unilateral ACL tears when compared to normal control groups; and less in women than in men (Anderson et al. 1987; Souryal, Moore and Evans 1988; Souryal and Freeman 1993).

Menstrual Cycle

It has been proposed that females are more vulnerable for ACL tears during certain times in their menstrual cycle (Arendt, Bershadsky and Agel 2002). The ACL has receptor sites for two sex hormones: estrogen and progesterone (Hewett 2000). Yu and others (1999) reported that these hormones might influence the composition and mechanical properties of the ACL. Specifically, estrogen and progesterone may decrease and/or disorganize the synthesis of collagen fibers thereby making the ACL more flexible and possibly weaker. Additionally, Postuma and her associates (1987) reported that estrogen decreases fine motor skills. This decline in neuromuscular protection may decrease stabilization of the knee joint.

Laxity

Laxity has been described as the combination of joint hypermobility and musculotendinous flexibility (Toth and Cordasco 2001). There's data demonstrating that females have more joint and muscle laxity than males (Wojtys, Huston and Ashton-Miller 1998). These data suggest that the differences in musculotendinous elasticity between males and females may lead to decreased knee stability.

Shoe/Playing Surface Interaction

The relationship between an athlete's shoes, the playing surface and the potential risk of ACL injury is a complex one because of the number of variables that play a role (such as cleat design and location, weather conditions and hardness of surface). Some studies suggest that a high level of friction between a player's shoes and the playing surface increase the risk for non-contact ACL injury (Lambson, Barnhill and Higgins 1996; Myklebust et al. 1997).

Knee Bracing

The American Academy of Orthopaedic Surgeons (1999) and the American Academy of Pediatrics Committee on Sports Medicine (1990) concluded there's no evidence that prophylactic knee braces prevent non-contact ACL injury. Because of the large number of variables that affect studies on knee bracing in athletics, however, further research may be needed using larger sample sizes of homogeneous individuals.

Summary

These anatomical, physiological and environmental factors may have merit in explaining why females suffer significantly more ACL injuries than their male counterparts. However, there's much conflicting data and little consensus regarding what role and to what extent each play. Further investigation with larger sample sizes, the latest technology and concise methodology that provides accurate and reproducible results are needed. Because these factors are largely uncontrollable, the practitioner's focus shifts to factors that can be significantly affected.

PRACTICALLY CONTROLLABLE FACTORS

There appears to be differences in muscle strength, muscle activation and movement patterns between females and males. These characteristics share a complex interplay that ultimately affects the risk of non-contact ACL injuries.

Muscle Strength

Huston and Wojtys (1996) showed that female athletes have weaker quadriceps (the muscle on the front of the thigh) and hamstrings (the muscle on the back of the thigh) than males, even with corrections for bodyweight. Anderson and his co-workers (2001) reported that anterior tibial translation (a forward gliding of the shin bone) can be reduced considerably by maximum contraction of the knee musculature. But because of the weakness of these muscles, it has been theorized that females have lower load-bearing capacity and are subjected to higher ACL strain during sport performance when compared to males (Anderson et al. 2001).

In addition to the quadriceps and hamstrings, the strength of the gluteals (the muscles that comprise the buttocks) and calves appear important to the risk of non-contact ACL injury. The hamstrings and calves assist in keeping the knee in a safe alignment. Additionally, it has been reported that weak gluteal musculature in females causes a more erect hip and trunk posture, increased quadriceps activation and higher forces transmitted through the knees (Colby et al. 2000; Toth and Cordasco 2001). The combined forces of the gluteals, hamstrings and calves contribute to counteract impact and energy when decelerating from a jump or cut. Weakness in any of these three major muscles may mean less stability and more undesirable forces through the knee joint.

Possibly even more important than absolute strength is muscular balance — specifically between the hamstrings and quadriceps. To decrease the chance of ACL injury, it has been suggested that the strength of the hamstrings should be at least 65% of the strength of the quadriceps (Hewett, Paterno and Noyes 1999). According to some calculations, the quadriceps — under certain conditions — can produce enough force to pull the tibia forward and tear the ACL (Stauber 1989). The hamstrings help offset quadriceps force and control forward movement of the tibia (Norkin and Levangie 1983). The unfortunate reality is that many females have been shown to have significantly weaker hamstrings than quadriceps. For instance, Hewett and his associates (1996) found that female athletes had hamstrings-to-quadriceps peak torque ratios of less than 50%. Dr. Hewett, currently the Director of Applied Research at the Cincinnati Sports Medicine Research and Education Foundation, stated that athletes who demonstrate an imbalance that's this significant may be at a high risk for sustaining non-contact ACL tears (Metz 1999).

The combined forces of the gluteals, hamstrings and calves contribute to counteract impact and energy when decelerating from a jump or cut. (Photo by Tim "Red" Wakeham)

Recommendations

To reduce the potential for ACL injury, it's important to strengthen all of the muscles in the lower body, paying special attention to the gluteals, hamstrings and calves. For optimal strengthening, make the muscles work systematically harder over time. Four common methods to accomplish this goal are to progressively increase the weight, repetitions or sets, or to decrease the time taken between work bouts.

It's difficult to be sure whether there are "optimal" weight-training exercises for providing maximal transfer of strength to different sport movements in healthy individuals. Studies seeking to definitively find this answer are difficult to conduct because of the number of uncontrollable variables. Many sport scientists report a significant drop in measurable strength from training to performance (Wakeham 2001). The drop in carryover is seen because there are too many differences between weight-room exercises and sport performance, including the force of contraction; speed of contraction; type of contraction; joint angles; range of motion; postural positions; neuromuscular patterning (path of movements); environmental pre-

To reduce the potential for ACL injury, it's important to strengthen all of the muscles in the lower body, paying special attention to the gluteals, hamstrings and calves. (Photo by Tim "Red" Wakeham)

dictability (open versus closed); context of situation; and type of equipment (Kanehisa and Miyashita 1983; Rushall and Pyke 1991; Kraemer and Newton 1994). The significant drop in carryover can be explained by the theory of specificity. Briefly, the theory states that maximum benefits of a training stimulus are only obtained when it *replicates* the movements and energy systems involved in the sport (Rushall and Pyke 1991). Even though many researchers conclude that large drops in transfer occur because of the many different variables between the weight room and performance, it may be advantageous to try and match as many "like" variables as possible. For example, some sportsmedical professionals hypothesize that prescribing ground-based, multi-joint, resistance exercises that bring athletes through the three cardinal planes may provide meaningful transfer of strength to "like" or "similar" sport performances. Currently, however, there's little scientific evidence to directly validate this supposition. But if there's any chance to increase the amount of strength carryover — thereby decreasing risk of injury — it's recommended.

Muscle Activation

Hewett and his colleagues (1996) found that females activate their calves and hamstrings considerably less than males when decelerating from a jump. Decreased hamstring and gastrocnemius activation can allow for more inward (varus) or outward (valgus) bending at the knee. This type of landing stance is a less stable position for the knees (Noyes et al. 1992). Other researchers have determined that females tend to be "quad dominant" during both jumping and cutting activities (Colby et al. 2000; Chappell et al. 2002). The expression "quad dominant" describes the propensity to produce high levels of force with the quadriceps and low levels of force with the gluteals, hamstrings and calves during a variety of sport movements. Preferential activation of the quadriceps and low activation of the gluteals, hamstrings and calves may be the result of a different muscle recruitment order or a delayed motor signal.

One specific hypothesis is that sudden stimuli or circumstances during competition may be responsible for disrupting an athlete's coordination (Boden et al. 2000). The loss of coordination then produces recovery through an awkward movement that preferentially activates the quadriceps or at least the quadriceps first. Whether preferential or first activation of the quadriceps while decelerating from a jump or sprint is learned or reactionary, non-contact ACL risk is thought to increase (Boden, Griffin and Garrett 2000).

Recommendations

To reduce the potential for ACL injury, strengthen the hip extensor musculature to allow bending at the hips, knees and ankles; consciously try to keep the knees in alignment between the first and second toes; land softly from jumps with toe-to-heel "rocker" landings; and use several small steps while decelerating from a sprint. Research demonstrates that these changes may increase gluteal, hamstring and gastrocnemius activation while decreasing quadricep activation and peak landing and shear forces through the knees (Nisell 1985; Buff, Jones and Hungerford 1988; Bobbert 1991; Chappell et al. 2002). Furthermore, females should be instructed to focus on preferentially using their gluteals, hamstrings and calves to decelerate and pivot.

To decrease "quad dominance" caused by a loss of coordination and balance, follow the ensuing suggestions: Identify high-risk positions, postures and movements. Additionally, become aware of sport-performance surroundings (players and play) and where the limbs and joints are in relation to the rest of the body during play. Awareness of high-risk movements and the performance environment makes it easier to anticipate play and safely react and coordinate the body and specific joints when stopping, landing or pivoting suddenly.

Non-specific balancing movements may lower the risk of ACL injury. (Photo by Tim "Red" Wakeham)

Enhance sport-specific balance and coordination through purposeful practice. Specifically, practice safe joint positions, stability and spatial orientation by performing general and sport-specific balance exercises under controlled circumstances. The sport-specific (exact) movements probably provide the greatest transfer to sport performance. However, Caraffa and his associates (1996) have shown that even non-specific balancing movements may lower the risk of ACL injury. The specific mechanism of the decreased risk of ACL injury from general balance exercises wasn't fully understood.

Hewett and his co-workers (2002) suggested that practicing sport-specific balance and coordination tasks may develop into re-flexive memorized motor patterns that can be involuntarily called upon to control acceleration and deceleration if suddenly put into similar scenarios. In theory, practicing recovery movements from unexpected stimuli trains athletes to quickly recognize, orient and safely stabilize. The hope is that this education and practice provides safe avoidance or quick recruitment of the proper knee musculature to provide knee stabilization and protection from ground reaction forces.

Progressive sport-specific resistance training may enhance dynamic stability around the knee. (Photo by Tim "Red" Wakeham)

To decrease "quad dominance" because of delayed motor signal to the hip extensor musculature, condition these muscles in a sport-specific manner. Wojtys and his colleagues (1996) compared the effects of agility exercises, isotonic and isokinetic resistance training on anterior tibial translation. The group who performed the agility exercises improved the reaction time of their hamstrings and calves during anterior tibial translation. The other two forms of resistance training did not. The ability of the hamstrings and calves to quickly activate to provide a stabilization force in response to sudden lower leg stress and during deceleration may significantly protect against non-contact ACL injury during sport performance (Huston and Wojtys 1996).

Summary

Absolute strength along with a balance of strength between the hip extensors and the quadriceps and hip flexors appear to be important in preventing non-contact ACL injury. Progressive sport-specific resistance training may enhance dynamic stability around the knee.

Early or full activation of the quadriceps with delayed or absence of high activation from the gluteals, hamstrings and calves ("quad dominance") during deceleration from jumps and sprints may lead to amplified ground-impact forces, increased shear forces within the knee, increased trunk and knee extension and forward forces on the tibia (Colby et al. 2000). Enhanced strength, body control and awareness along with sport-specific balance and agility training may be the optimal prescription to improve neuromuscular stabilization.

CONCLUSIONS

The dramatic number of female non-contact ACL tears each year is a statistic with which to be concerned. There are great emotional, physical and monetary costs to the injured individual. Many researchers have attempted to better understand the underlying mechanisms. Currently, there's little consensus regarding the anatomical, physiological and environmental factors relating to non-contact ACL injury in females. Further investigation is warranted. Based on current anatomical and hormonal evidence, modification of activity or restriction from sport for females isn't warranted.

Research regarding biomechanical risk factors of ACL injury appears interrelated. Muscle strength, balance and activation all play a significant role in non-contact female ACL etiology. A well-designed and implemented strength and conditioning plan may be able to overcome problems in these areas. In addition, preparation screening is a great opportunity to identify athletes at risk for non-contact ACL injury. Screening may include muscle strength testing and biomechanical analysis.

Education regarding high-risk positions, postures and movements is another purposeful injury-prevention strategy. Furthermore, teaching avoidance techniques and recovery strategies from precarious situations may help ensure athlete safety.

Non-contact ACL injury in females is a multi-factorial problem that may be controlled through education and training. Based on current evidence, injury-prevention program design and implementation for females should be different than their male counterparts.

REFERENCES

Adams, E. 2002. *An increased risk of ACL rupture in female athletes.* Midwest Institute of Sports Medicine. Epidemiology.

American Academy of Orthopaedic Surgeons. 1997. The use of knee braces. Document number 1124. Available at http://www.AAOS.org/wordhtml/papers/position/kneebr.htm.

American Academy of Pediatrics Committee on Sports Medicine. 1990. Knee brace use by athletes. *Pediatrics* 85 (2): 228.

Anderson, A. F., A. B. Lipscomb, K. J. Liudahl and R. B. Addlestone. 1987. Analysis of the intercondylar notch by computed tomography. *The American Journal of Sports Medicine* 15 (6): 547-552.

Anderson, A. F., D. C. Dome, S. Gautam, M. H. Awh and G. W. Rennirt. 2001. Correlation of anthropometric measurements, strength, anterior cruciate ligament size, and intercondylar notch characteristics to sex differences in anterior cruciate ligament tear rates. *The American Journal of Sports Medicine* 29 (1): 58-66.

Arendt, E., and R. Dick. 1995. Knee injury patterns among men and women in collegiate basketball and soccer: NCAA data and review of literature. *The American Journal of Sports Medicine* 23 (6): 694-701.

Arendt, E. A., B. Bershadsky and J. Agel. 2002. Periodicity of noncontact anterior cruciate ligament injuries during the menstrual cycle. *Journal of Gender-Specific Medicine* 5 (2): 19-26.

Arms, S. W., M. H. Pope, R. J. Johnson, R. A. Fischer, I. Arvidsson and E. Eriksson. 1984. The biomechanics of anterior cruciate ligament rehabilitation and reconstruction. *The American Journal of Sports Medicine* 12 (1): 8-18.

Bobbert, M. F. 1991. Drop jumping as a training method for jumping ability. *Sports Medicine* 9 (1): 7-22.

Boden, B. P., L. Y. Griffin and W. E. Garrett Jr. 2000. Etiology and prevention of noncontact ACL injury. *The Physician and Sportsmedicine* 28 (4): 53-60, 107-108.

Boden, B. P., G. S. Dean, J. A. Feagin Jr and W. E. Garrett Jr. 2000. Mechanisms of anterior cruciate ligament injury. *Orthopedics* 23 (6): 573-578.

Buff, H. U., L. C. Jones and D. S. Hungerford. 1988. Experimental determination of forces transmitted through the patello-femoral joint. *Journal of Biomechanics* 21 (1): 17-23.

Caraffa, A., G. Cerulli, M. Projetti, G. Aisa and A. Rizzo. 1996. Prevention of anterior cruciate ligament injuries in soccer: a prospective controlled study of proprioceptive training. *Knee Surgery, Sports Traumatology, Arthroscopy* 4 (1): 19-21.

Chappell, J. D., B. Yu, D. T. Kirkendall and W. E. Garrett. 2002. A comparison of knee kinetics between male and female recreational athletes in stop-jump tasks. *The American Journal of Sports Medicine* 30 (2): 261-267.

Colby, S., A. Francisco, B. Yu, D. Kirkendall, M. Finch and W. Garrett Jr. 2000. Electromyographic and kinematic analysis of cutting maneuvers: implications for anterior cruciate ligament injury. *The American Journal of Sports Medicine* 28 (2): 234-240.

Cross, M. J. 1998. Anterior cruciate ligament injuries: treatment and rehabilitation. In *Encyclopedia of sports medicine and science*, ed. T. D. Fahey. Internet Society for Sport Science. Available at http://sportsci.org. (February 26).

Feagin Jr, J. A., and K. L. Lambert. 1985. Mechanism of injury and pathology of anterior cruciate ligament injuries. *Orthopedic Clinics of North America* 16 (1): 41-45.

Griffin, L. Y. 2000. Better understanding of ACL injury prevention. *The NCAA News* 10 (9).

Griffin, L. Y., J. Agel, M. J. Albohm, E. A. Arendt, R. W. Dick, W. E. Garrett, J. G. Garrick, T. E. Hewett, L. Huston, M. L. Ireland, R. J. Johnson, W. B. Kibler, S. Lephart, J. L. Lewis, T. N. Lindenfeld, B. R. Mandelbaum, P. Marchak, C. C. Teitz and E. M. Wojtys. 2000. Noncontact anterior cruciate ligament injuries: risk factors and prevention strategies. *Journal of the American Academy of Orthopaedic Surgeons* 8 (3): 141-151.

Haycock, C. E., and J. V. Gillette. 1976. Susceptibility of women athletes to injury: myths vs reality. *Journal of the American Medical Association* 236 (2): 163-165.

Hewett, T. E. 2000. Neuromuscular and hormonal factors associated with knee injuries in female athletes: strategies for intervention. *Sports Medicine* 29 (5): 313-327.

Hewett, T. E., A. L. Stroupe, T. A. Nance and F. R. Noyes. 1996. Plyometric training in female athletes: decreased impact forces and increased hamstring torques. *The American Journal of Sports Medicine* 24 (6): 765-773.

Hewett, T. E., M. V. Paterno and F. R. Noyes. 1999. Differences in single leg balance on an unstable platform between female and male normal and ACL deficient and ACL reconstructed knees. Paper presented at the American Orthopaedic Society for Sports Medicine Annual Conference.

Hewett, T. E., G. D. Myer, K. R. Rord and M. V. Paterno. 2002. The gender gap. *Rehab Management* 6: 1-3.

Huston, L. J., and E M. Wojtys. 1996. Neuromuscular performance characteristics in elite female athletes. *The American Journal of Sports Medicine* 24 (4): 427-436.

Huston, L. J., B. Vibert, J. A. Ashton-Miller and E. M. Wojtys. 2001. Gender differences in knee angle when landing from a drop-jump. *American Journal of Knee Surgery* 14 (4): 215-219.

Hutchinson, M. R., and M. L. Ireland. 1995. Knee injuries in female athletes. *Sports Medicine* 19 (4): 288-302.

Ireland, M. L., and C. Wall. 1990. Epidemiology and comparison of knee injuries in elite male and female US basketball athletes. *Medicine and Science in Sports and Exercise* 22: 582.

Kanehisa, H., and M. Miyashita. 1983. Specificity of velocity in strength training. *European Journal of Applied Physiology* 52 (1): 365-371.

Kraemer, W. J., and R. U. Newton. 1994. Training for improved vertical jump. *Sports Science Exchange* 7 (6): 1-5.

Lambson, R. B., B. S. Barnhill and R. W. Higgins. 1996. Football cleat design and its effect on anterior cruciate ligament injuries: a three year prospective study. *The American Journal of Sports Medicine* 24 (2): 155-159.

Malinzak, R. A., S. M. Colby, D. T. Kirkendall, B. Yu and W. E. Garrett. 2001. A comparison of knee joint motion patterns between men and women in selected athletic tasks. *Clinical Biomechanics* 16 (5): 438-445.

Metz, G. 1999. Restoring the balance. *Training & Conditioning* 9 (3): 10-19.

Moore, J. R., and G. Wade. 1989. Training for muscle balance: prevention of anterior cruciate ligament injuries. *National Strength & Conditioning Journal* 11 (3): 35-40.

Myklebust, G., S. Maehlum, L. Engebretsen, T. Strand and E. Solheim. 1997. Registration of cruciate ligament injuries in Norwegian top level team handball: a prospective study covering two seasons. *Scandinavian Journal of Medicine and Science in Sports* 7 (5): 289-292.

Nisell, R. 1985. Mechanics of the knee: a study of joint and muscle load with clinical applications. *Acta Orthopaedica Scandinavica* Supplement 216 (56): 1-42.

Norkin, C. C., and P. K. Levangie. 1983. *Joint structure and function: a comprehensive analysis.* Philadelphia, PA: F. A. Davis Co.

Noyes, F. R., P. A. Mooar, D. S. Matthews and D. L. Butler. 1983. The symptomatic anterior cruciate-deficient knee. Part I: the long-term functional disability in athletically active individuals. *Journal of Bone and Joint Surgery* (American) 65 (2): 154-62.

Noyes, F. R., O. D. Schipplein, T. P. Andriacchi, S. R. Saddemi and M. Weise. 1992. The anterior cruciate ligament-deficient knee with varus alignment: an analysis of gait adaptations and dynamic joint loadings. *The American Journal of Sports Medicine* 20 (6): 707-716.

Posthuma, B. W., M. J. Bass, S. B. Bull and J. A. Nisker. 1987. Detecting changes in functional ability in women with premenstrual syndrome. *American Journal of Obstetrics and Gynecology* 156 (2): 275-278.

Rozzi, S. L., S. M. Lephart, W. S. Gear and F. H. Fu. 1999. Knee joint laxity and neuromuscular characteristics of male and female soccer and basketball players. *The American Journal of Sports Medicine* 27 (3): 312-319.

Rushall, B. S., and F. S. Pyke. 1991. *Training for sports and fitness.* Melbourne, Australia: MacMillian Company.

Schnirring, L. 1997. What's new in treating active women. *The Physician and Sportsmedicine* 25 (7): 91.

Silvers, H. J., and B. R. Mandelbaum. 2002. Are ACL tears preventable in the female athlete? *Medscape Orthopaedics & Sports Medicine* (6) 2.

Souryal, T. O., H. A. Moore and J. P. Evans. 1988. Bilaterality in anterior cruciate ligament injuries: associated intercondylar notch stenosis. *The American Journal of Sports Medicine* 16 (5): 449-454.

Souryal, T. O., and T. R. Freeman. 1993. Intercondylar notch size and anterior cruciate ligament injuries: a prospective study. *The American Journal of Sports Medicine* 21 (4): 535-539.

Stauber, W. T. 1989. Eccentric action of muscles: physiology, injury, and adaptation. *Exercise and Sport Science Reviews* 17: 157-185.

Toth, A. P., and F. A. Cordasco. 2001. Anterior cruciate ligament injuries in the female athlete. *Journal of Gender-Specific Medicine* 4 (4): 25-34.

Wakeham, T. 2001. Training for the game. *Training & Conditioning* 11 (3): 41-47.

Wojtys, E. M., L. J. Huston, P. D. Taylor and S. D. Bastian. 1996. Neuromuscular adaptations in isokinetic, isotonic, and agility training programs. *The American Journal of Sports Medicine* 24 (2): 187-192.

Wojtys, E. J., L. J. Huston and J. A. Ashton-Miller. 1998. Active knee stiffness differs between young men and women. Presented at the annual meeting of the American Orthopaedic Society for Sports Medicine. Vancouver, British Columbia.

Yu, W. D., S. H. Liu, J. D. Hatch, V. Panossian and G. A. Finerman. 1999. Effect of estrogen on cellular metabolism of the human anterior cruciate ligament. *Clinical Orthopaedics* 366: 229-238.

9

Improving Flexibility

Rachael E. Picone, M.S.

Flexibility can be defined as "the range of motion (ROM) that's available at a specific joint or group of joints." When applied to the physical attributes of an athlete, flexibility describes the capability to bend or flex freely through a normal and full ROM without injury. Each movable joint in the body has a ROM that can be measured, evaluated and improved until an optimal range is met.

In a sports program, flexibility is only one of many interrelated components of conditioning that plays a crucial role in functioning as an athlete. Flexibility complements cardiovascular endurance and muscular strength. Without it, total fitness cannot be achieved. Unfortunately, flexibility is often misunderstood and neglected by coaches and athletes alike. Both tend to undervalue the true potential of an effective stretching program and often lack patience to view it as anything more than a time-consuming nuisance. This may be due, in part, to the fact that stretching is a low-intensity activity and its results aren't visible through physical appearance.

Flexibility is only one of many interrelated components of conditioning that plays a crucial role in functioning as an athlete. (Photo courtesy of Ben Barnhart Photo Services)

Athletes must understand, however, that maintaining a flexible body is important as it has the potential to maximize performance while minimizing injury. On a professional or amateur level, goals of optimal performance can be attained through a balanced, synchronized, commonsense approach to fitness. Athletes will function at their personal best only when flexibility training becomes a serious part of their overall program.

WHAT DETERMINES RANGE OF MOTION?

Restriction of movement is controlled by multiple internal and external factors including genetics, physiological changes, specific diseases and lifestyle habits. When you consider all of the determining factors that affect flexibility, it becomes easy to see why each joint — as well as each athlete — has such a

Regular, moderate-level activities — such as walking and jogging — along with stretching promote greater flexibility. (Photo courtesy of James Cleaver)

distinct ROM. Indeed, some athletes have great shoulder flexibility but lack hamstring flexibility. It's also quite common for some athletes to have bilateral differences in flexibility — that is, one side of the body is more flexible than the other. While there's not much to be done about traits with which an athlete is predisposed and, consequently, cannot be controlled, some factors can be controlled. Coaches and athletes need to be aware that these should be considered of primary importance and focus. The following breakdown of factors and their influence on optimal flexibility will help foster an understanding of how the most effective training program can be developed.

Activity Level

Physical activity — which is, by far, the most influential controllable factor of flexibility — has the capability of restoring, improving and maintaining a healthy ROM. Conversely, inactivity promotes a loss of flexibility, increasing the chances of injury. Regular, moderate-level activities — such as walking and jogging — along with stretching promote greater flexibility. The frequency, intensity, duration and technique of the stretching program will determine its effectiveness.

Age

The relationship between age and flexibility still remains unclear. Research data are often difficult to interpret and compare due to factors such as a lack of testing-method standardization, large variations in population studies, joint-specificity differences and ranges of physiological growth. Although it appears that children are quite flexible, research generally demonstrates that only younger children possess high levels of flexibility. During the school years, flexibility decreases until puberty — possibly as a result of bone growth — which may cause tightness around joints. This childhood period of rapid growth and lowered flexibility potentially increases a young athlete's susceptibility to injuries due to overextension of muscles and joints. Flexibility levels have been shown to increase throughout adolescence, level off at physical maturity and finally decrease in adulthood. It has been proposed that when body tissues — such as ligaments and tendons — reach maturity in late adolescence, a plateau of flexibility is reached.

By comparison, older adults see a decline in flexibility and have a tendency to become stiff and tight. As part of the normal aging process, unwelcome changes occur: The musculoskeletal system grows weaker, discs in the spine begin to deteriorate, hormone levels decrease and connective tissues lose elasticity. The unfortunate end result is joint stiffness and pain along with a decline in mobility and stability. Although it's never too late in life to begin a program of flexibility training, the best time to educate athletes about the many benefits of stretching is unquestionably while they are young.

Anatomy

Since joints are regularly pushed and pulled, they must be stabilized so that they don't stretch beyond their optimal range and dislocate. Therefore, the natural characteristics of joints, ligaments, tendons, muscles and bones restrict ROM. The specific type and shape of the joint structure determines the extent of movement that it allows. Ball-and-socket joints — such as those in the hips and shoulders — offer extensive circumduction motion as compared with the knee, which is designed to permit only angular, hinge-like movement. The shape and positioning of bones also determines joint motion. It isn't possible, for example, to turn the ankle completely and place the side of the foot on the ground because bone impinges on bone and motion is stopped. The size, position and elasticity of ligaments, muscles, tendons and skin also play a role in determining flexibility. The number of stabilizing ligaments will affect joint movement to a large degree; more ligaments equal a stronger joint.

Body Composition

Excessive amounts of body fat impose restriction of motion simply by interfering with the ability of the body to move and stretch in certain positions. Excess abdominal fat, for instance, has been shown to interfere with the ROM in a Sit-and-Reach Test. Naturally, a reduction of body fat will usually lead to improvements in flexibility.

Body Temperature

Elevating the temperature of deep muscle tissue increases fiber elasticity, helping muscles to become more pliable and supple. As muscles and connective tissues are more easily lengthened, ROM improves. Increasing blood flow and warming a joint through dynamic movements — such as walking or cycling — improves flexibility and, therefore, positively affects athletic performance. Stretching cold muscles isn't only ineffective but may also present the risk for injury.

Disease

Joint disease commonly affects ROM due to the pain, stiffness and inflammation that it causes. Arthritis, as an example, reduces ROM in several ways. In rheumatoid arthritis, the joint becomes severely inflamed causing pain and stiffness. Osteoarthritis is characterized by degeneration of the joint: The protective cartilage between the two connecting bones begins to wear away, leaving the bone ends exposed and unprotected which results in painful distortion of joints. Other conditions that may affect ROM include neurological disease or injury, orthopedic spinal conditions, bone cancer, osteomalacia and chronic fatigue syndrome.

Gender

Females generally seem to have greater flexibility than males, attributed in part to anatomical differences in joint structure. For instance, the female pelvis exhibits many differences — such as broader hips and a shallower pelvic cavity — that lead to greater pelvic ROM. Compared to males, females may also be more inclined to partake in activities such as dance and gymnastics that emphasize the flexibility component of fitness. It has also been speculated that the cyclical effects of a woman's hormones contribute to increased laxity of the joint.

Females may be more inclined to partake in activities that emphasize the flexibility component of fitness. (Photo courtesy of Rutgers University Sports Media Relations and Information)

Hypermobility

Being hypermobile — or overflexible — is used to describe those who are considerably more flexible than normal. The term "double-jointed" is also commonly used, though these athletes don't have any extra anatomical joints as the name might suggest. Because the joint ligaments and capsules have greater laxity, the joints can move much further than normal. Hypermobility may be seen in all the joints throughout the body or at specific joints. The degree of joint laxity may be affected by a combination of factors including muscle tone and muscle-belly length, connective tissues, temperature, hormones, training, gender and genetics. Though maintaining joint stability through strength training is critical — especially with increasing age — hypermobility may not necessarily impose a problem or disadvantage

Injury

Depending upon their severity, injuries to muscles, connective tissues, and bones can limit movement. Symptoms of pain and swelling are often restricting factors in limiting ROM. Acute ligament sprains and muscle/tendon strains occur when the tissue is simply overstretched, usually by either a sudden twisting motion or a direct blow. In chronic and repetitive-motion injuries — such as bursitis and tendinitis — the pain leads to disuse. Inactivity further impairs ROM by shortening connective tissues and opposing the healing of inelastic scar tissue. An athlete may experience complete loss of function with more severe injuries such as bone fractures, tendon ruptures, ligament tears and dislocations. Flexibility levels and functional movement will vary over the course of rehabilitation.

THE VALUE OF STRETCHING

The benefits of having a normal or high degree of ROM are numerous and diverse. Most athletes are aware they should be stretching but many fail to do so — or fail to do so *properly*. Perhaps the best way to convince athletes to spend quality time stretching their muscles is to explain and continually emphasize how flexibility directly relates to their athletic performance and personal health. Understanding all of the benefits derived from developing and maintaining optimal flexibility will educate athletes and, in turn, help them stay motivated to continue with a program of regular stretching. The benefits include:

An athlete depends upon a large degree of functional flexibility for successful sports participation. (Photo courtesy of Katie Vetland)

• *Improvement in skills and sports performance.* An athlete depends upon a large degree of functional flexibility for successful sports participation. Stretching promotes a greater ROM which makes executing skills easier and improves the quality of movement. Due to less resistance in the joint, motions require less energy and are simply more efficient. Flexibility training can also increase neuromuscular coordination and fine-tune the agonist/antagonist relationship. An increase in flexibility has the potential to directly enhance and refine technique which will invariably lead to improved athletic performance.

• *Prevention, decreased severity and treatment of injury/disease.* Injury prevention is one of the main reasons that stretching becomes so vitally important for women who participate in sports. Stretching — which increases and maintains ROM — protects against injuries that may result from the physical demands imposed by athletics. Tight muscles are weak; they offer no joint protection and may contribute to cramping. If one area of the body is tight and inefficient, other parts of the body will attempt to compensate and the risk of injury increases.

In addition to decreasing the initial risk for injury, the severity of a sustained injury will — in all likelihood — be less if the woman has been conditioned with an effective flexibility program. This translates into less pain and less recovery time for an athlete. Rehabilitation from an injury always involves stretching. Even with gentle ROM exercises, early mobilization — that is, moving the tissue — increases circulation to the joint, may decrease pain and greatly aids in recovery. For an athlete to return to participation, a full ROM is essential and must be re-gained through rehabilitation.

- *Improvement in posture and muscle symmetry.* Posture affects energy level, appearance, efficiency and freedom of movement as well as sports performance. Sitting and standing habits, occupational tasks, bone density and muscular strengths and weaknesses directly influence posture. Poor posture may increase vulnerability to problems including low-back, neck and shoulder pain — all of which affect sports performance. Stretching — which emphasizes proper body alignment and posture awareness — minimizes stress to the spine and such problems.

    Tight muscles caused by exercise, aging or stress can also affect posture by creating muscular imbalances. An imbalance occurs when muscles on one side of a joint become far weaker — or less flexible — than muscles on the opposing side of a joint. Maintaining a balance between the strength and flexibility of each muscle group is the key to improving posture and achieving muscular symmetry. Restoring the muscles to their optimal lengths and balancing the opposing muscle groups strengthens the working condition and efficiency of an athlete.

- *Alleviation of delayed-onset muscular soreness.* Vigorous physical activity often causes delayed-onset muscular soreness, commonly referred to as "DOMS." Symptoms — inevitable to some degree with strenuous athletics — usually appear when athletes have been overworked or overstressed to a point that they haven't yet adapted. Typical symptoms of DOMS include stiffness, weakness, reduced ROM and muscle tenderness. Pain develops 6 - 12 hours after exercise, peaking at 24 - 48 hours. Dynamic movement and stretching have been shown to reduce the pain associated with DOMS.

Vigorous physical activity often causes delayed-onset muscular soreness, commonly referred to as "DOMS." (Photo courtesy of Image Extreme)

- *Prevention of decreased ROM associated with aging.* As joints are exercised through their full ROM, tissue temperature increases and a supply of blood — which is rich in nutrients — is circulated throughout the joint structure. Within the joint capsule itself, the synovial fluid decreases in thickness and increases in quantity, fully lubricating the joint and allowing a greater ROM. More nutrients can then be transported to the articular cartilage as both the joint circulation and the quality of the synovial fluid improves. This combined effect opposes the loss of elasticity and joint deceleration that's often seen with aging.

- *Reduction in low-back pain and injury.* It has been estimated that at one time or another, painful and debilitating low-back problems are experienced by 60 - 80% of the entire population. Most low-back problems develop gradually from multiple causes including low levels of muscular strength and flexibility, muscular imbalances, poor posture, repetitious work and psychological stress. When muscles and ligaments in the spine become stressed and mechanical imbalances occur, the soft tissues that support the lower back become vulnerable to strains. Movement and stretching nourish the spine and help preserve a natural curvature. This allows greater freedom and efficiency of movement in all directions, improvement in posture and less muscular tension. A balanced, consistent stretching program that focuses on the muscles of the hamstrings and lower back is recommended to prevent and reduce low-back pain.

- *Decreased muscular tension and stress.* Everyday physical and emotional stress in our lives damages many systems in our bodies. In response to stress, we tense our muscles. Unconscious habits of contracting muscles can cause chronic discomfort including low-back, shoulder, jaw and neck pain; headaches; fatigue; and vulnerability to injury and illness. Awareness of varying levels of tension — the first step towards relaxation — is better understood through stretching. As a stretch is held and attention is directed to the way the body feels, muscular tension is gradually released.

   Excessive stress prior to — or during — athletic competition can also result in acute tightening of muscles and may negatively affect athletic performance. Mental concentration may be hindered as well. Stretching purely for relaxation — rather than as an attempt to increase flexibility — is commonly recommended to diminish competition-related anxiety. An athlete should incorporate deep breathing and progressive relaxation techniques along with stretching to further promote relaxation. Returning the body to its natural, relaxed, balanced state helps normalize physical, mental and emotional processes.

- *Improved health benefits in women.* Stretching often relieves muscular cramps, backache and general fatigue associated with the female menstrual cycle. Exercises should focus on proper posture to minimize stress on the spine. Slow stretching and proper breathing will further promote relaxation. Gentle stretching is encouraged throughout the day as often as needed.

WARMING UP

Since warming up and stretching can both be carried out prior to an activity, the terms have mistakenly been used. Stretching isn't inclusively considered a warm-up; it is, however, part of the entire warm-up process which usually includes one to three distinct phases. The three phases of a warm-up are discussed in detail in the subsequent paragraphs and summarized in Figure 9.1.

Phase One

Increasing the blood flow to the muscles and slightly elevating the core temperature is the goal of Phase One; steady-state, full-body, aerobic exercise best accomplishes this general warm-up. Low- to moderate-intensity activity — such as walking, cycling or jumping rope — should be done for approximately five minutes or until an individual breaks a light sweat. The activity should gradually increase in intensity and sufficiently warm up the body without creating fatigue. A general warm-up is recommended for both fitness enthusiasts and serious athletes.

It's imperative to stretch prior to a conditioning session that calls for the immediate and extreme physical demands for which an athlete must be prepared to meet. (Photo courtesy of the University of Massachusetts Media Relations)

Phase Two

In Phase Two, general dynamic exercises are performed in order to continue preparing the synovial joints for more vigorous activity. After the general warm-up, mobility exercises can include the following: neck, shoulder, hip, ankle and wrist rotations; shoulder rolls; knee lifts; trunk flexion/extension; and partial squats. These dynamic movements should be slow and controlled through a complete and natural ROM, gradually increasing in speed and intensity with the purpose of loosening up muscles and joints. One or two sets of approximately 6 - 15 repetitions will be adequate for a sports-conditioning program.

Pre-activity stretching — which is also included in Phase Two — is only intended to prepare the body for activity and shouldn't be viewed as a means of increasing flexibility. It's imperative to stretch prior to a conditioning session that calls for the immediate and extreme physical demands for which an athlete must be prepared to meet. Pre-competition stretching is also a good idea, since the length of a stride or stroke can be crucial to performance. Stretching prior to weight-bearing activity should focus on the lower back, hamstrings, calves, chronically tight muscles and areas most susceptible to injury. Pre-stretching isn't always necessary if an individual is exercising purely for fitness benefits and the workout includes low- to moderate-intensity activities such as walking, cycling or jogging.

Phase Three

Sport-specific movements and stretches — depending upon the type and level of activity to be done — comprise the third phase of a comprehensive warm-up. Gymnasts, for example, would practice handstands and pike jumps along with performing positions such as splits and scales. The sport-specific

PHASE	TYPE	PURPOSE	METHOD
One	general warm-up	• increase the blood flow to the muscles and elevate the core temperature	• perform full-body, aerobic exercise
Two	dynamic exercises	• continue to prepare the muscles and joints for more vigorous activity	• do mobility exercises (such as shoulder rotation)
	pre-activity stretching	• prepare the body for activity	• stretch the lower back, hamstrings, calves, chronically tight muscles and areas susceptible to injury
Three	sport-specific movements and stretches	• rehearse movements physically and mentally	• do sport-specific activity

FIGURE 9.1: THE THREE PHASES OF A WARM-UP

phase of a warm-up gives an athlete time to rehearse both physically and mentally.

The best time to improve long-term flexibility, however, is at the end of a workout when the muscles are "tight" (from being exercised) and are still warm and pliable. An effective post-activity stretching program also harmonizes the mind and body, creating a calming mood and positive shift of focus to conclude a training session.

TYPES OF STRETCHES

Although limiting factors do exist, improvements in flexibility result when ROM is progressively overloaded by elongating the tissue beyond its resting length. This can be accomplished by several distinct — but somewhat controversial — methods. Although variations and combinations exist, the three basic types of stretches to increase flexibility include ballistic, static and proprioceptive neuromuscular facilitation. Stretches that are aimed at improving the available ROM are designed to reduce the internal resistance of the muscles and connective tissues. Decreasing the resistance is accomplished two ways: by increasing the length of connective tissue or attaining a greater degree of relaxation within the muscle. Careful application of a relaxed, low-force, pro-

Static stretching is the preferred technique because it imposes less risk of overstretching the tissues and may result in less muscular soreness when compared to other methods. (Photo courtesy of Image Extreme)

longed stretch utilizes both of these methods. The best way may depend upon an athlete's physical condition and whether or not there's a desire to increase or maintain ROM.

Ballistic Stretching

Ballistic stretching is a high-force, short-duration stretch that utilizes repetitive bouncing movements to create a stretch. For example, an athlete assumes a seated straddle position and then bounces towards the floor to stretch her hamstrings. Though well intentioned, ballistic stretching presents the risk for serious injury. The movements are uncontrolled and rapid and have the potential to overstretch soft tissues beyond their normal limits, thereby causing damage to the muscle. The excessive momentum and extreme stretch of a ballistic motion may cause the body to react with the "stretch reflex" by contracting (or shortening) the target muscle that's trying to be stretched. Attempting to stretch a muscle that's contracted is dangerous and contradictory to the goal of increasing flexibility. For this reason, ballistic stretching isn't advisable.

Static Stretching

Static stretching — the most common technique for flexibility training that's practiced by athletes — is simple, convenient, safe and effective. Slow, deliberate movements teach awareness of body position and posture as well as muscle tension and relaxation. Learning to recognize limits of flexibility — an important factor in avoiding injury — is another value of static stretching.

To benefit from static stretching, a muscle is pulled slightly beyond its resting length and held at a point of slight tension; force is then slowly applied to produce further stretching. Since active stretching doesn't always produce enough force to increase muscle length, passive assistance — self-assisted or partner-assisted — is usually necessary. A towel, stretching strap, resistance tubing or the hands can be used to apply additional passive assistance. For instance, an athlete assumes a quadricep stretch to the point of light tension; additional torque is then passively applied by gently pulling her foot toward her buttocks. The position is held and the body relaxes to stretch even further. The movement is never pulled to the point of pain but is mild and executed gradually, carefully and under complete control.

Static stretching is of such low force that the muscles and connective tissues require a greater time to elongate. Although it requires a longer time than a high-force ballistic stretch, the proportion of lengthening that remains is greater. Slow, sustained, static stretching also diminishes the stretch reflex. Static stretching is the preferred technique because it imposes less risk of overstretching the tissues and may result in less muscular soreness when compared to other methods.

Proprioceptive Neuromuscular Facilitation

As its name implies, proprioceptive neuromuscular facilitation (PNF) is slightly more complex than static stretching and can intimidate a coach or an athlete who isn't familiar with the term or the theories behind its practice. It was originally designed in the 1950s to rehabilitate paralysis patients and is successfully used today by many top athletes. PNF goes one step beyond static stretching by incorporating an isometric contraction of either the muscle being stretched or it's opposite.

Various forms of PNF stretching are used, depending upon the condition of the person and the situation. Two common techniques are contract-relax (CR) and contract-relax-antagonist-contract (CRAC).

In a three-step CR sequence — also known as "hold-relax" (HR) — with passive assistance (that is, resistance of one's own hands or a partner's), the tight muscle group is first gently stretched; this is followed by an isometric contraction of the same muscle group for approximately 6 - 15 seconds. The muscle is then relaxed and again, using passive assistance, immediately taken into a greater ROM. The reasoning behind the CR technique is rooted in the "inverse stretch reflex"; the contraction is thought to produce a relaxation phase in the same muscle.

Based upon concepts of reciprocal inhibition, the "contract-relax-antagonist-contract" (CRAC) technique follows the same sequence as CR with one modification: A 6- to 15-second contraction of the antagonist — or the muscle opposite the one that an athlete wishes to stretch — follows the relaxation phase; an athlete actively moves the limb into a new ROM and then proceeds with a second contraction to elicit reciprocal inhibition of the target muscle, allowing a deeper stretch. Isometric contractions shouldn't be explosive but should gradually build to a less-than-maximal contraction. PNF sequences are usually repeated several times with at least 20 seconds of rest between repetitions.

PNF stretches are at least as effective — if not superior — to other techniques in developing flexibility. This may be the preferred method when trying to improve flexibility, especially in extremely tight muscles. Although PNF may be modified to use individually, a partner usually assists with the contraction and final stretch phases. Coaches, athletic trainers and training partners have successfully applied PNF techniques but it's imperative that partners are adequately instructed in the technique to prevent injury. Subjects need to give verbal feedback to the partner and, in turn, partners must use caution in the amount of force that they provide.

DESIGNING A FLEXIBILITY PROGRAM

Undoubtedly, individual safety is the primary consideration in designing a flexibility-training program. But personal goals, level of maturity, experience and physical condition should also be taken into consideration. Training can be personalized to meet different needs, though programs should be designed with the same overall goal: to keep muscles and connective tissue supple, healthy and functional while maintaining the strength and integrity of the joint. Since there are different approaches to increasing flexibility, it's important to find a method with which an athlete is comfortable. Keep in mind that personal preferences and rates of progress will vary from one athlete to another.

Stretching as a group or team can promote camaraderie while giving athletes a chance to perform stretches with a partner (if necessary). It's strongly suggested that coaches view stretching as a *part* of practice and allow athletes ample time for flexibility training. Coaches should be certain that athletes actually take the necessary time to stretch by providing supervision as well as ensuring that stretching movements are performed safely and correctly.

Frequency, Intensity and Duration

Although the debate concerning the frequency, intensity and duration of stretching continues, athletes are encouraged to follow a few general guidelines. In terms of frequency, mobility and flexibility training should be included at least three days per week, preferably on a daily basis. Spontaneous stretching throughout the day isn't enough to improve flexibility; a consistent stretching program can mean the difference between making progress and not. Athletes need to stretch before and after training and may benefit from additional stretching on their own time.

The intensity of stretching may greatly depend upon whether or not an athlete is attempting to rehabilitate, increase or maintain ROM. During stretching, intensity — which is subjective — involves two factors: body position and the force or torque applied. Stretching positions can be modified for the beginner, intermediate and advanced athlete, thus varying intensity. Stretches should be gradual and gentle and only to the point of mild discomfort. Athletes should progress into a greater ROM simply by applying slightly more force.

It's generally recommended that each stretch be held for a duration of about 15 - 60 seconds. The use of a clock or stopwatch is highly suggested to initially help athletes learn an appropriate amount of time to spend in a stretch. Athletes should stay in the stretched position as long as it feels comfortable, taking extra time whenever needed. To make the stretch more effective, athletes should be encouraged to focus on feeling their muscles release and relax. For maximum results, the stretches can be repeated up to four times with an increase in repetitions as training progresses.

TEN TIPS FOR PROPER STRETCHING

1. Evaluate flexibility and monitor progress. Specifically, attempt to maintain

or improve upon the ROM in the previous workout.

2. Wear comfortable clothing that doesn't restrict movement. Removing footwear may be helpful to stretch the muscles of the lower body — that is, the quadriceps, hamstrings, calves, dorsi flexors and those in the feet.

3. Work at your own pace. Begin slowly and listen to your body. Since flexibility will vary greatly from one person to the next, stretching should never be competitive and should always be practiced within one's own limits. Overstretching beyond the body's natural limits will only weaken joints, making an individual more susceptible to injury.

4. Perform the movements through a comfortable, pain-free ROM.

5. Always include a general warm-up before pre-activity stretching. Perform flexibility exercises at the end of a workout when the core temperature is elevated and the tissues are warm and pliable.

6. Do a balanced routine that includes at least one stretch for each muscle group. Because flexibility is specific to each joint, it cannot be easily improved or maintained with one or two quick stretches. A core routine should include stretches for the gluteals, inner thigh, hamstrings, quadriceps, calves, chest, upper back, shoulders, arms, wrists, abdominals, lower back and neck. Stretch opposing muscles and emphasize chronically tight areas such as the lower back and hamstrings.

7. Incorporate sport-specific stretches into the warm-up that will be used during physical activity or sport participation.

8. Concentrate on technique by focusing on proper body alignment and isolating the target muscles involved in the stretch.

9. Become aware of your breathing rhythm. Inhale and exhale properly by taking deep, slow breaths that originate from the abdomen. Don't hold your breath while stretching.

10. Relax before and during the stretch. A relaxed muscle will move through a greater ROM.

REFERENCES

Corbin, C. B., R. Linsey and G. Welk. 2000. *Concepts of physical fitness. 10th ed.* New York, NY: McGraw-Hill.

O'Connor, B., K. Fasting, D. Dahm and C. Wells. 2001. *Complete conditioning for the female athlete: a guide for coaches & athletes.* Terre Haute, IN: Wish Publishing.

Picone, R. E. 2000. Improving functional flexibility. In *Maximize your training: insights from leading strength and fitness professionals*, ed. M. Brzycki, 355-387. New York, NY: McGraw-Hill/Contemporary.

10

The Female Athlete Triad

Rachael E. Picone, M.S.

Whether you're an elite competitive athlete, someone who's just physically active or an individual who's associated with training athletes, it's likely that you've never before heard the term "female athlete triad." This is a relatively new disorder and has only been discussed within the athletic and sportsmedical communities since the 1990s. The triad — which relates to physically active girls and women — was acknowledged and defined in 1992 as members of the Women's Task Force of the American College of Sports Medicine (ACSM) revealed that female athletes were being afflicted with a combination of problems that resulted in harmful consequences.

This new "syndrome" is really a set of symptoms that produces damaging physical and psychological consequences. The female athlete triad is comprised of three linked medical conditions that occur in sequence: disordered eating, menstrual irregularities and premature osteoporosis. As a result of disordered eating or inadequate nutrition, for example, the hypothalamus — which is responsible for regulating the endocrine gland — affects menses and the production of estrogen. The lack of protective estrogen, in turn, leads to weakened bones and significantly increases the prevalence of injury — a condition that's usually only thought of as a disease of the elderly. The reason this becomes such a major concern is because the first two decades of life are absolutely critical for bone development. Anything that disrupts bone growth in young females who haven't yet achieved a peak in bone density can be devastating. Adolescents and young adults must maximize bone density early in life for optimal skeletal health.

Adolescents and young adults must maximize bone density early in life for optimal skeletal health. (Photo courtesy of Katie Vetland)

THE ROOT OF THE PROBLEM

If physical activity — especially weight-bearing activity — has been shown to greatly benefit girls and women, then why are females at such risk? The causes — and effects — of this disorder aren't completely understood. It's a complicated issue arising from a combination of physiological, psychological and sociological factors. At the underlying core of the female athlete triad appear to be both external and internal pressures that cause an athlete to have a heightened focus on thinness. Expectations to fit a specific body image can come from parents, coaches, judges, sports agents or teammates. The Western culture only exacerbates the dilemma; today's "healthy" look — unattainable by most — is "thin" and girls and women are constantly subjected to society's acceptable message that being thin equates with happiness and success. Young female athletes are driven to excel yet they're under enormous pressure to meet an unrealistic standard of thinness. They receive two conflicting messages: Be strong, aggressive and assertive; and continue to maintain an "ideal bodyweight and shape" (which, in most cases, resembles that of a 10-year-old girl). The message they should be receiving, however, is that the healthiest and best-fueled athlete will, in fact, triumph.

The female athlete triad has now been recognized across all sports and all fitness levels including physically active girls and women who aren't competing. (Photo courtesy of Image Extreme)

Although endurance athletes, gymnasts and dancers seem to be more at risk, the triad has now been recognized across all sports and all fitness levels including physically active girls and women who aren't competing. Pre-adolescent and adolescent girls as well as young adults face an increased risk. At the time of puberty, concerns about body image range from normal interest to excessive anxiety. It's not uncommon for a young girl who develops an eating disorder — and, ultimately, the triad — to feel out of control, imperfect and inadequate. The American Psychiatric Association states that the average age of onset for an eating disorder is 17 and that it's often associated with a stressful life event such as leaving home for college. Given the pressures to achieve or maintain a certain bodyweight, society's message that "thin is in," concerns about body image during adolescence and external psychological stresses, it's not surprising that many turn to disordered eating as a primary coping strategy.

PREVALENCE OF THE TRIAD

The extent of the female athlete triad in athletes and dancers isn't known at this time. Research studies conducted since the late 1980s have given us a clearer understanding of how the components of the triad are related, how they can be prevented and how the triad can be treated. The research and knowledge about this inchoate issue is limited, however. Eating disorders are particularly challenging to study and are often underreported and significantly underdiagnosed. Individuals may feel threatened or be embarrassed about revealing their eating patterns and, therefore, aren't honest in completing health questionnaires and surveys.

Within the general population, the prevalence of females in late adolescence and early adulthood that meet the full criteria for anorexia nervosa is approximately 0.5 - 1.0%. More common may be individuals who are sub-threshold for the disorder or those who fall into the category of "eating disorder not otherwise specified." Bulimia nervosa is estimated to occur within 1 - 3% of young adult females in the general population and may be as high as 10% among college females. In the athletic population, disordered eating behaviors are reported to occur between 15 - 62%. Disordered eating is also reported to have high recurrence rates (up to 50%). In the general population, the extent of amenorrhea has been estimated at 2 - 5% and — depending on the definition used — at 3 - 66% among athletes. The incidence is high among gymnasts, distance runners, ballet dancers, figure skaters, equestrian participants and divers. The prevalence of premature osteoporosis in the female athletic population is unknown.

ATHLETES AT RISK

Several typical characteristics exist for girls and women that increase their risk of developing one or more of the triad components. The pressure to excel often drives these competitive and dedicated athletes. Perfectionism and self-critical behavior combined with low self-esteem and depression may set the stage for grappling with the female athlete triad.

Although the disorder can potentially be found across all levels of athletics, those who feel external and internal pressures to achieve or maintain a certain physique are at the highest risk. Participation in sports that emphasize a thin or lean appearance may cause undue anxiety for the athlete. For instance, striving to achieve what's considered to be an optimal bodyweight or body fat — by the athlete, parent or coach — may directly affect the risk for developing the triad. This may be perpetuated in the athletic community by misconceptions that low bodyweight and body fat automatically enhance athletic performance. What starts out as harmless dieting in an attempt to improve performance may result in a long-term pattern of self-destructive behavior.

A young athlete may also be driven to unhealthy nutritional habits from casual remarks made by those around her. Comments or jokes by a team member, coach or parent such as "it looks as if you've gained a little weight" or "maybe you should lose a few pounds" may unintentionally cause humiliation and an obsession with weight. Also at greater risk are adolescents and young adults who struggle with puberty and concerns about their body images; endurance athletes who expend more calories than they consume; and those who are mismatched with their sport.

Within the next few years, it's possible that other sports will adopt eligibility criteria that are similar to that which the International Tennis Federation and the Women's Tennis Council has for their players: In addition to increasing the age for competition, a mandatory annual medical exam and a minimal level of body fat are among the new proposed conditions for participation.

The ACSM Position Stand on the Female Athlete Triad outlines five categories of sports that emphasize a low bodyweight and, therefore, carry a greater risk for the triad. The categories are sports in which . . .

Sports that emphasize a low bodyweight carry a greater risk for the triad. (Photo courtesy of Tanda Tucker)

1. performance is scored subjectively (such as dance, figure skating, diving, gymnastics and aerobics);
2. a low bodyweight is emphasized (such as distance running, cycling and cross-country skiing);
3. body contour-revealing clothing is required for competition (such as volleyball, swimming, diving, cross-country running, cross-country skiing, track and cheerleading);
4. weight categories are used for participation (such as horse racing, rowing, wrestling and some types of martial arts); and
5. a prepubertal body habitus is emphasized for performance success (such as figure skating, gymnastics and diving).

MEDICAL CONDITIONS OF THE TRIAD

As stated earlier, the female athlete triad has three medical conditions that are interconnected and occur in sequence. These conditions are disordered eating, menstrual irregularities and premature osteoporosis.

Disordered Eating

Before the athletic community was even aware of their existence, eating disorders were known within the psychological community; the condition of self-starvation was identified as early as 1694 and binging and purging — though recognized much later — eventually became listed as a psychiatric disorder in 1980. The American Psychiatric Association has since outlined diagnostic criteria as well as associated features of each disorder.

Various biological, psychological and sociocultural factors may predispose an individual to develop an eating disorder. Major risk factors include one or more of the following: female gender; perfectionistic personality traits and a high need for control; poor self-esteem; a sense of loneliness; external and internal pressures to succeed; external and internal pressures to attain an ideal bodyweight and/or optimal body fat; genetic predisposition (such as family history of obesity, eating disorders, substance abuse and depression); dieting; and a personal history of physical or sexual abuse, teasing and harassment. According to the National Association of Anorexia Nervosa and Associated Disorders, the onset of illness occurs by age 20 in 86% of the cases. At the time of puberty, an adolescent struggles with a changing body, body-image preoccupation and peer pressure. Many young girls who "survive" their adolescent years without an eating disorder may become more at risk during their early collegiate years when the pressure to succeed — academically, athletically and socially — intensifies. In moments of overwhelming stress, eating for comfort or attempting to become thinner as a magical way to gain acceptance from peers may be the unhealthy way that some choose to cope.

Types of Disorders

A wide spectrum of conditions has been noted on the continuum of disordered eating. At one end are problems that carry a lower risk such as poor nutrition and improper or "fad" dieting; at the other end exist devastating, clinically defined, chronic illnesses. Early phases of an eating disorder — or "pre-conditions" — often precede a full-blown illness. Binging at night, for example, may occur for several weeks before a patient begins a cycle of binging and purging. Behaviors of a disorder may also intensify over time.

The American Psychiatric Association currently categorizes eating disorders as follows: anorexia nervosa, bulimia nervosa and eating disorders not otherwise specified (which includes binge-eating disorder).

Anorexia nervosa. In patients with anorexia nervosa — a condition of self-starvation — bodyweight is at or below 15% of normal weight for age and height (that is, less than 85% of what would be expected) or a body-mass index (BMI) that's equal to or below 17.5 kilograms per meter squared (kg/m²). Anorexics exhibit a refusal to maintain a minimally normal bodyweight and have an intense and irrational fear of gaining weight or becoming fat. They're often quite thin and visibly underweight yet continue to lose weight. Although an obsession with food and weight exists, denial of hunger and refusal to eat are characteristic behaviors. Diagnostic criteria for anorexia nervosa also include distress about body image, weight and shape or denial of the seriousness of the current low bodyweight and the absence of at least three consecutive menstrual cycles (in girls who have been menstruating normally).

There are two subtypes of anorexia nervosa: restricting and binge-eating/ purging. The restricting type of anorexia nervosa refers to individuals who haven't regularly engaged in binge eating or purging but use dieting, fasting or excessive exercise as their primary means of weight loss; the binge-eating/purging type of anorexia nervosa, however, refers to individuals who have regularly engaged in binge eating or purging or both. Extreme weight loss causes medical risks such as anemia, amenorrhea, dehydration, electrolyte imbalance, decreased body temperature and damage to major organs. Death may result from starvation, electrolyte imbalances (cardiac arrest) or suicide.

Bulimia nervosa. This eating disorder was once classified as "Dietary Chaos Syndrome" due to the peculiar behaviors associated with it. In bulimia — which means "great hunger" — patients become caught in a binge-and-purge cycle. During recurrent episodes of uncontrollable, secretive and rapid binge eating, the bulimic consumes large quantities of food — typically high-calorie "junk food" — in a limited amount of time (usually less than two hours). After overeating, the bulimic is often consumed by feelings of anxiety, guilt and depression. In order to prevent weight gain, the individual subsequently engages in unhealthy behaviors by using one or more of the following methods: self-induced vomiting, laxatives or diuretics, starvation (fasting) or compulsive exercising. About 80 - 90% of the individuals with bulimia nervosa use self-induced vomiting and roughly 33% abuse laxatives to prevent weight gain. For a diagnosis of bulimia, binge-and-purge behaviors must both occur on the average of at least twice a week over a period of three months and the bulimia must not occur exclusively during episodes of anorexia nervosa.

There are two subtypes of bulimia nervosa: purging and non-purging. The non-purging type of bulimia nervosa refers to individuals who may fast or exercise excessively but don't engage in purging behaviors such as self-induced vomiting or the use of laxatives or diuretics. Binging and purging often lead to malnutrition, dehydration, gastrointestinal problems and amenorrhea as well as psychological difficulties. Potentially fatal complications include esophageal tears, gastric rupture and cardiac arrhythmias.

In contrast to anorexics, those with bulimia nervosa are often at a normal — though fluctuating — bodyweight and, therefore, are harder to recognize. For example, the purging type of bulimia nervosa differs from the binge-eating/purging type of anorexia nervosa because bulimics will maintain normal bodyweights. Bulimics also tend to realize that their behavior is abnormal while anorexics are unable to realize that a problem exists. Though both are obsessed with food, bulimics turn toward food, not away from it. As with anorexics, bulimics also have a fear of gaining weight and critically judge themselves by how they feel about their bodyweights and shapes and often harshly compare themselves to others.

Eating disorders not otherwise specified (NOS). This final category encompasses any other severe disturbances in eating behavior that don't fit the full diagnostic criteria for one of the specifically defined illnesses. For instance, an individual may meet all of the criteria for anorexia nervosa except for amenorrhea. Binge-eating disorder — referred to as "compulsive overeating" — is included as part of NOS. It's similar to bulimia nervosa but isn't associated

- Distorted and unrealistic body image/preoccupation with body, bodyweight and weight loss (such as body dissatisfaction; obsessing about thinness and weighing on a scale; fear of gaining weight; and abnormal weight loss)
- Unusual changes in behavior patterns related to food (such as continuous dieting; refusal to eat; denial of appetite/hunger; counting every calorie and fat gram that's eaten; obsessing about cooking/cookbooks; obsessing with diets/diet books/preparation and serving of food; and hiding food)
- Desire to be alone while eating
- Emaciation (excessively thin) and fluctuation in bodyweight
- Unusual devotion to school work
- Depression, mood swings, irritability, anxiety and social withdrawal
- Decline in athletic performance
- Threats of self-destruction and reckless behavior
- Substance abuse or dependence
- Binging/self-induced vomiting
- Use of laxatives, diuretics and/or diet pills
- Menstrual irregularities
- Hair loss
- Hypercarotenemia (yellowing of the skin)
- Decreased body temperature (sensitivity to cold, excessive facial/body hair and cold hands/feet)
- Swollen salivary glands (swollen face) and sore throat
- Broken blood vessels in eyes
- Erosion of tooth enamel
- Lightheadedness, exhaustion and fainting
- Hyperactivity
- Excessive exercise
- Sleep problems and insomnia

FIGURE 10.1: WARNING SIGNS OF AN EATING DISORDER

with the regular use of inappropriate compensatory behaviors such as purging, fasting or excessive exercise.

Warning Signs of an Eating Disorder

Although some warning signals may be secretive, all perceptible and possible signs of an eating disorder must be taken seriously. Not all individuals will exhibit all symptoms for their particular disorder. While obsessed with her weight, for example, an athlete with anorexia may not complain about being cold. And although it's a diagnostic criterion for anorexia nervosa, amenorrhea happens in some individuals before weight loss and in others only after a sub-

- Cessation of menstruation
- Chronic dehydration
- Abnormal loss of bodyweight
- Decrease in basal metabolic rate
- Decrease in hormone levels
- Abnormal thyroid and adrenal hormone functions
- Chronic kidney problems/failures and liver damage
- Irregular heart rhythms and ECG changes (which can lead to cardiac arrest)
- Weakened heart muscle and cardiovascular disease
- Decreased blood pressure
- Elevated cholesterol
- Enzymatic changes (pancrease)
- Irritation, tears and bleeding in the esophagus
- Infected and swollen salivary glands (from frequent vomiting)
- Erosion of tooth enamel and increased cavities (from malnutrition and frequent vomiting)
- Electrolyte imbalance, water retention and general swelling
- Vitamin and mineral deficiencies
- Increased levels of uric acid in the blood
- Hypokalemia (potassium deficiency)
- Hypoglycemia (low blood sugar)
- Anemia (iron-poor blood)
- Lightheadedness, exhaustion and fainting
- Sensitivity to the cold
- Dry skin and dehydration (from reduced fluid intake and excessive fluid elimination)
- Thinning scalp hair
- Abdominal pain, gastrointestinal problems, intestinal ulcers and diminished appetite
- Stomach bloating (from electrolyte imbalance and insufficient protein intake)
- Dulled intestinal nerves (from laxative abuse)
- Loss of muscle mass
- Calcium loss from bone, osteoporosis and stress fractures
- Memory loss and disorientation
- Decreased sex drive (hypothalamus)
- Decreased body temperature and growth of lanugo (fine hair on the surface of the body)
- Fine rash (from frequent vomiting) and pimples (from laxative abuse)
- Constipation (failure to take in or retain a sufficient amount of fluid and food)
- Neurological abnormalities
- Death

FIGURE 10.2: PHYSICAL CONSEQUENCES OF AN EATING DISORDER

stantial amount of weight has been lost. Bulimics are often harder to recognize because they may be at normal bodyweights. Keep in mind that prior to the onset of illness, less significant signs such as continuous dieting may appear. Be alert for these behavioral signs and physical symptoms and remember that early recognition and intervention is vital for saving lives. The most common warning signs of an eating disorder are shown in Figure 10.1.

Physical Consequences of an Eating Disorder

As a result of self-starvation and binge-purge cycles, the body undergoes severe physical changes both hormonally and metabolically. The physiological complications for an athlete who has an eating disorder can indeed be significant and even life threatening. Not only can symptoms such as muscle loss, bone loss and dehydration interfere with athletic performance but damage to other body systems — such as the kidney and intestines — may be irreversible. Bulimics suffer more from purging (self-induced vomiting) than from binging and frequently experience malnourishment, permanent loss of dental enamel, esophageal irritation and swollen salivary glands. Dehydration and electrolyte imbalances in both anorexics and bulimics lead to further problems such as muscle cramps, fatigue, changes in the electrical rhythm of the heart, decreased blood pressure and edema (swelling). The effects of eating disorders are complex and dangerous; girls and women must be educated about the life-long damage that they may be inflicting on their bodies as well as how their athletic capacities and performances may be impaired. The physical consequences of an eating disorder are shown in Figure 10.2.

Psychological Consequences of an Eating Disorder

Unfortunately, the effects of an eating disorder aren't limited to physical problems. As a secondary result of the disorder, psychological issues also arise. Some of the psychological concerns — such as depression, for instance — may be caused as a direct result of physiological semi-starvation while others are the result of the behaviors associated with the disorder. If, for example, a bulimic adopts a particular strategy for binging and purging, she may exhibit a lack of spontaneity and may be afraid to change her daily routine or may fear social situations. Bulimics are typically ashamed of their eating behavior, which leads to bingeing and purging in secrecy. Feelings of guilt and shame usually follow. Since the self-esteem of patients with an eating disorder is based highly on their bodyweight, gaining weight — or not being able to control their weight — may be viewed as failure. The ensuing self-criticism, mood swings, "all-or-nothing" thinking and obsessions and compulsions related to food only complicate matters for the athlete. Keep in mind that an individual may seek help because of her resulting psychological distress rather than for the eating disorder itself. Various psychological consequences of an eating disorder are given in Figure 10.3.

- Depression
- Anxiety
- Shame/guilt
- Mood swings
- Low self-esteem
- Withdrawal from family and friends and impaired relationships
- Restrained emotional expression
- Feelings of ineffectiveness
- Fear of change in daily routine
- Perfectionism, "all-or-nothing" thinking and compulsive behavior(s)
- A need to control one's environment
- Obsessions and compulsions related to food
- Suicidal thoughts

FIGURE 10.3: PSYCHOLOGICAL CONSEQUENCES OF AN EATING DISORDER

Menstrual Irregularities

Although at one time believed to be a sign of fitness in female athletes, the dangers and negative consequences of menstrual irregularities have now become apparent. Amenorrhea — the cessation of menstruation — can be caused by a number of conditions that are unrelated to the triad such as pregnancy, hormonal imbalance, psychological stress, the use of anabolic steroids, changes in the use of birth control pills and premature menopause. In the second part of the female athlete triad, however, changes in the menstrual cycle are due to an eating disorder or an energy imbalance when the caloric expenditure of activity exceeds the caloric consumption of food. Premature osteoporosis and increased risk for stress fractures and broken bones are the subsequent effects of amenorrhea. As an example, the risk for stress fracture in amenorrheic female runners tends to be 4.5 times higher when compared to eumenorrheic (normally menstruating) athletes. Another new preliminary yet alarming finding in young runners has also linked amenorrhea with early cardiovascular disease.

Amenorrhea can occur in varying degrees: primary, secondary and oligomenorrhea.

Primary Amenorrhea

The onset of menstruation — known as "menarche" — occurs in girls around the age of 12 or 13. Primary amenorrhea — or delayed menarche — is characterized by a pre-adolescent who hasn't had a menstrual period by the age of 16 or has gone two years following the development of secondary sex characteristics without menarche. Though genetics seem to play a major role in determining the timing of menarche, eating disorders and inadequate nutrition may lead to this delay.

Pre-Selection in Sports Participation

Recent studies indicate that growth and development aren't affected — positively or negatively — by sports and training. A longitudinal British study called the "Training of Young Athletes" (TOYA) investigated the relationship between sports participation, growth and sexual maturity. Gymnasts, swimmers and soccer and tennis players aged 8 - 17 were followed over a three-year period. The results suggested that regular training doesn't adversely affect growth or sexual maturation. Rather, sport-specific selection occurs.

This acknowledged "pre-selection" for specific sports reflects a probable biological and sociological selection among young athletes. For instance, a basketball or volleyball coach may approach taller girls to inquire about their interest in participation. Pre-selection for athletic success may favor either a late- or early-maturing child, depending on the specific size demands of a sport.

Pre-selection for athletic success may favor either a late- or early-maturing child, depending on the specific size demands of a sport. (Photo courtesy of Tanda Tucker)

Although the onset of menstruation is related to factors such as genetics, medical health and environment, the hypothesis that intensive training at a young age causes a delay in biological maturation has persisted. Based on this theory, it has been suggested that young girls shouldn't participate in sports. But sport-specific selection is cited as a reason that young girls appear to be delayed in menarche. Activities in which girls may be inclined to participate and compete in — such as dance and gymnastics — may favor a late-maturing girl. Those who naturally experience earlier changes in body composition and stature may be socialized away from sports that are biased toward a pre-menarcheal (before puberty) body type. The triad may develop in girls who wish to excel in sports such as these but who didn't inherit body types that are favorable for success; unfortunately, they end up feeling pressure to change their bodies and an eating disorder may be the outcome. But there are currently no concrete data to implicate physical activity as a cause of delayed sexual maturity — or primary amenorrhea — in girls.

Secondary Amenorrhea and Oligomenorrhea

Secondary amenorrhea can be defined as "the absence of three or more consecutive menstrual cycles in a female who has previously had normal periods." In post-mancheal females, the absence of at least three consecutive menstrual cycles is part of the diagnostic criteria for anorexia nervosa. For most healthy women, the length of time for a normal menstrual cycle is approximately 28 days and ranges between 23 and 38 days. In oligomenorrhea, however, the menstrual cycle occurs at irregular, erratic intervals. It's critical to diagnose and treat oligomenorrhea as it may be a precursor to an even more serious secondary amenorrhea. Though the exact cause is uncertain, secondary amenorrhea and oligomenorrhea occur in bulimics due to undernourishment; fluctuation in weight caused by extreme dieting, fasting and purging; or emotional stress rather than abnormal weight loss. Remember, too, that menstrual cycles may be irregular for the first few years at the onset of menstruation and then again preceding menopause.

A Critical Balance

During the fertile or childbearing years, the pituitary hormones (follicle-stimulating hormone and luteinizing hormone) — which are controlled by the hypothalamus — and the ovarian hormones (estrogen and progesterone) act to control ovulation and the monthly release of a mature egg. In the female athlete triad, a loss of bodyweight results due to an underlying eating disorder or inadvertently because too few calories are being consumed for the amount of strenuous exercise being performed. The athlete becomes underweight and undernourished with too little body fat. The hypothalamus — which functions, in part, to regulate energy balance — senses this stress to the body and attempts to conserve energy by reducing hormone levels and essentially turning off the reproductive system. Fundamentally, a woman needs enough energy to become pregnant. When the hypothalamus recognizes that her body isn't prepared for a pregnancy, the menstrual cycle and ovulation are shut down as a protective mechanism to prevent pregnancy from occurring.

Self-starvation, bingeing and purging or excessive energy expenditure can all result in insufficient caloric intake, undernourishment, levels of body fat that are too low and energy imbalance. The amenorrheal athlete is then at a high risk for stress fractures and osteoporosis along with difficulty in reproduction, compromised immune function, impaired athletic performance and decreased concentration. To the young competitive athlete willing to push her limits, amenorrhea may not seem like a great threat so it's critical that coaches continue to take a serious and informed approach to this issue and intervene when appropriate.

Treating Amenorrhea

It's vital to note that some females may initially seek treatment because of a menstrual irregularity rather than for an eating disorder. Amenorrhea is one of the most telling signs of disordered eating but just as a cough is an indication of a cold, it's only a physical symptom. Therefore, any athlete who experiences an abnormal menstrual cycle should be screened for an eating disorder as well as osteoporosis and, if necessary, referred to counseling. Although the treatment of amenorrhea obviously depends on the cause, it should include a thorough medical evaluation, nutritional counseling from a professional who can evaluate energy needs and correct energy imbalances and malnutrition along with an evaluation from a coach who can help the athlete reduce her training regime and schedule. The athlete should also be made aware that menstrual cycles may not return to normal for approximately two to three months after gaining weight and improving nutrition and energy balance.

OSTEOPOROSIS

The third component of the female athlete triad associated with eating disorders and amenorrhea is premature osteoporosis, a dangerous bone disease that's characterized by low bone mass — referred to as "osteopenia" — and deterioration of bone. A malnourished athlete lacks the proper nutrition — that is, enough calcium and vitamin D — to foster healthy bone growth. A young woman also needs estrogen in order to build bones and develop a healthy skeleton. If delayed menarche, secondary amenorrhea or oligomenorrhea occurs and hormone levels are reduced, bone mass will also be decreased. The unfortunate end result for the athlete is this debilitating condition that normally only affects older menopausal women. Research has shown that in some cases, active young athletes and dancers with amenorrhea have skeletons similar to 50- or even 70-year-old women. At this time, it's unclear how much bone loss is irreversible.

The link between amenorrhea and incurred stress fractures is strong. Research has demonstrated that athletes with a history of stress fracture were significantly older at menarche, had a history of menstrual dysfunction and were more likely to engage in disordered eating. Studies on bone mineral density in athletes have also noted that even moderate menstrual irregularities, if allowed to persist, negatively influence bone density. In one study, for example, athletes who suffered with less severe oligomenorrhea were six times more likely to sustain a stress fracture; the risk increased to eight times if the athlete also exhibited restrictive eating patterns.

During the time that the athlete is experiencing abnormal menstrual cycles, a stress fracture or broken bone may eliminate the athlete from training and competing altogether. However, an even more serious problem — especially for a younger athlete who's still growing — is a decrease in peak bone density that will affect the lifetime health of her skeleton. As recently reported from a survey of high school ballet dancers and cross-country runners, 20% had a history of amenorrhea and 41% thought that it was healthy and acceptable to occasionally miss a period. A study of collegiate athletes at Ball State University during the 1998-99 season found that 36.6% of women reported current menstrual irregularities and that 36.6% had stress fractures in the previous season. Clearly, the need within the athletic population for education and prevention of amenorrhea remains high.

Disease Facts

At the Fourth International Symposium on Osteoporosis, the National Osteoporosis Foundation (NOF) raised the previous estimation of people affected with or at high risk of the disease from 25 - 28 million. Approximately 80% of those with the condition are women, many of whom endure fractures, hospitalization and a loss of independence. In 1991, there were more than one million osteoporotic bone fractures suffered by women. Fractures (which commonly occur at the wrist, spine and hip) are frequently the first symptom or indication to many that this silent but damaging — and often dangerous — condition is present. Fractures are quite critical and may prove fatal with one out of five women dying as a result of hip-fracture complications.

The attached economic price that the United States Healthcare system pays for osteoporosis has been estimated to be 10 billion dollars a year. In 1997, the NOF reported that certain expenditures were overlooked and raised that figure to a staggering 14 billion dollars a year. Osteoporosis has become a major life-threatening health problem for women and the elderly in America as well as other industrialized and growing nations. Over the next 30 years in America alone, the number of individuals age 65 and over will climb to 70 million. As the population continues to age, economic and personal costs will continue to multiply. Researchers predict that the number of Americans affected by the disease could reach 41 million by the year 2015 unless prevention and treatment strategies are seriously investigated and implemented at this time.

Women are four times more likely than men to sustain osteoporosis-related fractures. Females start out with less bone and muscle mass, can be affected by menstrual irregularities and are vulnerable to diets that may be deficient in calcium. At the stage of life known as "menopause," women also lose a great deal of bone mass due to a gradual decrease in the natural production of estrogen. This hormone acts to protect women against osteoporosis by slowing the loss of calcium from bone. In menopausal women, therefore, a loss of estrogen translates into a decrease in bone formation or a loss of bone. Low bone mass is the first phase of the disease. From this point, bones may become increasingly porous, brittle and fragile and women are placed at high risk for fracture from even the slightest day-to-day activities. Of course, menopause is a normal physiological consequence of aging and women can expect to live out half of their adult lives in this condition. By the age of 52, for instance, 85% of women will have reached menopause.

All women will inevitably be faced with menopause, the increased risk of osteoporosis and decisions about prevention and treatment of the disease during their lives. Preventing bone loss from occurring is the first line of defense in the prevention of osteoporosis.

Bone Mineral Accretion in Young Females

The target population for the prevention of osteoporosis may not be — as once widely believed — the older generations but, in fact, appears to be the young. Attaining a higher peak bone mass as a young female may delay the age at which a loss of bone from aging occurs and may decrease the severity of the disease once it develops.

Attaining Peak Bone Mineral Density

Bone mass (or bone density) continues to increase throughout the years of growth and development. A peak in bone mass — called the "peak bone mineral density" (PBMD) — is reached at a young adult age. Longitudinal studies report that females reach PBMD around their mid-to-late 20s. Recent research has found that total-body bone mineral density reaches adult values by approximately 18 years of age with the most rapid period of bone gain occurring between the ages of 12 and 14. The steady increase in bone from age 11 - 18 in white females results in a 40 - 50% gain of skeletal mass. Cross-sectional studies on bone accretion in females demonstrate that roughly 85% of adult bone mass is acquired by 14½ years of age.

In addition to genetics and the rate of bone loss later in life, the risk of fracture depends on the peak bone mass that's achieved by approximately age 20. It may be possible to delay the risk of fracture by maximizing bone mass as a young adult. Influencing bone mass during the first two decades of life in order to achieve a higher PBMD depends, in part, on preventing the female athlete triad in young athletes. Since preventing bone loss from occurring is the best defense against osteoporosis, the target population for prevention ought to be the younger generations. Fortunately, newer programs targeting young girls — such as "Powerful Bones. Powerful Girls. The National Bone Health Campaign™" — aim to provide education about the importance of strong and healthy bones.

PREVENTING AND TREATING THE FEMALE ATHLETE TRIAD

Over time, awareness, exposure and worldwide attention of the triad has occurred. It's known that the chain of events occurring with the triad not only impairs sports performance but also causes significant and potentially fatal medical complications. A fourth possible component of the triad recently identified — premature cardiovascular disease — has led many to believe that the triad may be even more dangerous than previously imagined. So how exactly is this life-threatening disorder managed? The first step in dealing with this must be to gain greater understanding of the causes and effects of the female athlete triad. For example, it's known that eating disorders are complex. They affect athletes both physically and psychologically and may cause irreparable damage. But do they increase the risk for soft-tissue injury among athletes? Further research is also needed to determine the true prevalence of the triad, diagnostic and treatment guidelines and prognosis.

Knowledge of the triad may be incomplete to some degree but it must become a priority for athletes, parents, coaches and athletic trainers to prevent, recognize and treat the female athlete triad. Preventing the triad can only hap-

The target population for the prevention of bone loss ought to be the younger generations. (Photo courtesy of Image Extreme)

pen through proper education. Coaches, athletic trainers, parents and athletes must be well informed about the female athlete triad. The ACSM position stand on the triad — which was introduced in 1997 — states that all physically active girls and women should be educated about proper nutrition, safe training practices and the warning signs and risks of the triad. Learning to recognize the warning signs of the triad is crucial. It's important to remember, however, that many individuals who have severe disordered eating practices will deny that a problem exists. They may first present with symptoms of weight loss, amenorrhea or a stress fracture. Although there's a lack of diagnosis and treatment guidelines, it's recommended that at the first sign of any of the components of the triad, the athlete should be referred for medical evaluation and screened for the other two components. Treatment must be a multidisciplinary approach that deals with the physical symptoms and addresses the underlying psychological issues. While successful treatment is possible, it's the responsibility of the athletic community to avert female athletes from encountering the triad in the first place. Supporting young female athletes in a safe and healthy manner and minimizing the risks to which they're exposed will allow athletes to continue reaping the many positive benefits that sports provide.

The female athlete triad can be prevented and treated in the following ways:

- Continue scientific research
- Mandate annual screening of the triad for female athletes/dancers
- Mandate preseason education
- Mandate education for parents of athletes who are 18 years of age or younger
- Mandate education for coaches and athletic trainers
- Clearly define referral guidelines
- Clearly define treatment guidelines
- Clearly define sports participation guidelines when components of the triad become present
- Promote healthy stress-management behaviors and tactics
- Promote community awareness of the triad through educational programs

PRACTICAL INFORMATION

Since the triad can appear across varying ages and levels of fitness and competition, using an individual approach toward each athlete will be optimal. Many feasible plans and procedures, however, can be used as general guidelines. Although an objective for the athletic community might be for girls and women to be well educated about the triad and to come forward with disordered- eating practices, that may remain unlikely for a significant number of individuals in the athletic population. Therefore, learning how to confront someone who may be struggling with a problem and knowing where to turn for reliable information is paramount for coaches, athletic trainers, parents and athletes alike.

How to Confront Someone with an Eating Disorder

Confronting someone who you suspect of having an eating disorder may feel like a monumental task. Knowing what steps to take and having a specific action plan in place will ease the responsibility. In a private and quiet setting, tell the person that you've observed behavior that's characteristic of an eating disorder. Try to be nonjudgmental, patient and respectful. To promote good communication, use a non-authoritative tone and ask open-ended questions. Although she may deny an existing problem, encourage her to seek help through a physical and psychological assessment as soon as possible. Suggest to her that meeting with a professional who specializes in eating disorders would be most beneficial. If the athlete is a minor, discuss your observations with school supervisors and her parents. Consult with professional organizations, particularly the National Association of Anorexia Nervosa and Associated Disorders (ANAD) for their specific plan called "Confront." The National Collegiate Athletic Association (NCAA) has also outlined a seven-step "Plan of Action" that athletic trainers and coaches can use if there's a concern that a student-athlete may be at risk because of an eating disorder.

A Note About Recovery

Treatment for a female athlete with an eating disorder must be an inter-related approach between family, friends, teachers, coaches, therapists, nutritionists and physicians. Since many deny that they're ill, family members and friends will play a central role in their recovery. For a successful recovery,

All physically active girls and women should be educated about proper nutrition, safe training practices and the warning signs and risks of the female athlete triad. (Photo courtesy of Jane Lybeck)

early detection of the illness is critical. The course of treatment varies but includes one or more of the following: individual therapy, group therapy, family therapy, patient education, medication, hospitalization, bone density screening/ treatment, outpatient programs, medical monitoring, nutritional counseling and supplementation, behavior modification and stress-management techniques. As long as an athlete receives medical clearance, physical activity can be continued throughout treatment. The most common technique that's used to assess bone density is dual-energy x-ray absorptiometry (DXA or DEXA). Athletes should be reassured that a DEXA scan is a painless, non-invasive and simple procedure with less radiation exposure than a typical chest x-ray. The length of treatment and recovery will vary.

Guidelines for Coaches, Athletic Trainers and Instructors

As stated in the ACSM Position Stand on the Female Athlete Triad, all sportsmedical professionals — including coaches and trainers — should be educated about preventing and recognizing the symptoms and risks of the triad. The athletic community shares the responsibility to prevent, recognize and treat the triad. If you're a coach, consider attending a seminar on eating disorders and the female athlete triad and get to know your athletes personally. In fact, in 1995, the WomenSport International Forum on the triad agreed that education for coaches *should* be mandatory. Coaches must re-learn how to create an environment that doesn't encourage the triad. Group weigh-ins and remarks about body size, for example, should be avoided. Understand that any female who has components of the triad faces serious physical and psychological issues. In order to help them fully recover, coaches need to be supportive and must appreciate that these athletes need professional help. A list of viable guidelines for coaches is shown in Figure 10.4.

Coaches must re-learn how to create an environment that doesn't encourage the triad. (Photo courtesy of Allen Yusufov)

Educational Resources

There are many health organizations that offer educational materials related to eating disorders and the female athlete triad: *The BodyWise Handbook* — which is available online from The National Women's Health Information Center (NWHIC) — offers educational information for physical education teachers, coaches and dance instructors; the National Eating Disorders Screening Program (NEDSP) includes a specific set of guidelines for coaches in their screening kit; the NCAA has produced a three-part video

- Avoid making bodyweight, body composition, food or calories an issue and avoid weigh-ins.
- Provide an accepting, non-threatening, open-minded environment. Promote the positive aspects and benefits of the sport.
- Encourage open discussion about eating disorders and the female athlete triad.
- Provide yearly (seasonal) presentations to athletic teams from health professionals about nutrition and the female athlete triad.
- Provide athletes with ongoing education including information on a local eating disorders program and where to go for help. Post information in a clearly visible place all year long and keep a library of pamphlets, books and videos accessible.
- Encourage healthy eating and exercise habits. Provide frequent water and snack breaks during exercise training and competitions.
- Avoid overtraining and have athletes keep training logs and health journals.
- Have athletes choose healthy role models to emulate.
- Encourage athletes to set realistic, healthy and attainable fitness goals.
- Avoid commenting — either positively or negatively — about body size, composition, shape or weight.
- Identify sources of personal stress in the lives of your athletes and be sensitive and understanding to their individual needs.
- Be tolerant of differences in genetics, bodyweight and body composition.
- Have team athletes choose a teammate as an "accountability partner."
- Discuss any matters related to an athletes' bodyweight in person and in private.
- If weight loss is required, refer the athlete to a qualified nutritionist and physician.
- If body-composition assessment is performed, emphasize the lean-body mass component. The range of error in body-fat testing should be made aware to athletes and positive goals — to *monitor* changes in body composition — should be established before any testing takes place. All testing and test results should remain private and confidential.
- In conjunction with the school nutritionist, mental health department and sportsmedical staff, have a written policy and referral system in place to follow if an athlete is suspected of or has been diagnosed with any components of the triad. Although it's not recommended to remove them completely from sports participation, their medical and psychological risks should be carefully evaluated and monitored under the care of a physician. Athletes who are non-compliant to treatment measures and those who might be at increased health risk will need to modify their sports participation status.

FIGURE 10.4: GUIDELINES FOR COACHES

series titled "Nutrition and Eating Disorders" (available at http://
www.karolmedia.com); and ANAD offers prevention/education packets for
schools. Visit NOVA Online for the PBS special broadcast "Dying To Be Thin."
Athletes should also be educated and screened for osteoporosis by taking a
simple risk profile questionnaire that includes a menstrual and medical history. (Contact the National Osteoporosis Foundation.) Another opportunity for
promoting awareness and prevention of the triad is during "National Eating
Disorders Awareness Week" which is held each year during the second week
of February. (Contact the National Eating Disorders Association.) For further
information on these and other programs, refer to the recommending reading
for this chapter.

RECOMMENDED READING

Benardot, D. 2000. *Nutrition for serious athletes*. Champaign, IL: Human Kinetics.

Otis, C. L., and R. Goldingay. 2000. *The athletic woman's survival guide: how to
win the battle against eating disorders, amenorrhea, and osteoporosis*. Champaign,
IL: Human Kinetics.

Otis, C. L., B. Drinkwater, M. Johnson, A. Loucks and J. Wilmore. 1997. ACSM
position stand on the female athlete triad. *Medicine and Science in Sports and
Exercise* 29 (5): i-ix.

REFERENCES

Allison, K. C., and R. I. Slupik (ed). 1996. *American Medical Association complete
guide to women's health*. New York, NY: Random House.

American Psychiatric Association. 1994. *Diagnostic and statistical manual of mental disorders. 4th ed*. Washington, DC: American Psychiatric Association.

Beals, K. A. 2001. Changes in the prevalence of risk factors for the female athlete triad among collegiate athletes over a two-year period. *Medicine and Science in Sports and Exercise* 33 (supplement): S285 [abstract].

Benardot, D. 2000. *Nutrition for serious athletes*. Champaign, IL: Human Kinetics.

Blimke, C. J. R., and O. Bar-Or, eds. 1995. *New horizons in pediatric exercise science*. Champaign, IL: Human Kinetics.

Boskind-White, M., and W. C. White Jr. 1983. *Bulimarexia: the binge/purge cycle*.
New York, NY: W. W. Norton & Company.

Bryant, C. X., and J. A. Peterson. 1995. Exercise and women's issues: increased
knowledge of the effects of exercise in women allows fitness professionals to
design exercise programs that meet women's specific needs. *Fitness Management* 11 (6): 26-29.

Drinkwater, B. L., S. K. Grimston, D. M. Raab-Cullen and C. M. Snow-Harter. 1995. ACSM position stand on osteoporosis and exercise. *Medicine and Science in Sports and Exercise* 27 (4): i-vii.

Joy, E., N. Clark, M. L. Ireland, J. Martire, A. Nattiv and S. Varechok. 1997. Team management of the female athlete triad: part I: what to look for, what to ask. *The Physician and Sportmedicine* 25 (3): 94.

_____. 1997. Team management of the female athlete triad: part II: optimal treatment and prevention tactics. *The Physician and Sportsmedicine* 25 (4): 55.

Lloyd, T., V. M. Chinchilli, D. F. Eggli, N. Rollings and H. E. Kulin. 1998. Body composition development of adolescent white females: the Penn State Young Women's Health Study. *Archives of Pediatric Adolescent Medicine* 152 (10): 998-1002.

Mayo, J., J. Alvarez, S. Sanders, T. Church, A. Foster and J. Painich. 2001. Knowledge of high school athletes about the female athlete triad. *Medicine and Science in Sports and Exercise* 33 (supplement): S286 [abstract].

Mazzeo, R. S., P. Cavanaugh, W. J. Evans, M. Fiatarone, J. Hagberg, E. McAuley and J. Startzell. 1998. ACSM position stand on exercise and physical activity for older adults. *Medicine and Science in Sports and Exercise* 30 (6): 992-1008.

Micheli, L. J., and M. D. Jenkins (contributor). 1990. *Sportswise: an essential guide for young athletes, parents and coaches.* Boston, MA: Houghton Mifflin Company.

Myszkewycz, L., and Y. Koutedakis. 1998. Injuries, amenorrhea and osteoporosis in active females. *Journal of Dance Medicine & Science* 2 (3): 88-94.

National Osteoporosis Foundation. 1997. *Fourth International Symposium on Osteoporosis.* Washington, D.C. June. [available at www.nof.org]

Nelson, M. E., and S. Wernick. 1998. *Strong women stay young.* New York, NY: Bantam Books.

Nelson, M. E., M. A. Fiatarone, C. M. Morganti, I. Trice, R. A. Greenberg and W. J. Evans. 1994. Effects of high-intensity strength training on multiple risk factors for osteoporotic fractures: a randomized controlled trial. *Journal of the American Medical Association* 272 (24): 1909-1914.

O'Connor, B., K. Fasting, D. Dahm and C. Wells. 2001. *Complete conditioning for the female athlete: a guide for coaches & athletes.* Terre Haute, IN: Wish Publishing.

Otis, C. L., and R. Goldingay. 2000. *The athletic woman's survival guide: how to win the battle against eating disorders, amenorrhea, and osteoporosis.* Champaign, IL: Human Kinetics.

Otis, C. L., B. Drinkwater, M. Johnson, A. Loucks and J. Wilmore. 1997. ACSM position stand on the female athlete triad. *Medicine and Science in Sports and Exercise* 29 (5): i-ix.

Petranick, K., and K. Berg. 1997. The effects of weight training on bone density of premenopausal, postmenopausal, and elderly women: a review. *Journal of Strength and Conditioning Research* 11 (3): 200-208.

Picone, R. E. 1999. Strength training for children. *Fitness Management* 15 (7): 32-35.

Riggs, B. L., and L. J. Melton III. 1995. The worldwide problem of osteoporosis: insights afforded by epidemiology. *Bone* 17 (supplement): 505S-511S.

Rourke, K. M., J. Bowering, P. Turkki, P. J. Buckenmeyer, F. D. Thomas, B. A. Keller and G. A. Sforzo. 1998. Bone mineral density in weight-bearing and nonweight-bearing female athletes. *Pediatric Exercise Science* 10 (1): 28-37.

Schnirring, L. 1997. What's new in treating active women. *The Physician and Sportsmedicine* 25 (7): 91.

Schoene, M., and C. Nelson. 2001. An ominous addition to the female athlete triad? *Sports Medicine Digest* 23 (7): 73.

Smith, A. D. 1996. The female athlete triad: causes, diagnosis, and treatment. *The Physician and Sportsmedicine* 24 (7): 67.

Stein, P. M., and B. C. Unell. 1986. *Anorexia nervosa: finding the life line*. Minneapolis, MN: CompCare Publications.

Tomten, S. E., J. A. Falch, K. I. Birkeland, P. Hemmersbach and A. T. Hostmark. 1998. Bone mineral density and menstrual irregularities: a comparative study on cortical and trabecular bone structures in runners with alleged normal eating behavior. *International Journal of Sports Medicine* 19 (2): 92-97.

Turner, L. W., D. Leaver-Dunn, R. DiBrezzo and I. Fort. 1998. Physical activity and osteoporotic fracture among older women. *Journal of Athletic Training* 33 (3): 207-210.

Wellness Encyclopedia, The University of California, Berkeley. Editors of the University of California, Berkeley Wellness Letter. Boston: Houghton Mifflin Company. 1991.

Yeager, K. K., R. Agostini, A. Nattiv and B. Drinkwater. 1993. The female athlete triad: disordered eating, amenorrhea, osteoporosis. *Medicine and Science in Sports and Exercise* 25 (7): 775-777.

INTERNET RESOURCES

Academy for Eating Disorders (AED): http://www.aedweb.org

Alliance for Eating Disorders Awareness: http://www.eatingdsorderinfo.org

American College of Sports Medicine (ACSM): http://www.acsm.org

American Dietetic Association (ADA): http://www.eatright.org

American Medical Association (AMA): http://www.ama-assn.org

Anorexia Nervosa and Related Eating Disorders, Inc. (ANRED):
  http://www.anred.com

Centers For Disease Control and Prevention (CDC): http://www.cdc.gov

Powerful Bones. Powerful Girls. The National Bone Health Campaign:
  http://www.cdc.gov/powerfulbones

Center for Science in the Public Interest (CSPI): http://www.cspinet.org

CNN Health: http://www.cnn.com/HEALTH

Eating Disorders Anonymous (EDA):
  http://www.eatingdisordersanonymous.org

Eating Disorders and Education Network (EDEN): http://comnet.org/eden

Eating Disorders Shared Awareness (EDSA): http://www.mirror-mirror.org

Gatorade Sports Science Institute: http://www.gssiweb.com

Harvard Eating Disorders Center (HEDC): http://www.hedc.org

Healthfinder: http://www.healthfinder.gov

International Association of Eating Disorders Professionals (IAEDP):
  http://www.iaedp.com

International Association for Dance Medicine and Science (IADMS):
  http://www.iadms.ord

International Eating Disorder Referral Organization:
  http://www.edreferral.com

National Association of Anorexia Nervosa and Associated Disorders (ANAD):
  http://www.anad.org

National Association for Girls and Women in Sport (NAGWS):
  http://www.aahperd.org/nagws/nagws_main.html

National Collegiate Athletic Association (NCAA): http://www.ncaa.org

National Eating Disorders Association:
  http://www.NationalEatingDisorders.org

National Eating Disorder Information Centre (Toronto-based) (NEDIC):
  http://www.nedic.ca

National Eating Disorders Screening Program (NEDSP):
  http://www.nmisp.org/eat.htm

National Institutes of Health (NIH): http://www.nih.gov

National Institute of Mental Health (NIMH): http://www.nimh.nih.gov

Weight-Control Information Network (WIN):
  http://www.niddk.nih.gov/health/nutrit/nutrit.htm

National Osteoporosis Foundation (NOF): http://www.nof.org

National Women's Health Information Center (NWHIC):
  http://www.4woman.gov/bodyimage

The BodyWise Handbook: http://www.4woman.gov/BodyImage/bodywise/bodywise.htm

National Women's Health Resource Center (NWHRC): http://www.healthywomen.org

Nemours Foundation: http://www.Nemours.org

NOVA Online: "Dying To Be Thin" (companion web site plus teacher's guide): http://www.pbs.org/wgbh/nova/thin

Penn State Sports Medicine Newsletter Homepage (subscriptions): http://cac.psu.edu/~hgk2

Physician and Sports Medicine Online: http://www.physsportsmed.com

Sports Doctor (*The Athletic Woman's Survival Guide* by C. Otis and R. Goldingay): http://www.sportsdoctor.com

Strong Women (*Strong Women Stay Young* by M. Nelson and S. Wernick): http://www.strongwomen.com

Support, Concern, and Resources for Eating Disorders (SACRED): http://www.eating-disorder.org

Tucker Center for Research on Girls & Women in Sport: http://education.umn.edu/tuckercenter

Tufts Nutrition: http://nutrition.tufts.edu

WomenSport International: http://www.de.psu.edu/wsi/index.htm

University of Massachusetts Center for Nutrition in Sport and Human Performance: http://www.umass.edu/cnshp

4 Girls Health: http://www.4girls.gov

11

Eating to Win

Matt Brzycki, B.S.

Nutrition is the process by which an individual selects, consumes, digests, absorbs and utilizes food. Unfortunately, this important aspect of overall training is either inadequately addressed or entirely overlooked.

Implementing good nutritional practices has several purposes. First of all, proper nutrition plays a critical role in the capacity to perform at optimal levels and to expedite recovery. Clearly, the ability to fully recuperate after an exhaustive activity directly affects future performances and the intensity of training. Nutritional habits are also a factor in the development of physical attributes such as muscular strength and aerobic fitness.

The knowledge base for nutritional training is very critical. Athletes can improve their nutritional skills by recognizing the desirable food sources, understanding the recommended intakes of those food sources and realizing the caloric contributions of the various nutrients. In addition, becoming familiar with caloric needs along with the principles and procedures for weight management — that is, gaining, losing or maintaining bodyweight — can provide support for nutritional planning. Moreover, knowing what foods/fluids to consume before and after vigorous activity will facilitate the objective to maximize performance as an athlete. Finally, good nutritional skills will help determine whether or not nutritional supplementation is warranted.

THE NUTRIENTS

Everything that a person does requires energy. The energy is obtained through the foods (or nutrients) that are consumed and is measured in calories (which, technically, are units of heat). Essentially, the foods that are eaten serve as a fuel for the body. Food is also necessary for the growth, maintenance and repair of biological tissues such as muscle and bone.

Foods are composed of six nutrients: carbohydrates, protein, fat, water, vitamins and minerals. These main constituents of food can be grouped as either macronutrients or micronutrients. In order to be considered nutritious, an athlete's food intake must contain the recommended amounts of the macronutrients as well as appropriate levels of the micronutrients. No single food satisfies this requirement. As a result, variety is the key to a balanced diet. (Here and in other discussions that follow, the term "diet" simply refers to a normal food intake, not a specialized regimen of eating.)

The primary function of carbohydrates (or "carbs") is to furnish an athlete with energy, especially during intense activity. (Photo by Pete Silletti)

The Macronutrients

As the name implies, macronutrients are needed in relatively large amounts. Three macronutrients — carbohydrates, protein and fat — provide and athlete with calories and, therefore, a supply of energy. Although it has no calories, water is also categorized as a macronutrient because it's needed in considerable quantities.

Carbohydrates

The primary function of carbohydrates (or "carbs") is to furnish an athlete with energy, especially during intense activity. The body breaks down carbohydrates into glucose (or "blood sugar"). Glucose can be used as an immediate form of energy during an activity or stored as glycogen in the liver and muscles for future use. Highly conditioned muscles can stockpile more glycogen than poorly conditioned muscles. If the glycogen stores are depleted, an athlete will feel overwhelmingly exhausted. For this reason, having greater glycogen stores can give an athlete a significant physiological advantage. It makes a great deal of sense, therefore, that the diet should be carbohydrate-based. In fact, at least 65% of the daily calories should be in the form of carbohydrates.

Carbohydrates are classified as either "simple" (which are sugars such as table sugar and honey) or "complex" (which are starches such as the starch in bread). Carbohydrate-rich foods include potatoes, cereals, pancakes, breads, spaghetti, macaroni, rice, grains, fruits and vegetables.

Protein

Protein is necessary for the growth, maintenance and repair of biological tissues, particularly muscle tissue. Additionally, protein regulates water balance and transports other nutrients. Protein can also be used as an energy source in the event that adequate carbohydrates aren't available.

When proteins are ingested as foods, they are broken down into their basic building blocks: amino acids. The body can manufacture most of the 22 known amino acids. Eight (or nine in the case of children and certain adults) must be provided in the diet and are termed "essential amino acids." When a food contains all of the essential amino acids in amounts that facilitate the growth and repair of muscle tissue, it's deemed a "complete protein." In addition, such foods are considered to have a high "biological value" meaning that a large portion of the protein is absorbed and retained. The biological value is an index in which all protein sources are compared to egg whites because they are the most complete protein. (Egg whites have a biological value of 100). All animal proteins — with the exception of gelatin — are complete proteins and, as a result, have a high biological value. Conversely, the protein found in vegetables and other sources is considered to be an "incomplete protein" — having a low biological value — because it doesn't include all of the essential amino acids. A white potato, for instance, has a biological value of 34.

Approximately 15% of the daily calories should be from protein. Good sources of this macronutrient are beef, pork, fish, poultry, eggs, liver, dry beans and dairy products.

Fat

It may be difficult to believe, but fat is actually vital to a balanced diet. First, fat serves as a major source of energy during low-intensity activities such as sleeping, reading and walking. Second, fat helps in the transportation and the absorption of certain vitamins. Third, fat adds substantial flavor to foods. This makes food much more appetizing — and also explains why fat is craved so much.

Foods that are high in fat include butter, cheese, margarine, meat, nuts, dairy products and cooking oils. Animal fats — such as butter, lard and the fat in meats — are referred to as "saturated fats" and contribute to heart disease; vegetable fats — such as corn, olive and peanut oils — are dubbed "unsaturated fats" and are less harmful. (At room temperature, saturated fats tend to be solid while unsaturated fats are usually liquid.)

There's really no need for athletes to add extra fatty food to their diets in order to obtain adequate fat. If anything, far too much fat is often consumed. The fact is that fat often accompanies carbohydrate and protein choices. In addition, foods are often prepared in such a way that the fat content is elevated. For example, baked potatoes have a negligible amount of fat — barely a trace of their calories; french-fried potatoes, on the other hand, have a considerable amount of fat — one half of their calories.

At most, 20% of the daily calories should be composed of fat. Keep in mind that this allotment of fat — as well as that of carbohydrates and protein — is to be distributed over the course of the day. So there's nothing wrong with eating a food that's more than 20% fat as long as this particular choice is offset by other foods consumed throughout the day that have a lower fat content.

Obviously, any fat that isn't used as energy is stored in the body as fat. If not used for energy, however, carbohydrates and protein are converted into fat and stored in that form as well.

Water

Since it's needed in rather large quantities, water is usually classified as a macronutrient. Water doesn't have any calories or provide an individual with any energy but it does play major roles in the body. Water lubricates joints and regulates body temperature. Also, water helps carry nutrients to the cells and waste products from the cells. Incredibly, almost two thirds of the bodyweight is water.

The best sources of water are milk, fruits, fruit juices, vegetables, soup and, of course, water. Athletes should consume about 16 ounces of water for every pound of bodyweight that they lose during their training.

The Micronutrients

Vitamins and minerals are classified as micronutrients because they are required in somewhat small amounts. Neither of these nutrients supplies an athlete with any calories or energy. But vitamins and minerals have many other important functions. (It's well beyond the scope of this chapter to provide an extensive overview of the functions and sources of vitamins and minerals. For more detailed information, athletes are encouraged to pursue other sources.)

Vitamins

The Polish chemist Casimir Funk coined the term "vitamine" in 1912. Vitamins are potent compounds that are required in very minute quantities. They occur in a wide variety of foods, especially in fruits and vegetables. An athlete can obtain an adequate intake of vitamins from a balanced diet that contains a variety of foods. Even though vitamins aren't a source of energy, they perform many different functions that are vital to an active lifestyle. Vitamins can be grouped as either fat-soluble or water-soluble.

Fat-Soluble Vitamins

The four fat-soluble vitamins — vitamins A, D, E and K — require proper amounts of fat to be present before transportation and absorption can take place. Excessive amounts of fat-soluble vitamins are stored in the body. Here's a brief listing of their functions and sources:

- Vitamin A (retinol) is required for normal vision (especially at night) and promotes bone growth, healthy hair, skin and teeth. Organ meats, dairy products, fish, eggs, carrots, spinach and sweet potatoes are good sources of this vitamin.

- Vitamin D (calciferol) enhances calcium absorption and is vital for strong bones and teeth. The "sunshine vitamin" can be found in fish, fortified milk products and cereals, dairy products and egg yolks.

- Vitamin E (tocopherol) acts as an antioxidant, aids in the formation of red blood cells and helps to maintain the muscles and other biological tissues. Once known as "the vitamin in search of a disease," good sources of it are poultry, seafood, eggs, vegetable oils, nuts, fruits, vegetables and meats.

- Vitamin K assists in blood clotting and bone metabolism. It's found in green leafy vegetables, brussel sprouts, cabbage, potatoes, plant oils, oats, margarine and organ meats.

Water-Soluble Vitamins

The eight B vitamins — biotin, cobalamin, folate, niacin, pantothenic acid, pyridoxine, riboflavin and thiamine — and vitamin C are considered to be water-soluble vitamins because they're found in foods that have a naturally high content of water. There's minimal storage of water-soluble vitamins in the body — excess amounts are generally excreted in the urine. Their functions and sources are summarized as follows:

- Biotin helps to synthesize glycogen, amino acids and fat. Rich sources of biotin are liver, fruits, vegetables, nuts, eggs, poultry and meats.

- Cobalamin (B_{12}) forms and regulates red blood cells, prevents anemia and maintains a healthy nervous system. This vitamin can be found in fortified cereals, meats, fish, poultry and dairy products.

- Folate (folic acid and folacin) is needed to manufacture red blood cells and aids in the metabolism of amino acids. Enriched cereal grains, fruits, dark green leafy vegetables, meats, fish, liver, poultry, enriched and whole-grain breads and fortified cereals are good sources of folate.

- Niacin (B_3) promotes normal appetite, digestion and proper nerve function and is required for energy metabolism. It's found in meats, fish, poultry, eggs, potatoes, enriched and whole-grain breads and bread products, orange juice, peanuts and fortified cereals.

- Pantothenic acid (B_5) helps in the metabolism of carbohydrates, protein and fat. Good sources of this vitamin are chicken, beef, potatoes, oats, cereals, tomato products, liver, kidney, yeast, egg yolks, broccoli and whole grains.

- Pyridoxine (B_6) assists in the formation of red blood cells and the metabolism of carbohydrates, protein and fat. Fortified cereals, organ meats, lean meats, poultry, fish, eggs, milk, vegetables, nuts and bananas are rich sources of this vitamin.

- Riboflavin (B_2) aids in the maintenance of skin, mucous membranes and nervous structures. This vitamin is found in organ meats, poultry, beef, lamb, fish, milk, dark green leafy vegetables, bread products and fortified cereals.

- Thiamine (B_1) maintains a healthy nervous system and heart and helps to metabolize carbohydrates and amino acids. Good sources of thiamine are enriched, fortified and whole-grain products, bread and bread products, ready-to-eat cereals, meats, poultry, fish, liver and eggs.

- Vitamin C (ascorbic acid) promotes healing, helps in the absorption of iron and the maintenance and repair of connective tissues, bones, teeth and cartilage. Citrus fruits, tomatoes, tomato juice, potatoes, brussel sprouts, cauliflower, broccoli, strawberries, watermelon, cabbage and spinach are rich sources of vitamin C.

Minerals

Minerals are found in tiny amounts in foods. Like vitamins, nearly all the minerals that are needed can be obtained with an ordinary intake of foods. Minerals can be divided into two subcategories: macrominerals and microminerals.

Macrominerals

As the name implies, macrominerals are required in relatively large amounts — specifically, more than 250 milligrams per day. The macrominerals are calcium, chloride, magnesium, phosphorus, potassium, sodium and sulfur. Here's a brief overview of their functions and sources:

- Calcium is essential in blood clotting, muscle contraction, nerve transmission and the formation of bones and teeth. Rich sources of this mineral are milk, cheese, yogurt, oysters, broccoli and spinach.
- Chloride is an electrolyte that regulates body fluids in to and out of the cells and helps to maintain a proper acid-base (pH) balance. It's found in table salt, milk, canned vegetables and animal foods.
- Magnesium is essential for healthy nerve and muscle function and bone formation. Green leafy vegetables, nuts, meats, poultry, fish, oysters, starches, milk and beans are good sources of magnesium.
- Phosphorus maintains pH, helps in energy production and is essential for every metabolic process in the body. Good sources are milk, yogurt, ice cream, cheese, peas, meats, poultry, fish and eggs.
- Potassium is an electrolyte that regulates body fluids in to and out of the cells and promotes proper muscular contraction and the transmission of nerve impulses. This mineral is found in citrus fruits, bananas, deep yellow vegetables and potatoes.
- Sodium is an electrolyte that regulates body fluids in to and out of the cells, transmits nerve impulses, maintains normal blood pressure and is involved in muscle contraction. Table salt, milk, canned vegetables and animal foods are good sources of sodium.
- Sulfur is needed to make hair and nails. It's found in beef, peanuts, clams and wheat germ.

Microminerals

As might be suspected, microminerals are needed in relatively small amounts — specifically, less than 20 milligrams per day. The microminerals are chromium, copper, fluoride, iodine, iron, manganese, molybdenum, selenium and zinc. (A number of other minerals — including arsenic, boron, cobalt, lithium, nickel, silicon, tin and vanadium — are probably essential in very small amounts but their roles in the human body are unclear and Recommended Dietary Allowances haven't been established.) This is a quick rundown of the functions and sources of the microminerals:

- Chromium functions in the metabolism of carbohydrates and fat and helps to maintain blood-glucose levels (homeostasis). Meats, poultry, fish and peanuts are good sources of chromium.

- Copper stimulates the absorption of iron and has a role in the formation of red blood cells, connective tissues and nerve fibers. Good sources are organ meats, seafood, nuts, beans, whole-grain products and cocoa products.

- Fluoride prevents dental caries and stimulates the formation of new bones. This mineral is found in fluoridated water, teas and marine fish.

- Iodine is necessary for proper functioning of the thyroid gland and prevents goiter and cretinism. Seafood, processed foods and iodized salt are good sources of this mineral.

- Iron is involved in the manufacture of hemoglobin and myoglobin (two proteins that transport oxygen to the tissues) and has a role in normal immune function. It's found in liver, fruits, vegetables, fortified bread and grain products, meats, poultry and shellfish.

- Manganese is involved in the formation of bones and the metabolism of carbohydrates. Good sources of manganese are nuts, legumes, coffee, tea and whole grains.

- Molybdenum helps to regulate the storage of iron. Dark green leafy vegetables, legumes, grain products, nuts and organ meats are good sources of this mineral.

- Selenium protects cell membranes. It's found in organ meats, chicken, seafood, whole-grain cereals and milk.

- Zinc has a role in the repair and growth of biological tissues. Good sources of this mineral are fortified cereals, meats, poultry, eggs and seafood.

DAILY SERVINGS

Consuming an assortment of foods helps to ensure that an individual has obtained adequate amounts of carbohydrates, protein and fat along with sufficient quantities of vitamins and minerals. According to the U. S. Department of Agriculture and Department of Health and Human Services, a variety of daily foods should include an appropriate number of servings from these six food groups (with the servings in parentheses):

An athlete's caloric needs depend upon a number of factors, including age, size, body composition, metabolic rate and level of activity. (Photo by Jason Gallucci)

- Bread, Cereal, Rice and Pasta (6 - 11)
- Vegetable (3 - 5)
- Fruit (2 - 4)
- Milk, Yogurt and Cheese (2 - 3)
- Meat, Poultry, Fish, Dry Beans, Eggs and Nuts (2 - 3)
- Fats, Oils and Sweets (use sparingly)

The exact number of servings that are suitable for athletes is contingent upon their caloric (energy) needs. An athlete's caloric needs depend upon a number of factors, including age, size, body composition, metabolic rate and level of activity.

The recommendations for daily servings are based upon the Food Guide Pyramid that was introduced by the U. S. Department of Agriculture and Department of Health and Human Services in 1992. Two professors at the Harvard School of Public Health have suggested a new pyramid with different daily servings. While their proposal is interesting, it has yet to gain wide acceptance by the scientific and medical communities. There are also a number of other "pyramids" including the Asian Diet Pyramid, the Latin American Diet Pyramid, the Mayo Clinic Healthy Weight Pyramid, the Mediterranean Diet Pyramid and the Vegetarian Diet Pyramid. Despite the differences in the names, all of these pyramids have much in common. Bottom line: The daily servings that are currently recommended by the U. S. Department of Agriculture and Department of Health and Human Services are appropriate for active individuals.

RECOMMENDED DIETARY ALLOWANCES

First published in 1943 and updated regularly, the Recommended Dietary Allowances (RDAs) were developed by the Food and Nutrition Board of the National Academy of Sciences/National Research Council. The RDAs are set by first determining the "floor" below which deficiency occurs and then the "ceiling" above which harm occurs. A margin of safety is included in the RDAs to meet the requirements of nearly all healthy people. In fact, the RDAs are designed to cover the biological needs of *97.5% of the population*. In other words, the RDAs exceed what most people require in order to meet the needs of those who have the highest requirements. So the RDAs don't represent minimum standards. And failing to consume the recommended amounts doesn't necessarily indicate that a person has a dietary deficiency. (The RDAs of selected vitamins and minerals for females aged 9 - 50 are given in Tables 11.1 and 11.2, respectively.)

CALORIC CONTRIBUTIONS

As mentioned previously, three macronutrients — carbohydrates, protein and fat — furnish an athlete with calories, albeit in different amounts. Carbohydrates and protein yield four calories per gram (cal/g). Fat is the most concentrated form of energy, containing nine cal/g. Armed with this information, the caloric contributions can be determined for each of the three energy-providing macronutrients in any food — provided that it's known how many grams of each macronutrient are in a serving.

As an example, consider a snack food such as Fritos® Brand Original Corn Chips (Frito-Lay, Incorporated). Examining the nutrition label reveals that a one-ounce serving of this product contains 15 grams of carbohydrates, 2 grams of protein and 10 grams of fat. To find the exact number of calories that are supplied by each macronutrient, simply multiply its number of grams per serving by its corresponding energy yield. In this example, each serving of the food has 60 calories from carbohydrates [15 g x 4 cal/g], 8 calories from protein [2 g x 4 cal/g] and 90 calories from fat [10 g x 9 cal/g]. Therefore, this food has a total of 158 calories per serving (which is rounded up to 160 on the nutrition label). As can be seen, this product has 50% more grams of carbohydrates than fat (15 compared to 10) — yet nearly 57% of the calories (90 of the 158) are furnished by fat. Moreover, consuming the entire contents of the 2.5-ounce bag will contribute 25 grams of fat — or 225 calories from fat — to an athlete's caloric budget.

Compare this to Baked Lays® Potato Crisps, another snack food by the same manufacturer. A one-ounce serving of this product has 23 grams of carbohydrates, 2 grams of protein and 1.5 grams of fat. Each serving of this food contains 92 calories from carbohydrates [23 g x 4 cal/g], 8 calories from protein [2 g x 4 cal/g] and 13.5 calories from fat [1.5 g x 9 cal/g]. So this food has a total of 113.5 calories per serving (which is rounded down to 110 on the nutrition label). This particular product, then, has more than 15 times as many grams of carbohydrates than fat (23 compared to 1.5) — and only 11.9% of the calories (13.5 of the 113.5) are supplied by fat. Furthermore, consuming 2.5 ounces of this product will add a mere 3.75 grams of fat — or 33.75 calories from fat — to an athlete's caloric budget.

Knowing the different caloric contributions of the macronutrients is also helpful in understanding information about fat content on the packaging of a product that could easily be misinterpreted. Case in point: A package that proclaims a product to be "99% fat free" means that it's 99% fat free by weight, not by calories. How critical is this distinction? Very. Placing one gram of fat into 99 grams of water forms a product that — in terms of weight — is "99% fat free." But since water has no calories, this particular "99% fat free" product would actually be — in terms of calories — 100% fat.

Although the preceding example was hypothetical, the fact is that this discrepancy actually occurs on the packaging of many products. Here are four illustrations of real products:

- A package of Hershey®'s Chocolate Drink (Hershey® Foods Corporation) states that it's "99% fat free." As would be expected, this leads many consumers to believe that a mere 1% of its calories come from fat. In reality, one serving of this product (eight ounces) has 129 calories of which 9 are from fat — meaning that it's 6.98% fat. (The numbers on the nutrition label are rounded up to 130 calories per serving with 10 calories from fat.)

- A package of Black Bear of the Black Forest™ Gourmet Cooked Ham (Black Bear Enterprises, Incorporated) notes that it's "98% fat free." Naturally, this prompts many consumers to think that only 2% of its calories are derived from fat. In actuality, one serving of this product (two ounces) has 49 calories of which 9 are from fat — meaning that it's 18.37% fat. (The values on the nutrition label are rounded up to 50 calories per serving with 10 calories from fat.)

- A package of Black Bear of the Black Forest™ Barbeque Flavor Breast of Chicken (Black Bear Enterprises, Incorporated) states that it's "96% fat free." This, of course, leads many consumers to conclude that only 4% of its calories come from fat. In reality, one serving of this product (two ounces) has 66 calories of which 18 are from fat — meaning that it's 27.27% fat. (The numbers on the nutrition label are rounded up to 70 calories per serving with 20 calories from fat.)

- A package of Oscar Mayer® Dinner Ham (Oscar Mayer Foods) notes that it's "96% fat free." Again, this leads many consumers to believe that only 4% of its calories are from fat. In actuality, one serving of this product (three ounces) has 83 calories of which 27 are from fat — meaning that it's 32.53% fat. (The values on the nutrition label are rounded down to 80 calories per serving with 25 calories from fat.)

While the percentages of fat calories for these four products aren't terribly bad, it's certainly a far cry from how the percentages on the package can be interpreted.

ESTIMATING YOUR CALORIC BUDGET

As mentioned earlier, an athlete's caloric needs are determined by several factors such as age, size, body composition, metabolic rate and level of activity. Another factor is gender: Everything else being equal, a woman has a lower caloric need than a man. During a resting state, an individual's caloric requirements can be established precisely by both direct and indirect calorimetry. Direct calorimetry measures the heat produced by the body in a small, insulated chamber; indirect calorimetry calculates the heat given off by the body based upon the amount of oxygen that's consumed and carbon dioxide that's produced. Unfortunately, both of these methods can be expensive and impractical for most people. For a quick and reasonably accurate estimate of a person's daily caloric needs, the U. S. Department of Agriculture suggests multiplying the bodyweight by a number that corresponds to the approximate level of activity. Essentially, this number represents the energy requirements in calories per pound of bodyweight (cal/lb). For women, the values are 14 if they're sedentary, 18 if they're moderately active and 22 if they're very active. To illustrate, a 150-pound woman who is very active requires about 3,300 calories per day (cal/day) to meet her energy needs [150 lb x 22 cal/lb]. Although this calculation has gray areas — such as the characterization of the term "moderately active" — it still results in a fairly good estimate.

Once the caloric budget has been estimated, it can be determined how many of these calories should come from carbohydrates, protein and fat. Using the previous example, someone who requires about 3,300 cal/day should consume roughly 536.25 grams of carbohydrates [3,300 cal/day x 0.65 ÷ 4 cal/g], 123.75 grams of protein [3,300 cal/day x 0.15 ÷ 4 cal/g] and 73.33 grams of fat [3,300 cal/day x 0.20 ÷ 9 cal/g]. Note that these numbers are based upon a diet that consists of 65% carbohydrates, 15% protein and 20% fat.

WEIGHT MANAGEMENT

Managing bodyweight — that is, gaining, losing or maintaining it — is simply a matter of arithmetic and can be likened to managing a savings account. If more calories are deposited (consumed) than withdrawn (expended), a caloric profit is produced and results in weight gain; if more calories are withdrawn (expended) than deposited (consumed), a caloric deficit is produced and results in weight loss; and lastly, if the same amount of calories are deposited (consumed) as withdrawn (expended), a caloric balance is produced and results in no change in weight. However, a closer inspection of weight management — specifically, gaining and losing it — is worthwhile.

Gaining Weight

Some female athletes will be healthier — and more competitive — if they increase their bodyweight. The potential to gain weight is determined by a number of things, the most important of which is an individual's genetic profile. A person whose ancestors had ectomorphic tendencies — that is, lean features with little in the way of muscular size — has the genetic destiny for that type of physique. This doesn't mean that a person with those inherited characteristics — who would be categorized as an "ectomorph" — is incapable of gaining weight. But it will be difficult for those who have a high degree of ectomorphy to achieve a significant increase in their bodyweight.

The primary goal of gaining weight is to increase lean-body (or muscle) mass. One pound of muscle has about 2,500 calories. Therefore, if an athlete consumes 250 cal/day above her caloric budget — a 250-calorie profit — it will take her 10 days to gain one pound of lean-body mass [2,500 cal ÷ 250 cal/day = 10 days]. So if the previously mentioned 150-pound athlete requires 3,300 cal/day to maintain her bodyweight, she must consume 3,550 cal/day — 250 calories above her need — to gain one pound of lean-body mass in 10 days. Keep in mind that this estimate must be recalculated on a regular basis to account for changes in bodyweight. After increasing her bodyweight to 151 pounds, for example, she'll now require 3,322 cal/day to meet her energy needs [151 lb x 22 cal/lb]. In order to gain another pound of lean-body mass in 10 days, she must increase her caloric consumption to 3,572 cal/day — 250 calories above her need.

The daily caloric profit shouldn't be more than about 350 - 700 calories above the normal daily caloric needs. If the weight gain is more than about 1% of the bodyweight per week, it's likely that some excess calories will be stored in the form of fat. However, if the weight gain is less than about 1% of the bodyweight per week and is the result of a demanding strength-training program in conjunction with a balanced nutritional intake, then it will probably be in the form of increased lean-body mass.

Gaining weight requires total nutritional dedication for seven days a week. Additional calories must be consumed daily on a regular basis until the desired gain in weight is achieved. The best way for the body to absorb food is when it's divided into several regular-sized meals intermingled with a few snacks. The body doesn't absorb one or two large meals as well — most of these calories are simply jammed through the digestive system. As a matter of fact, when consuming a large number of calories at one time, some of them will be diverted to fat deposits because of the sudden demand on the metabolic pathways. (This has been referred to as "nutrient overload.")

Besides what has been discussed, here are some additional tips for gaining weight:

- Set short-term goals that are realistic
- Keep a food/activity log or diary
- Eat at least three meals per day
- Eat at least three nutritious snacks per day
- Consume foods that are high in calories (but not high in fat)
- Eat dense fruit (such as bananas, pineapples and raisins)
- Eat dense vegetables (such as peas, corn and carrots)
- Drink juice and milk
- Increase the size of portions

Losing Weight

Some female athletes will be healthier — and more competitive — if they decrease their bodyweight. Like gaining weight, the potential to lose weight is primarily determined by a person's inherited characteristics. An individual whose ancestors had endomorphic tendencies — that is, round features with little in the way of muscular definition — has the genetic destiny for that type of physique. This doesn't mean that a person with those inherited characteristics — who would be categorized as an "endomorph" — is incapable of losing weight. But it will be difficult for those who have a high level of endomorphy to achieve a significant decrease in their bodyweight.

Understand that the numbers on height/weight charts and bathroom scales are poor indicators of whether or not a woman should lose weight. The need for weight loss should be determined by body composition rather than bodyweight, especially in the case of an athlete. For the most part, athletes tend to be larger and have more lean-body mass than the general population. To illustrate, think about two women who stand five feet, seven inches tall and weigh 150 pounds. If their heights and weights are considered without regard for their body compositions, it might be concluded that they're both a bit overweight. But what if one woman had 20% body fat and the other had 30% body fat? If this was the case, then only one woman might need to lose weight — the one with the higher percentage of body fat. As such, determining the need to lose weight should be based upon body composition.

As long as athletes consume a variety of foods that provide adequate calories and nutrients, there's no need for them to take nutritional supplements. (Photo by Pete Silletti)

A variety of methods can be used to measure body composition such as air displacement plethysmography (ADP), bioelectrical impedance analysis (BIA), computerized tomography (CT), dual energy x-ray absorptiometry (DEXA), hydrostatic (underwater) weighing and near infrared reactance. But perhaps the most popular method of assessing body composition is using skinfold calipers. In general, this is considered to be the most practical and least expensive method of assessment without sacrificing much in the way of accuracy (assuming that the tester is reasonably skilled and the formula is reliable). The average woman should maintain a body fat of about 16 - 25%; a normal body fat for a female athlete is a bit lower than her non-athletic counterpart — about 12 - 22%. (Body fats in excess of 32% in women are considered to be unhealthy.) In most sports, a low percentage of body fat is desirable; in some sports, however, a high percentage of body fat is actually advantageous. For instance, long-distance swimmers obtain increased buoyancy and thermal insulation from higher levels of body fat.

The primary goal of losing weight is to decrease body fat. One pound of fat has about 3,500 calories. As such, if an athlete consumes 250 cal/day below her caloric budget — a 250-calorie deficit — it will take her 14 days to lose one pound of fat [3,500 cal ÷ 250 cal/day = 14 days]. So if the 150-pound athlete in the ongoing example needs 3,300 cal/day to maintain her bodyweight, she must consume 3,050 cal/day — 250 calories below her need — to lose one pound of fat in 14 days. Remember that this estimate must be recalculated on a regular basis to account for changes in bodyweight. After decreasing her bodyweight to 149 pounds, for example, she'll now require 3,278 cal/day to meet her energy needs [149 lb x 22 cal/lb]. In order to lose another pound of fat in 14 days, she must decrease her caloric consumption to 3,028 cal/day — 250 calories below her need.

Actually, a caloric deficit can be achieved by decreasing caloric consumption, increasing caloric expenditure (through additional activity) or a combination of the two. In fact, proper weight loss should be a blend of consuming less calories and expending more calories.

The daily caloric deficit shouldn't be more than about 500 - 1000 calories below the normal daily caloric needs. If the weight loss is more than about 1% of the bodyweight per week, it's likely that some of this weight reduction will be the result of decreased lean-body mass and/or water rather than body fat. However, if the weight loss is less than about 1% of the bodyweight per week and is the result of a rigorous training program in conjunction with a reduced caloric intake, then it will probably be in the form of decreased body fat.

Losing weight must be a carefully planned activity. Skipping meals — or all-out starvation — isn't a desirable method of weight loss, since sufficient calories are still needed to fuel an active lifestyle. Oddly enough, losing weight should be done in a fashion similar to that of gaining weight: Frequent — but smaller — meals spread out over the course of the day will suppress the appetite. It's also a good idea to drink plenty of water before, during and after meals. This creates a feeling of fullness without providing any calories.

Besides what has been discussed, here are some additional tips for losing weight:

• Set short-term goals that are realistic
• Keep a food/activity log or diary
• Read the nutrition labels
• Eat a moderate amount of sugars
• Eat foods that are low in fat
• Reduce the intake of saturated fats
• Eat more fruits and vegetables
• Chew your food slowly
• Decrease the size of portions

PRE-ACTIVITY FOODS/FUELS

A meal that's consumed prior to an activity — whether it's a training session or a competition — should accomplish several things such as removing hunger pangs, readying the body with fuel for the upcoming activity and relaxing the psychological state. There's no food that athletes can consume before an activity that will directly improve their performance. But there are certain foods that athletes can consume before an activity that can impair their performance and, for that reason, should be avoided. For instance, fats and meats are digested slowly and, therefore, shouldn't be eaten prior to training or competing. Other foods to omit include those that are greasy, highly seasoned and flatulent (gas-forming) along with any specific foods that athletes may personally find distressful to their digestive systems. If anything, the choices for the pre-activity meal should be almost bland, yet appetizing enough so that an athlete wants to eat it.

Prior to an activity, foods that cause a sharp increase in the levels of blood glucose should also be avoided. Here's why: In response to highly elevated blood-glucose levels, the body increases its blood-insulin levels to maintain a stable internal environment (known as "homeostasis"). As a result of this biochemical balancing, blood glucose is sharply reduced. This leads to hypoglycemia (or "low blood sugar") which decreases the availability of blood glucose as a fuel and causes an athlete to feel severely fatigued. Although this condition is usually temporary, it remains an important consideration.

The idea, then, is to consume foods that elevate or maintain blood glucose without triggering a dramatic response by blood insulin. At one time, it was thought that simple carbohydrates (sugars) increase blood glucose more rapidly than complex carbohydrates (starches). A more recent trend of thought has been to consider the Glycemic Index (GI) of a food. The GI dates back to 1981 when it was conceptualized by a group of scientists as a way to help determine which foods were best for people with diabetes. The GI is a system of quantifying the carbohydrates in foods based upon how they affect blood glucose. A value is assigned to a food that correlates to the magnitude of the increase in blood glucose. For instance, a food with a GI of 25 means that it elevates blood glucose to a level that is 25% as great as consuming the same amount of pure glucose. Incidentally, the GI isn't related to portion size. So the GI is the same whether a person consumes 10 grams of a particular food or 110 grams. (The number of calories, of course, would differ according to the size of the portion.)

Before an activity, it's best to consume foods that are easy to digest and high in carbohydrates — specifically, those with a low GI. These foods help to keep blood-glucose levels within a desirable range.

Don't simply assume that a sugary food raises blood glucose more than a starchy food. Indeed, honey (58) has a lower GI than a bagel (78) and, given these two options, would be a better choice for a pre-activity food. Foods with a relatively low GI include roasted peanuts (14), cherries (22), pure fructose (23), grapefruit (25), milk (34), pears (36), plain pizza (36), apples (38), apple juice (40), spaghetti (40), oranges (43), grapes (43), macaroni (46), oatmeal (55) and orange juice (55).

Water is perhaps the best liquid for an athlete to drink before training or competing. The fluid intake should be enough to guarantee optimal hydration during the activity.

The timing of the pre-activity meal is also crucial. To ensure that the digestive process doesn't impair an athlete's performance, the pre-activity meal should be eaten at least three hours prior to training or competing. In short, the pre-activity meal should include foods that are familiar to an athlete and are well tolerated — preferably carbohydrates with a low GI.

POST-ACTIVITY FOODS/FLUIDS

After an intense activity, proper nutrition accelerates recovery and better prepares athletes for their next physical challenge. The idea is to replenish their depleted glycogen stores and to expedite the recovery process as soon as possible after they train or compete.

Following an activity, it's best to consume foods that are high in carbohydrates — specifically, those with a high GI. These foods will help to restore muscle glycogen in the quickest fashion. Foods with a relatively high GI include bananas (60), table sugar (65), watermelon (72), waffles (76), rice cakes (77), Rice Krispies® (82), pretzels (83), corn flakes (84), white rice (88), baked potatoes (93), white bread (95), glucose (100) and buckwheat pancakes (103).

Because appetite is suppressed immediately after intense efforts, it may be more practical for an athlete to initially consume fluids rather than solid food or a meal. Cold fluids also help to cool the body. Commercial sports drinks can be excellent post-activity fluids. In terms of recovery, there are two important components of a sports drink: carbohydrates and electrolytes (sodium and potassium). Since all sports drinks are different, the nutrition labels should be read to be sure of their exact contents. As an example, 12 ounces of Gatorade® Energy Drink (The Gatorade Company) has 78 grams of carbohydrates which provide 312 calories; the same amount of Gatorade® Thirst Quencher contains 21 grams of carbohydrates which provide 84 calories. Both products have adequate amounts of electrolytes and a high GI but vastly different levels of carbohydrates and calories.

According to Nancy Clark, M. S., R. D. — an internationally known sports nutritionist and author — athletes should consume 0.5 grams of carbohydrates per pound of their bodyweight (g/lb) within two hours of completing an intense activity. This should be repeated again within the next two hours. For instance, an individual who weighs 150 pounds needs to ingest about 75 grams of carbohydrates — or 300 calories of carbohydrates — within two hours after an intense activity and another 75 grams of carbohydrates during the next two hours [0.5 g/lb x 150 lb].

There's some evidence to suggest that combining the carbohydrates with a small amount of protein can expedite recovery by improving the rate at which the glycogen stores are replenished. However, it appears that simply increasing the quantity of post-activity carbohydrates will have the same results. Nonetheless, consuming a small amount of protein following an intense activity may aid in the repair of muscle tissue.

Finally, it's also important to rehydrate after an activity. Athletes should consume about 16 ounces of water for every pound of bodyweight that they lose during their training.

NUTRITIONAL SUPPLEMENTS

Skillful promoters regularly tout nutritional supplements — including protein, vitamins and minerals — with almost supernatural powers, having the ability to do practically everything imaginable. Athletes are frequently tempted, teased and seduced by their brilliant promises to "lose flab," "gain muscle," "get stronger" and "improve performance." Because of this, many athletes don't give a second thought to spending huge sums of their money on a never-ending parade of nutritional supplements — or the more trendy buzzword "neutraceuticals." Unfortunately, most of the claims concerning nutritional supplements are purely speculative and anecdotal with little or no scientific or medical basis.

Protein Supplements

Many athletes think that they need to consume additional protein in order to increase their muscular strength and lean-body mass and, for that reason, take protein supplements. A number of studies have shown that the protein needs of athletes may be higher than those of sedentary individuals. But this need has been drastically exaggerated and overrated by health-food manufacturers and promoters.

The fact of the matter is that individuals who consume adequate calories generally obtain sufficient protein. Recall that an athlete's caloric requirements are determined by several factors including size and level of activity. Larger, more active individuals require and consume more calories than the average person. With these additional calories comes additional protein. In other words, the increased protein need of athletes is met by an increased caloric intake. Dr. Gail Butterfield, a registered dietician and fellow of the American College of Sports Medicine, states, "I am not convinced that even with the initiation of a [strength-training] program that protein requirement is increased as long as [caloric] intake is increased."

For adults, the RDA for protein is 0.8 grams per kilogram of bodyweight per day (g/kg/day). Assuming a sufficient caloric intake, 1.2 - 2.0 g/kg/day (about 150 - 250% of the RDA for adults) is present in any mixed diet that contains 15% of its calories as protein. Recall the 150-pound athlete in the ongoing example who must consume 3,300 cal/day to maintain her bodyweight. If 15% of these calories came from protein, she would be receiving 495 calories from protein or 123.75 grams [495 cal ÷ 4 cal/g]. Based upon the RDA of 0.8 g/kg/day, this athlete would be consuming enough protein to meet the daily needs of a woman who weighed a little more than 340 pounds [123.75 g/day ÷ 0.8g/kg/day x 2.2 lb/kg = 340.31 lb]. This amount of protein is actually about 2.15 g/kg/day — or about 2.5 times the RDA. And remember, this is without the athlete making any effort to consume extra protein. So even if the requirement for athletes may be greater, it's likely that they're already consuming enough protein to ensure proper levels of consumption. If an athlete is concerned that she isn't getting enough protein in her diet, she can obtain sufficient amounts by simply consuming more foods that are high in protein.

While on the subject, understand that an excessive intake of protein carries the potential for numerous unwanted side effects. An intake of protein that's in excess of the needs for growth, maintenance and repair of tissue is either stored as fat or excreted in the urine. When excessive protein is urinated, it places a heavy burden on the liver and kidneys and may damage those organs. An excessive intake of protein also increases the risk of dehydration which, in turn, increases the risk of developing a heat-related disorder such as heat exhaustion, heat stroke or heat cramps. Other potential side effects from a high intake of protein include an excessive loss of calcium in the urine, diarrhea, cramping and gastrointestinal upset.

Vitamin and Mineral Supplements

Many athletes believe that their foods don't supply sufficient micronutrients and, therefore, they take vitamin and mineral supplements. There's no unbiased, scientific evidence to suggest that those who consume a balanced diet need vitamin and mineral supplementation in excess of the RDA; likewise, there's no unbiased, scientific evidence to suggest that an increased consumption of vitamins and minerals improves performance. Recall that athletes typically require and consume more calories than the average person. With these additional calories come additional vitamins and minerals. In truth, even a marginal diet provides adequate vitamins and minerals. Understand, too, that your liver is a storehouse for vitamins and minerals. This organ can quickly compensate for a temporary dietary shortfall by releasing its stored nutrients as needed and then replenishing its reservoirs when the opportunity arises.

That being said, vitamin and mineral supplements may be needed by those who don't consume adequate diets. For example, a multi-vitamin and -mineral supplement may be warranted for vegetarians and women who are pregnant or lactating. Supplementation may also be appropriate for athletes who restrict their caloric intakes because their sports have aesthetic demands (such as ballet, dance, gymnastics and figure skating) or weight classifications (such as boxing, competitive weightlifting, judo, lightweight crew and wrestling). Since women are at an increased risk for iron and calcium deficiency, supplementation may be justified for those two minerals. Finally, a folate (folic acid) supplement may be warranted for women of childbearing age.

Whenever possible, it's better to get vitamins from foods rather than pills because the high concentration of a vitamin or a mineral in pill form may interfere with the absorption of some other nutrients. Also keep in mind that supplements containing more than 150% of the RDA are for disease treatment and should never be used unless a competent health professional has diagnosed their need. Professional advice concerning nutritional supplementation should be sought from a registered dietitian (R.D.) or a sports nutritionist.

VITAMIN (units)	Females (divided by age group)					Pregnancy		Lactation	
	9-13	14-18	19-30	31-50	51-70	19-30	31-50	19-30	31-50
Vitamin A (mcg)	600	700	700	700	700	770	770	1,300	1,300
Vitamin D (mcg)	5	5	5	5	10	5	5	5	5
Vitamin E (mg)	11	15	15	15	15	15	15	19	19
Vitamin K (mcg)	60	75	90	90	90	90	90	90	90
Vitamin C (mg)	45	65	75	75	75	85	85	120	120
Biotin (mcg)	20	25	30	30	30	30	30	35	35
Choline (mg)	375	400	425	425	425	450	450	550	550
Folate (mcg)	300	400	400	400	400	600	600	500	500
Niacin (mg)	12	14	14	14	14	18	18	17	17
Pantothenic Acid (mg)	4	5	5	5	5	6	6	7	7
Riboflavin (mg)	0.9	1.0	1.1	1.1	1.1	1.4	1.4	1.6	1.6
Thiamin (mg)	0.9	1.0	1.1	1.1	1.1	1.4	1.4	1.4	1.4
Pyridoxine (mg)	1.0	1.2	1.3	1.3	1.5	1.9	1.9	2.0	2.0
Cobalamin (mcg)	1.8	2.4	2.4	2.4	2.4	2.6	2.6	2.8	2.8

TABLE 11.1: RECOMMENDED DIETARY ALLOWANCES (RDAS) OF SELECTED VITAMINS FOR FEMALES AGED 9 - 50

When consumed in reasonable doses, vitamins and minerals pose no health or safety risks. The American Dietetic Association — the largest and most established organization devoted to both practice and research in nutrition — reports that megadoses of vitamins and minerals pose a risk of toxicity that can create adverse side effects and may lead to serious medical complications. When taken in megadoses — any dose greater than 10 times the RDA — the vitamins that are in excess of those needed to saturate the enzyme systems function as free-floating drugs instead of receptor-bound nutrients. Like all drugs, high

VITAMIN (units)	Females (divided by age group)					Pregnancy		Lactation	
	9-13	14-18	19-30	31-50	51-70	19-30	31-50	19-30	31-50
Calcium (mg)	1300	1300	1000	1000	1200	1000	1000	1000	1000
Chromium (mcg)	21	24	25	25	20	30	30	45	45
Copper (mcg)	700	890	900	900	900	1000	1000	1300	1300
Flouride (mg)	2	3	3	3	3	3	3	3	3
Iodine (mcg)	120	150	150	150	150	220	220	290	290
Iron (mg)	8	15	18	18	8	27	27	9	9
Magnesium (mg)	240	360	310	320	320	350	350	310	320
Manganese (mg)	1.6	1.6	1.8	1.8	1.8	2.0	2.0	2.6	2.6
Molybdenum (mcg)	34	43	45	45	45	50	50	50	50
Phosphorus (mg)	1250	1250	700	700	700	700	700	700	700
Selenium (mcg)	40	55	55	55	55	60	60	70	70
Zinc (mg)	8	9	8	8	8	11	11	12	12

TABLE 11.2: RECOMMENDED DIETARY ALLOWANCES (RDAS) OF SELECTED MINERALS FOR FEMALES AGED 9 – 50

doses of vitamins and minerals have the potential for adverse side effects.

Of greatest concern is excessive intake of the fat-soluble vitamins — particularly vitamins A and D — which can be extremely toxic and may have undesirable side effects. Consuming large doses of vitamin A can result in decalcification of the bones (resulting in fragile bones), an increased susceptibility to disease, enlargements of the liver and the spleen, muscle and joint soreness, vomiting, cessation of menstruation (amenorrhea), stunted growth, loss of appetite, loss of hair, irritability, double vision, skin rashes, headaches, nausea, drowsiness and diarrhea. Consuming large doses of vitamin D can result in nausea, loss of hair, loss of weight, vomiting, decalcification of the bones (resulting in fragile bones), drowsiness, diarrhea, headaches, hypertension, elevated cholesterol and loss of appetite.

Excess amounts of the B vitamins and vitamin C are generally excreted in the urine (which prompts many authorities to suggest that supplementation with water-soluble vitamins leaves a person with nothing more than expensive urine). This action, places an inordinate amount of stress on the liver and kidneys. Though mainly excreted, excess amounts of the water-soluble vitamins may still have toxic effects. For example, megadoses of vitamin C can be harmful while in the body. Potential side effects from an excessive intake of vitamin C include kidney stones, diarrhea, bladder irritation, intestinal problems, destruction of red blood cells, nausea, stomach cramps, an increase in plasma cholesterol, ulceration of the gastric wall, leaching of calcium from the bones and gout.

FOOD FOR THOUGHT

As long as athletes consume a variety of foods that provide adequate calories and nutrients, there's no need for them to take nutritional supplements. By investing their money in high-quality foods instead of purchasing expensive nutritional supplements, athletes will achieve greater success in maximizing their physical potential in a much safer manner. Remember, there are no shortcuts on the road to proper nutrition.

REFERENCES

Barron, R. L., and G. J. Vanscoy. 1993. Natural products and the athlete: facts and folklore. *Annals of Pharmacotherapy* 27 (5): 607-615.

Brand-Miller, J., S. Colagiuri, T. M. S. Wolever and K. Foster-Powell. 1999. *The glucose revolution*. New York, NY: Marlowe & Company.

Bryant, C. X., J. A. Peterson and R. J. Hagen. 1994. Weight loss: unfolding the truth. *Fitness Management* 10 (May): 42-44.

Bubb, W. J. 1992. Nutrition. In *Health fitness instructor's handbook, 2nd ed*, by E. T. Howley and B. D. Franks, 95-114. Champaign, IL: Human Kinetics Publishers, Inc.

_____. 1992. Relative leanness. In *Health fitness instructor's handbook, 2nd ed*, by E. T. Howley and B. D. Franks, 115-130. Champaign, IL: Human Kinetics Publishers, Inc.

Burke, L. M., G. R. Collier and M. Hargreaves. 1993. Muscle glycogen storage after prolonged exercise: effect of the glycemic index of carbohydrate feeding. *Journal of Applied Physiology* 75 (2): 1019-1023.

Butterfield, G. 1991. Amino acids and high protein diets. In *Perspectives in exercise science and sports medicine, volume 4*, ed. D. R. Lamb and M. Williams, 87-122. Indianapolis, IN: Brown & Benchmark.

City of New York Department of Consumer Affairs. 1992. *Magic muscle pills!! Health and fitness quackery in nutrition supplements*. New York, NY: Department of Consumer Affairs.

Clark, N. 1990. *Nancy Clark's sports nutrition guidebook*. Champaign, IL: Leisure Press.

Clarkson, P. M., and E. S. Rawson. 1999. Nutitional supplements to increase muscle mass. *Clinical Reviews in Food Science and Nutrition* 39 (4): 317-328.

Coleman, E. 2000. Does whey protein enhance performance? *Sports Medicine Digest* 22 (7): 80, 82.

_____. 2001. Being supplement savvy. *Sports Medicine Digest* 24 (4): 46-47.

Cummings, S., E. S. Parham and G. W. Strain. 2002. Position of the American Dietetic Association: weight management. *Journal of the American Dietetic Association* 102 (8): 1145-1155.

Ernst,E. 1998. Harmless herbs? A review of the recent literature. *The American Journal of Medicine* 104 (February): 170-178.

Farley, D. 1993. Dietary supplements: making sure hype doesn't overwhelm science. *FDA Consumer* 27 (November): 8-13.

Fink, K. J., and B. Worthington-Roberts. 1995. Nutritional considerations for exercise. In *The Stairmaster fitness handbook, 2nd ed*, ed. J. A. Peterson and C. X. Bryant, 205-228. St. Louis, MO: Wellness Bookshelf.

Guthrie, H. A. 1983. *Introductory nutrition. 5th ed*. St. Louis, MO: The C. V. Mosby Company.

Herbert, V., and G. J. Subak-Sharpe, eds. 1990. *The Mount Sinai School of Medicine complete book of nutrition*. New York, NY: St. Martin's Press.

Houston, M. E. 1999. Gaining weight: the scientific basis of increasing skeletal muscle mass. *Canadian Journal of Applied Physiology* 24 (4): 305-316.

Ivy, J. L. 1991. Muscle glycogen synthesis before and after exercise. *Sports Medicine* 11 (1): 6-19.

_____. 2001. Dietary strategies to promote glycogen synthesis after exercise. *Canadian Journal of Applied Physiology* 26 (supplement): S236-S245.

Jakicic, J. M., K. Clark, E. Coleman, J. E. Donnelly, J. Foreyt, E. Melanson, J. Volek and S. L. Volpe. 2001. ACSM position stand on the appropriate intervention strategies for weight loss and prevention of weight regain for adults. *Medicine and Science in Sports and Exercise* 33 (12): 2145-2156.

Lowenthal, D. T., and Y. Karni. 1990. The nutritional needs of athletes. In *The Mount Sinai School of Medicine complete book of nutrition*, ed. V. Herbert and G. J. Subak-Sharpe, 396-414. New York, NY: St. Martin's Press.

Lukaski, H. C. 1995. Micronutrients (magnesium, zinc, and copper): are mineral supplements needed for athletes? *International Journal of Sports Nutrition* 5 (supplement): S74-S83.

Manore, M. M., Barr, S. I., and G. E. Butterfield. 2000. Joint position statement by the American College of Sports Medicine, American Dietetic Association and Dieticians of Canada on nutrition and athletic performance. *Medicine and Science in Sports and Exercise* 32 (12): 2130-2145.

McArdle, W. D., F. I. Katch and V. L. Katch. 1986. *Exercise physiology: energy, nutrition and human performance. 2nd ed.* Philadelphia, PA: Lea & Febiger.

McCarthy, P. 1989. How much protein do athletes really need? *The Physician and Sportsmedicine* 17 (5): 170-175.

National Collegiate Athletic Association [NCAA]. 1991. No miracles found in many "natural potions." *NCAA News* 28 (July 17): 7.

NCAA Committee on Competitive Safeguards and Medical Aspects of Sports. 1992. Ergogenic aids and nutrition. Overland Park, KS: NCAA memorandum (August 6).

National Research Council, Committee on Diet and Health, Food and Nutrition Board. 1989. *Diet and health: implications for reducing chronic disease risk.* Washington, D. C.: National Academy Press.

Philen, R. M., D. I. Ortiz, S. B. Auerbach and H. Falk. 1992. Survey of advertising for nutritional supplements in health and bodybuilding magazines. *Journal of the American Medical Association* 268 (8): 1008-1011.

Rasmussen, B. B., K. D. Tipton, S. L. Miller, S. E. Wolf and R. R. Wolfe. 2000. An oral essential amino acid-carbohydrate supplement enhances muscle protein anabolism after resistance exercise. *Journal of Applied Physiology* 88 (2): 386-392.

Scrimshaw, N. S., and V. R. Young. 1976. The requirements of human nutrition. *Scientific American* 235 (3): 50-64.

Singh, A., F. M. Moses and P. A. Deuster. 1992. Chronic multivitamin-mineral supplementation does not enhance physical performance. *Medicine and Science in Sports and Exercise* 24 (6): 726-732.

Smith, N. J. 1984. Nutrition. In *Sports medicine,* ed. R. H. Strauss, 468-480. Philadelphia, PA: W. B. Saunders Company.

Sparling, P., R. Recker and T. Lambrinides. 1994. Position statement to football players from Cincinnati Bengals Training Staff and nutrition consultant.

St. Jeor, S. T., B. V. Howard, T. E. Prewitt, V. Bovee, T. Bazzarre and R. H. Eckel. 2001. Dietary protein and weight reduction. *Circulation* 104 (15): 1869-1874.

Taylor, M. R. 1993. *The dietary supplement debate of 1993: an FDA perspective.* Presented at the Federation of American Societies for Experimental Biology Annual Meeting. New Orleans, LA.

Telford, R., E. Catchpole, V. Deakin, A. Hahn and A. Plank. 1992. The effect of 7 to 8 months of vitamin/mineral supplementation on athletic performance. *International Journal of Sports Nutrition* 2 (2): 135-153.

Weight, L. M., T. D. Noakes, D. Labadorios, J. Graves, D. Haem, P. Jacobs and P. Berman. 1988. Vitamin and mineral status of trained athletes including the effects of supplementation. *American Journal of Clinical Nutrition* 47 (2): 186-191.

Willett, W. C., and M. J. Stampfer. 2003. Rebuilding the food pyramid. *Scientific American* 288 (1): 64-71.

Williams, M. H. 1992. *Nutrition for fitness and sport*. Dubuque, IA: Brown & Benchmark.

12

20 Questions ... and 20 Answers

Matt Brzycki, B.S.

This chapter examines a number of frequently asked questions concerning the training of female athletes. No doubt, many readers have the same or similar questions.

1. Are there telltale signs of overtraining?

Yes. Overtraining is a result of overstressing the body. Generally speaking, the excessive stress is produced by excessive activity. Symptoms of overtraining include chronic fatigue, appetite disorders, insomnia, depression, anger, substantial weight loss or gain, prolonged muscular soreness, anemia and an elevated resting heart rate.

The most obvious indicator of overtraining, however, is a lack of progress in an athlete's level of strength and conditioning. An athlete can identify a lack of progress by keeping accurate records of her performances.

The best cure for overtraining is to obtain sufficient rest in order to allow the body the opportunity to recover. This may necessitate reducing the volume of activity that's performed (in terms of workouts, exercises and/or sets). Taking some time off periodically from exercising also helps to avoid overtraining.

2. How can shin splints be avoided?

"Shin splints" is a general term used to describe a variety of painful conditions on the anterior (front) part of the lower leg. The pain — often typified as a dull ache — is usually located on the lower two-thirds of the tibia (the shin bone) and is felt during dorsi flexion and plantar flexion.

Shin splints are considered to be an overuse injury and, for the most part, have two main causes. In some cases, there's a strength imbalance between the muscles of the lower leg. Specifically, the dorsi flexors on the anterior part of the lower leg are weaker than the calf muscles on the posterior part of the lower leg. In effect, the stronger calf muscles overpower the weaker dorsi flexors and produce an injury. This situation can be remedied by doing two things: performing exercises for the dorsi flexors and reducing exercises for the calves. Shin splints can also result from high-impact forces that exceed the structural integrity of the lower leg. There are a number of ways to lessen this orthopedic stress. First of all, athletes should wear proper shoes that provide adequate support and shock-absorbing qualities. It's also important to decrease the number of weightbearing activities that are performed and increase the non-weightbearing ones. If possible, weightbearing activities should be done on softer, more yielding surfaces.

If an athlete has shin splints, she can alleviate the pain and swelling by applying ice to the inflamed area. The ice treatment should last about 20 minutes and be done as soon as possible after she has completed her activity.

3. Is there a certain way that a person should breathe when lifting weights?

Yes. It's important for people to breath properly when they perform a strenuous activity such as strength training — especially during intense efforts. Holding the breath during exertion creates an elevated pressure in the abdominal and thoracic cavities which is referred to as the "Valsalva maneuver." The elevated pressure interferes with the return of blood to the heart. This may deprive the brain of blood and can cause an individual to lose consciousness.

To emphasize correct breathing, exhale when the resistance is raised and inhale when it's lowered. Or simply remember EOE — Exhale On Effort. As it turns out, inhaling and exhaling naturally usually results in correct breathing.

4. If an athlete stops lifting weights her muscles will turn to fat, right?

Wrong. It's a common misconception that muscle can turn into fat. In truth, muscle cannot be changed into fat — or vice versa — any more than gold can be changed into lead. Muscle tissue consists of special contractile proteins that allow movement to occur. It's about 70% water, 22% protein and 7% fat. (The remaining 1% or so includes inorganic salts such as calcium, potassium and sodium.) Conversely, your fatty (or adipose) tissue is composed of spherical cells that are specifically designed to store fat. Fatty tissue is about 22% water, 6% protein and 72% fat. Since muscle and fat are two different and distinct types of biological tissue, a muscle cannot turn into fat if an athlete stops lifting weights. Similarly, lifting weights — or doing any other type of physical activity — will not change fat into muscle. The fact is that muscles hypertrophy (or become larger) from physical activity and muscles atrophy (or become smaller) from physical inactivity.

5. Will lifting weights make women less flexible and more bulky?

Not necessarily. One of the biggest misconceptions in strength training is the belief that women — and men, for that matter — who lift weights will lose flexibility. If anything, performing repetitions throughout a full range of motion against a resistance will maintain or even improve flexibility. Women who have residual fears about becoming less flexible can perform a series of flexibility movements both before and after their strength training. As an added measure, they can also stretch the muscles that were involved in an exercise immediately after it's completed. (Flexibility training is discussed in great detail in Chapter 9.)

Another popular misconception in strength training is the belief that women will develop large, unsightly muscles. Understand that increases in muscular strength are often accompanied by increases in muscular size. While this is true for both men and women, increases in muscular size are much less pronounced in women. Since the early 1960s, research has shown that most women can achieve significant improvements in their muscular strength without concomitant gains in their muscular size. One researcher, for example, found that a group of 47 women increased their strength in the leg press by nearly 30% after 10 weeks of exercising yet the largest increase in muscular size that was

The overwhelming majority of women can gain considerable muscular strength from lifting weights yet have little or no change in their muscular size. (Photo by Pete Silletti)

experienced by any of them was *less than one-quarter inch*. Clearly, strength training doesn't lead to excessive muscular bulk in the majority of women.

There are several physiological reasons that prevent or minimize the possibility that women will significantly increase the size of their muscles. First of all, most women are genetically bound by an unfavorable and unchangeable ratio of muscle to tendon (that is, short muscle bellies coupled with long tendinous attachments). In addition, most women have relatively low levels of serum testosterone. The low levels of this growth-promoting hormone restrict the degree to which women can increase their muscular size.

A final physiological factor that prevents or minimizes the possibility that women will significantly increase their muscular size is their percentage of body fat. Quite simply, women tend to inherit higher percentages of body fat than do men. For example, the average 18- to 22-year-old woman is about 22 - 26% body fat, whereas the average man of similar age is about 12 - 16%. The higher the percentage of body fat, the lower the percentage of muscle mass. This extra body fat also tends to soften or mask the effects of strength training. Women who possess very little body fat appear to be more muscular than they actually are because their muscles are more visible. Likewise, the appearance of more muscle mass may not be the result of muscular hypertrophy. Rather, a decrease in body fat may simply make the same amount of muscle mass become more noticeable.

If you're wondering about female bodybuilders, they've inherited a greater potential to increase the size of their muscles than the average woman. Highly competitive female bodybuilders have developed large muscles because of their genetic potential — not simply because they lifted weights. Keep in mind, too, that female bodybuilders look much more muscular while posing on stage than they actually are in a relaxed state. Prior to a competition, female bodybuilders have restricted their caloric intakes — often severely — thereby reducing their body fat and body fluids. Immediately prior to posing on stage, they've also "pumped" their muscles. This engorges their muscles with blood and makes them temporarily bigger. Finally, the stage lighting as well as their tans and clothing — and even the oil that's rubbed on their bodies — all contribute to making female bodybuilders appear as if they have much more muscular size than they really do.

There are a relatively small number of women who have inherited the ingredients necessary to experience significant increases in their muscular size from lifting weights. However, the overwhelming majority of women can gain considerable muscular strength from lifting weights yet have little or no change in their muscular size. In short, it's physiologically improbable for the average woman to develop large muscles that are unsightly or unfeminine.

6. How often should athletes "max out" to check their progress in the weight room?

Workouts often morph into versions of a weightlifting contest with numerous sets leading to one-repetition maximum (1-RM) attempts. Unless an athlete happens to be a competitive weightlifter, there's no need for her to "max out" to determine how much weight she can lift for one repetition. And even if she's a competitive weightlifter, she doesn't have to perform low-repetition sets until she gets close to a contest.

One reservation with performing a 1-RM is that it's a highly specialized skill that requires proper warm-up, instruction, supervision and practice. This time and effort could be used elsewhere such as perfecting skills that will actually be used in athletic competition. The main concern with doing a 1-RM, however, is an increased risk of musculoskeletal injury. Attempting a 1-RM with a maximal or near-maximal weight can place an inordinate and unreasonable amount of stress on the muscles, connective tissues and bones. An injury occurs when this stress exceeds the structural integrity of those components. Any injury that occurs from attempting a 1-RM is simply inexcusable.

Performing a 1-RM isn't really necessary to monitor an athlete's progress. If an athlete is recording her workout data — and she should — she can simply check her workout card or log to evaluate her levels of strength.

Over the years, a number of prediction equations have been developed and used to estimate a 1-RM based upon the relationship between muscular strength and muscular endurance. By using a prediction equation, a 1-RM can be estimated in a safe and practical — yet reasonably accurate — manner without having to "max out." The following equation can be used to predict a 1-RM based upon repetitions-to-fatigue (where "X" equals the number of repetitions performed):

Predicted 1-RM = weight lifted ÷ (1.0278 - 0.0278X)

To illustrate the equation, suppose that an athlete was able to do 8 repetitions to the point of muscular fatigue with 150 pounds. Inserting these values into the equation yields a predicted 1-RM of about 186 pounds [0.0278 x 8 = 0.2224; 1.0278 - 0.2224 = 0.8054; 150 ÷ 0.8054 = 186.24]. In other words, she can do 8 repetitions with about 80.54% (or 0.8054) of her predicted 1-RM.

In a study that involved 48 subjects, researchers found that this equation had a high correlation for predicting a 1-RM bench press (r=0.99) and squat (r=0.96); in a study that involved 67 subjects, researchers showed that this equation had a high correlation for predicting a 1-RM in all three of the competitive powerlifts: the bench press (r=0.993), squat (r=0.969) and deadlift (r=0.956).

It should be noted that this equation is most accurate for predicting a 1-RM when the number of repetitions-to-fatigue is 10 or less. In a study that involved 220 subjects, researchers compared six different equations and found that the aforementioned equation was the only one of the six in which the predicted bench press didn't differ significantly from the actual bench press when 10 or fewer repetitions were completed (r=0.98; t=0.99).

At any rate, a test of muscular endurance — though not a direct measure of pure maximal strength — is much safer than a 1-RM lift because it involves a submaximal load. (Because genetic factors — particularly predominant muscle-fiber type — play a major role in muscular endurance, prediction equations aren't accurate for everyone. However, they're still very practical for much of the population.)

7. Do higher repetitions build muscular endurance instead of muscular strength?

It has been believed that doing higher repetitions (with a lighter weight) builds muscular endurance and doing lower repetitions (with a heavier weight) builds muscular strength. Actually, muscular endurance and muscular strength are directly related. If an athlete increases her muscular endurance, she will also increase her muscular strength. Here's an example: Suppose that an athlete's one-repetition maximum (1-RM) in the bench press is 100 pounds and you can do 10 repetitions with 75% of it (75 pounds). And after several months of strength training with higher repetitions — say, within a range of about 8 - 12 — suppose that she has progressed to the point where she can do 90 pounds for 10 repetitions. Given that she increased the amount of weight that she could lift for 10 repetitions in the bench press by 20% — from 75 to 90 pounds — would her 1-RM strength now be greater than, less than or equal to her previous 1-RM effort of 100 pounds? The odds are that it will be greater than her previous 1-RM. So even though she exercised with higher repetitions, she increased her muscular strength.

By the way, it works the other way as well. If an athlete increases her muscular strength, she will also increase her muscular endurance. Here's why: As she gets stronger, she needs fewer muscle fibers to sustain a sub-maximal effort (muscular endurance). This also means that she has a greater reserve of muscle fibers available to extend the sub-maximal effort.

8. Should women do higher repetitions to tone their muscles and lower repetitions to bulk them?

There's no scientific evidence that higher repetitions increase muscular definition or "tone" and lower repetitions increase muscular size or "bulk." In one 10-week study, there were no significant differences in muscular size (and strength) between a group who did sets of four repetitions and a group who did sets of 10 repetitions.

If a woman performs the same program — that is, the same exercises as well as the same number of sets and repetitions — as someone else for a period of time, chances are that they will not end up looking like physical clones of each other. The next time you're in the weight room, observe different pairs of training partners. You'll see that people who exercise together usually have different builds — despite using the same exercises and performing the same number of sets and repetitions.

People respond differently because each person — except for identical twins — is a unique genetic entity with a different genetic potential for achieving muscular size. Some people are predisposed toward developing highly defined physiques while others are predisposed toward developing heavily muscled physiques. Therefore, the belief that doing high repetitions with light weights will increase muscular definition and doing low repetitions with heavy weights will increase muscular size is entirely anecdotal with no factual basis whatsoever. Whether sets consist of low repetitions, high repetitions or intermediate repetitions, a woman is still going to develop according to her genetic (or inherited) blueprint — provided that the sets are done with similar levels of intensity.

If an athlete increases her muscular endurance, she will also increase her muscular strength. (Photo by Pete Silletti)

So, an athlete's response from strength training isn't necessarily due to a particular program. Following the program of a successful bodybuilder doesn't mean that she will develop the same level of muscular size; likewise, following the program of a successful weightlifter doesn't mean that she will develop the same level of physical strength. If it were that simple, then millions of people would have award-winning physiques and awe-inspiring strength. Yet, millions of people make a terrible mistake by trying to heroically implement the programs of the current physique stars and strength athletes — programs that are usually impractical, inefficient and, in some cases, unsafe.

The truth is that heritability dictates trainability. The main determinant of an athlete's response to strength training is her genetics. The cumulative effect of her inherited muscular, mechanical, hormonal and neural qualities is what determines her physical potential. A woman who has inherited a high percentage of fast-twitch fibers, long muscle bellies coupled with short tendinous attachments, high levels of testosterone, favorable lever lengths, mesomorphic tendencies, low points of tendon insertions and an efficient neurological system would prove to be incredibly strong as well as physically impressive. Compared to the average woman, this genetic marvel would be capable of almost unbelievable feats of strength. There are a few individuals like that but most people aren't so fortunate. But this doesn't mean that an athlete cannot get stronger or improve her physique. Indeed, an athlete should be encouraged and challenged to progress as much as possible within her genetic profile.

9. Should athletes do high-velocity repetitions to recruit their fast-twitch fibers?

No. The selective recruitment of muscle fibers is physiologically impossible. Muscle fibers are recruited — or "innervated" — by the nervous system in an orderly fashion according to the intensity or force requirements and not by the speed of movement. Demands of low muscular intensity are met by slow-twitch fibers. Intermediate fibers are recruited once the slow-twitch fibers are no longer able to continue the task. The fast-twitch fibers are finally recruited only when the other fatigue-resistant fibers have severely depleted their energy stores and cannot meet the force requirements. All fibers are working when the fast-twitch fibers are being used. The orderly recruitment pattern remains the same regardless of whether the repetition speed was fast or slow.

This pattern is consistent with the "size principle" of recruitment that was proposed by Dr. Elwood Henneman in the 1950s. He described the experimental basis of his principle in 18 related articles that were published in the *Journal of Neurophysiology* over the course of 25 years. According to this principle — which is widely accepted by neurophysiologists and regarded by them as one of the most important advances ever in the field of motor control — motoneurons are recruited based upon increasing size: The motor unit with the smallest motoneuron is recruited first and the motor unit with the largest motoneuron is recruited last. (A motor unit consists of a motoneuron and all the muscle fibers that it innervates.) In general, the smallest motoneurons innervate slow-twitch fibers and the largest motoneurons innervate fast-twitch fibers. Therefore, slow-twitch fibers are recruited first and fast-twitch fibers are recruited last.

The orderly pattern of recruitment has another important exercise implication: If an athlete wants to engage as many fast-twitch fibers as possible, then it's critical that she exercises to the point of muscular fatigue.

10. Is it true that lifting weights in an explosive manner will increase speed, power and quickness?

No it's not. Lifting weights at rapid speeds of movement is only a *demon-*

stration of power — not an *adaptation*. There's absolutely no scientific evidence to suggest that "explosive" lifting in the weight room leads to "explosive" performance in the athletic arena. Keep in mind, too, that fast speeds of movement make an exercise less effective and more dangerous.

11. Isn't periodization the most effective way of gaining strength?

Also referred to as "cycling," periodization is a theoretical schedule of pre-planned workouts that has been popularized by competitive weightlifters as their preferred method of training to peak for a one-repetition maximum (1-RM) during their contests. Essentially, the idea is to change or "cycle" program variables such as the number of sets and repetitions, the workloads (which are based upon percentages of a 1-RM) and the recovery intervals between the sets/exercises. These variables are manipulated during rigidly defined "phases" of training which usually are designated as "hypertrophy," "basic strength," "strength-power," "peaking," "maintenance" and "active rest." It's thought that by manipulating the variables, athletes can selectively target specific physiological functions.

Here's a relatively simple example of a classic (linear) model of periodization that's divided into two seven-week "cycles" or "periods" (to supposedly develop strength and power): During the first three weeks of each cycle, an athlete is required to do 2 - 3 sets of 8 - 10 repetitions in each exercise with 50 - 70% of her 1-RM; during the fourth and fifth weeks of each cycle, she must do 3 - 4 sets of 6 repetitions in each exercise with 70 - 85% of her 1-RM; and during the sixth and seventh weeks of each cycle, she must do 3 - 5 sets of 1 - 4 repetitions in each exercise with 85 - 95% of her 1-RM.

There are several issues and concerns relating to the use of periodization. Perhaps first and foremost is the fact that there's no legitimate scientific evidence to support the wild claim that doing different numbers of sets and repetitions with different percentages of a 1-RM while taking different intervals of recovery between sets will specifically influence hypertrophy, strength, strength-power or anything else.

Second, periodization is overly — and unnecessarily — complicated and correspondingly confusing. The use of pseudoscientific terminology coupled with pre-planned workouts that specify inflexible instructions to vary the sets, repetitions, workloads and recovery intervals in rigidly defined phases adds to the confusion. Equally confusing is the notion of "active rest" — a contradiction in terms if there ever was one. Strength training is actually quite simple: Overload the muscles by increasing the resistance and/or repetitions from one workout to the next.

Third, periodization is far too inflexible because of the precise nature of pre-planned workouts. The reality is that athletes often get sick or injured and are forced to miss workouts. In the event of a missed workout, do they renew their training according to their pre-planned schedule? If not, at what point in the pre-planned schedule do they resume? Essentially, "periodization" is a sexy word for "variety." But incorporating variety into a program — which is certainly important — can be done as needed in a manner that's far less regimented and much more informal.

Fourth, periodization requires all athletes to perform specific numbers of repetitions with certain percentages of their 1-RMs. For instance, athletes might be required to do 8 repetitions with 70% of their 1-RMs. Because of wide variations in muscular endurance, however, such a prescription might be far too easy for some and literally impossible for others. Therefore, preplanned workouts that demand the same number of repetitions be done with a specific percentage of a maximal load are only effective for the relatively small segment of the population that has inherited a particular level of muscular endurance that corresponds exactly to the specifications and parameters of the training schedule.

The sole factors that determine an athlete's response from strength training are her genetic profile and her level of effort — not the equipment that she used. (Photo by Pete Silletti)

Fifth, periodization makes some sense for competitive weightlifters since — for the most part — they only peak for two or three contests a year. But it makes little sense for other athletes such as softball or basketball players who might have to peak two or three times a week for two or three months. Indeed, for what competitions do they peak? Isn't every one important? Imagine an athlete saying apologetically, "Sorry about my performance today, coach, but I'm not scheduled to peak in my Strength-Power Phase for two more weeks." Remember, too, that references to the training methods or techniques of competitive weightlifters are irrelevant and, therefore, don't apply to any athletes other than competitive weightlifters. The question that an athlete must ask herself is, "Am I training to become a better athlete or a better weightlifter?"

To summarize: Besides being confusing, trying to implement periodization with athletes other than competitive weightlifters is impractical, irrelevant, illogical and unnecessary. There are other ways to address an athlete's needs that are considerably less complicated as well as more practical, relevant and logical.

12. What's ground-based training?

The notion of "ground-based training" has received a good bit of attention since the mid 1990s. Essentially, ground-based training is the belief that since athletes do many physical activities with their feet in contact with the ground then that's how they should lift weights. In other words, it's the belief that exercises should be done while standing on the ground. For instance, proponents of ground-based training contend that the barbell squat is more functional than the leg press because it's done in the standing position.

In response to the notion of ground-based training, Jeff Watson — the Strength and Conditioning Coach at Villanova University — once asked, "Does this mean that you cannot get stronger while sitting or lying down?" Obviously, an athlete *can* get stronger in an exercise even though it's not done in the standing position. Many athletes know this from their personal experiences because they've improved their muscular strength in exercises that aren't performed while standing such as the leg press, bench press and lat pulldown — not to mention exercises that are done with their bodyweight in which their feet aren't in contact with the floor such as dips and chin-ups.

13. Do athletes need to do any warm-up sets prior to a set in which they exercise to the point of muscular fatigue?

Great question. Just because an athlete didn't do any warm-up sets doesn't mean that she isn't warmed up. From a physiological perspective, an adequate warm-up is one in which the core temperature is increased by one degree. If an athlete does a relatively high number of repetitions and lifts the weight in a deliberate, controlled fashion without any explosive or jerking movements, then she will actually warm-up as she does the exercise. Think about it: If an athlete does a set of 10 repetitions with a speed of movement that's roughly six seconds per repetition, she will have exercised her muscles for about one minute before she reaches muscular fatigue. After one minute of exercising, there's little doubt that she will be adequately warmed up and prepared — both physiologically and psychologically — to exercise to muscular fatigue.

An exception to this would be someone such as a competitive weightlifter who does low-repetition sets. In this case, one or more warm-up sets should be done prior to the low-repetition efforts to reduce the risk of injury.

14. Will athletes respond differently if they do the seated press with a machine rather than the seated press with a barbell?

Not really. In truth, any exercise that progressively applies a load on the muscles will stimulate improvements in muscular size and strength. The seated (or shoulder) press — whether it's done with a machine or a barbell — addresses the same major muscles, namely the anterior deltoid and triceps. Although balancing a barbell requires a greater involvement of synergistic muscles, it doesn't appear as if this results in a significantly greater response. Indeed, studies have shown that there are no significant differences in the development of strength when comparing groups who used free weights and groups who used machines. The bottom line is that the muscles don't have eyes, brains or cognitive ability. Therefore, they cannot possibly know whether the source of resistance is a barbell, dumbbells, a selectorized machine, a plate-loaded machine or another human being. The sole factors that determine an athlete's response from strength training are her genetic profile and her level of effort — not the equipment that she used.

15. What's the best exercise for getting rid of the fat around the mid-section?

The abdominal area probably gets more attention than any other body part. Many people perform countless repetitions of sit-ups, knee-ups and other abdominal exercises — sometimes more than once per day — with the belief that this will give them a highly prized set of "washboard abs." In exercise-physiology parlance, the belief that exercise causes a localized loss of body fat is known as "spot reduction."

A litmus test for evaluating the notion of spot reduction is to examine whether a significantly greater change occurs in an active or exercised body part compared to a relatively inactive or unexercised body part. In one study, researchers evaluated the effects of a 27-day sit-up program on the fat-cell diameter and body composition of 13 subjects. Over this four-week period, each subject performed a total of 5,004 sit-ups (with the legs bent at a 90-degree angle and no foot support). Fat biopsies from the abdominal, subscapular and gluteal sites revealed that the sit-up program reduced the fat-cell diameter at all three sites to a similar degree. In other words, exercising the abdominal muscles didn't preferentially affect the fat in the abdominal area more than the gluteal or subscapular areas.

Abdominal exercises certainly involve the abdominal muscles. However, the exercises have little effect on the subcutaneous fat that resides over the abdominal muscles (and below the skin). The reason why fat cannot be selectively lost from an isolated area is that when individuals exercise, fat (and carbohydrate) stores are drawn from throughout their bodies as a source of fuel — not just from one specific area. So, an athlete can do an endless amount of abdominal exercises but these Olympian efforts will not automatically trim her mid-section. Quite simply, spot reduction is physiologically impossible.

The abdominals should be treated like any other muscle. Once an activity for the abdominals exceeds about 70 seconds in duration, it becomes an increasingly greater test of aerobic (or muscular) endurance rather than muscular strength. The abdominals can be targeted effectively in a time-efficient manner by exercising them to the point of concentric muscular fatigue within about 8 - 12 repetitions (or about 50 - 70 seconds).

16. Will plyometrics improve performance in the vertical jump?

Not necessarily. Since the mid 1960s, plyometrics have been romantically endorsed as a way to "bridge the gap" between strength and speed. In the United States, the first reference to these types of exercises in the athletic literature appears to have been in 1966 by the Soviet author Yuri Verhoshanski (whose surname has also been spelled "Verkhoshansky"). However, the term "plyometrics" seems to have been coined in 1975 by Fred Wilt who was an American track and field coach.

Plyometrics apply to any exercise or jumping drill that uses the myotatic (or stretch) reflex of a muscle. This particular reflex is triggered when a muscle is pre-stretched prior to a muscular contraction, resulting in a more powerful movement than would otherwise be possible. For instance, just before jumping vertically — such as for a rebound — an athlete bends at her hips and knees. This "countermovement" pre-stretches her hip and leg muscles allowing her to generate more force than if she performed the jump without first squatting down. Plyometrics for the lower body include bounding, hopping and various box drills such as depth jumping (in which an athlete steps off a box and, upon landing, immediately does a vertical jump); plyometrics for the upper body include ballistic (or "drop") push-ups and often incorporate medicine balls to induce the stretch reflex.

Understand that the use of plyometrics has been highly controversial for quite some time. It's important to know that most of the support for plyometrics is based upon anecdotal — not scientific — evidence. The truth of the matter is that there's little unbiased research that convincingly and consistently proves plyometrics are effective.

Although some research has shown that plyometrics are effective, roughly an equal amount of research has shown that they're no more effective than regular strength-training or jumping activities when it comes to improving performance in the vertical jump (as well as strength, speed and power, for that matter). For example, a study that involved 26 subjects found no significant improvement in the vertical jump in those who performed depth jumps two times per week. In a study that involved 38 subjects, researchers found no significant difference in the vertical jump between a group that trained with an isokinetic leg press and a group that trained with depth jumps. In a study that involved 44 subjects (in two different experiments), researchers concluded that depth jumps (of varying heights) are no more effective than "other more common training methods" for improving the vertical jump. A study that involved 50 subjects found no significant differences in the vertical jump between one group that did strength training and two groups that did plyometrics. And in a study that involved 24 subjects, researchers found no significant difference in the vertical jump between a group that performed a strength-training program and a group that performed a strength-training program and plyometrics.

One other bit of research deserves special note: In a study that involved 30 subjects, researchers found that as the height of the depth jump increased the performance in the vertical jump (and maximal vertical power output) decreased in a linear fashion. Actually, the greatest performances were produced by depth jumping from a height of only *4.72 inches*. Given this information, it's difficult to understand why depth jumping is even done.

So while the mechanical output of a muscle is certainly increased by the pre-stretch mechanism, it doesn't necessarily follow that a physiological or neurological adaptation/alteration occurs. Even if there was indisputable evidence that plyometrics were an effective way to improve performance in the vertical jump — or anything else — it's extremely important to consider the risks. Frankly, the potential for injury from plyometrics is enormous. A large number of strength and fitness professionals have questioned the safety of plyometrics for many years. When performing plyometrics, the musculoskeletal system is exposed to repetitive trauma and high-impact forces. The extreme biomechanical loading places an inordinate amount of stress on the muscles, bones and connective tissues. Research has suggested that the stress from the impact forces increases the potential for injury. This is particularly true of plyometrics that have a large vertical component such as depth jumping.

The most common plyometric-related injuries in the lower body are patellar tendinitis ("jumper's knee"), stress fractures, shin splints, muscle strains, heel bruises and sprains of the knee and ankle. Other potential injuries include compression fractures, ruptured tendons and meniscal (cartilage) damage. Another area that's highly susceptible to injury from plyometrics is the lower back. Several studies have found that depth jumping results in "spinal shrinkage" — that is, a loss of stature — presumably from compression of the intervertebral discs. It's reasonable to think that decreases in the height of the discs increases the potential for injury to the spine. And performing depth jumps from greater heights or with added weight significantly increases the impact forces and spinal shrinkage. Doing so may also cause athletes to alter their landing strategies as a protective mechanism thereby increasing the potential for other injuries. Young athletes are especially vulnerable because their musculoskeletal systems are relatively immature.

When aerobic dancing was introduced years ago, most fitness enthusiasts eagerly accepted this activity with little or no reservation. Within a short period of time, untold numbers of participants suffered injuries that were directly attributable to the high-impact forces that were absorbed by their musculoskeletal systems. The concerns about these inherent dangers ushered in the development and acceptance of low-impact aerobics. If a multitude of injuries resulted from jumping up and down several *inches*, how many injuries can be expected from jumping up and down several *feet*? Also consider this: Most authorities recommend that athletes should stretch under control without any bouncing or ballistic movements to reduce their risk of injury. The fact that plyometrics are an extremely violent form of stretching is a blatant contradiction to these safety concerns.

It's no surprise, then, that many individuals in the sportsmedical community view plyometrics as "an injury waiting to happen." According to Dr. Ken Leistner — who has treated his share of injuries in his New York office — plyometrics "are not safe under any circumstances, nor for any particular athlete, no matter how 'advanced' he or she may be." Adds Dr. Leistner, " . . . plyometrics are dangerous stuff and it is not fair, right or ethical for a coach to impose plyometrics on his or her athletes. Plyometrics are dangerous in themselves and will also do things to the body that will increase the probability of injuries during future events."

Before plyometrics can be accepted as an appropriate method of training, research must show that they're effective and safe on a more convincing and consistent basis. At this point in time, a compelling number of scientific studies have found that plyometrics are no more effective than regular strength-training and jumping activities. Moreover, plyometrics carry an unreasonably — and unjustifiably — high risk of injury.

That being said, it's important to understand that some plyometric drills are actually nothing more than glorified agility drills that are intended to improve specific skills, kinesthetic awareness and anaerobic conditioning. When these drills have a small vertical component and involve a low amount of impact forces, they're an effective and safe method of training. But when these drills have a large vertical component and involve a high amount of impact forces that aggressively pre-stretch muscles in an attempt to make the stretch reflex more responsive, they're an ineffective and dangerous method of training.

An athlete can improve her vertical jump in a much safer manner by simply practicing her jumping skills and techniques in the same way that they're used in her sport or activity and by strengthening her major muscle groups, especially the hips and legs.

Sooner or later, jumping off a plyometrics box will send you limping to a doctor's office. The bottom line: Look before you leap.

17. Isn't low-intensity activity more effective for fat loss than high-intensity activity?

Not necessarily. There's often a debate over which level of intensity (or effort) is the most effective for losing fat. Specifically, the issue revolves around whether high-intensity activity is better for fat loss than low-intensity activity.

During physical activity, there are three possible sources of energy (or fuel) available for an athlete to use: carbohydrates, fat and protein. Of these three energy sources, the body doesn't like to use protein as a fuel. In fact, protein is used as a last resort. Remember, protein is located in the muscles and if an athlete is in a situation where she must rely on it as an energy source, then she's literally cannibalizing herself. So, that leaves carbohydrates and fat as the main energy sources.

Exactly which energy source is preferred during physical activity is based upon the level of intensity that's required. Exercising with a relatively high level of intensity uses a greater percentage of carbohydrates as an energy source; exercising with relatively low level of intensity uses a greater percentage of fat as an energy source. (Carbohydrates are a more efficient source of energy. However, fat is used as an energy source because the body doesn't need to be efficient at lower levels of intensity.)

This is not to say that carbohydrates and fat are the sole sources of energy during activity of high and low intensity. Rather, they're both used but to different degrees: During high-intensity activity, carbohydrates are the principal energy source but fat is also used; during low-intensity activity, fat is the principal energy source but carbohydrates are also used.

These physiological facts have led to the mistaken belief that low-intensity (or "fat-burning") activity is better than high-intensity (or "carbohydrate-burning") activity when it comes to "burning" fat as well as expending calories and losing weight. Furthermore, this misconception has spawned the hyped-up notion that people should exercise within their "fat-burning zones."

The concept of exercising with a low level of intensity in order to mobilize and selectively utilize a higher percentage of fat may sound logical but it doesn't hold up mathematically and has never been verified in a laboratory setting. In truth, even though a greater *percentage* of fat calories are used during low-intensity activity, a greater *number* of fat calories (and total calories) are used during high-intensity activity.

During any activity, the rate of caloric expenditure is directly related to the intensity of effort — the higher the intensity, the greater the rate of caloric expenditure. In the case of running, for example, intensity is directly associated with speed: The faster that an athlete runs, the greater her rate of caloric expenditure. The time of the activity is also a factor: The longer that an athlete performs a given activity, the greater the total caloric expenditure.

The American College of Sports Medicine offers equations for determining oxygen consumption and caloric expenditure during walking (an activity of relatively low intensity) and running (an activity of relatively high intensity). Based upon these equations, a 150-pound woman who walks three miles in 60 minutes on a level surface will utilize roughly 3.936 calories per minute (cal/min). Over the course of the 60-minute walk, her total caloric usage would be about 236 calories [3.936 cal/min x 60 min]. If that same individual ran those three miles in 30 minutes on a level surface, she would use about 12.164 cal/min. (Note the higher rate of caloric expenditure.) During her 30-minute effort, she would have used about 365 total calories [12.164 cal/min x 30 min]. So, exercising with a higher level of intensity utilized significantly more calories than exercising with a lower level of intensity [365 cal compared to 236 cal]. This is true despite the fact that the activity of lower intensity was performed for twice as long as the activity of higher intensity [60 min compared to 30 min].

These calculations have been corroborated by research performed in the laboratory. In one study, a group of subjects walked on a treadmill at an average speed of 3.8 miles per hour (mph) for 30 minutes. In this instance, the subjects used an average of about 8 cal/min for a total caloric expenditure of 240 calories [8 cal/min x 30 min]. Of these 240 calories, 59% [144 cal] were from carbohydrates and 41% [96 cal] were from fat. As part of the study, the same group also ran on a treadmill at an average speed of 6.5 mph for 30 minutes. At this relatively higher level of intensity, the subjects used an average of about 15 cal/min for a total caloric expenditure of 450 calories [15 cal/min x 30 min]. Of these 450 calories, 76% [342 cal] were from carbohydrates and 24% [108 cal] were from fat. In other words, exercising with a higher level of intensity resulted in a greater total caloric expenditure than exercising with a lower level of intensity [450 cal compared to 240 cal] and also used a greater number of calories from fat in the same length of time [108 cal compared to 96 cal]. Additional studies have also demonstrated that more calories are expended when running a given distance than walking the same distance.

The intent behind advocating low-intensity activity of long duration is to enhance safety and improve compliance in the non-athletic population. However, low-intensity activity isn't more effective for fat loss — or weight loss — than high-intensity activity. But suppose that low-intensity activity was better for losing fat and weight. Since activities of lowest intensity require the greatest percentage of fat as the energy source, this would suggest that the best activity for fat/weight loss would be sleeping.

In terms of losing weight, more calories must be expended than consumed in order to produce a caloric deficit. Whether carbohydrates or fat are used to produce this caloric shortfall is immaterial. A caloric deficit created by the selective use of fat as an energy source doesn't necessarily translate into greater fat loss compared to an equal caloric deficit created by the use of carbohydrate as an energy source. The main determinant of fat and weight loss is *calories*, not *composition*.

Researchers who perform studies and review the scientific literature in the area of exercise and weight loss generally agree that it probably doesn't matter whether an individual uses fat or carbohydrates while exercising in order to lose weight. Finally, it's unlikely that low-intensity activity would elevate the heart rate enough to improve the level of aerobic fitness.

So regardless of the type of physical activity, an athlete should use the highest possible level of effort. Hard work should be a standard part of an athletic lifestyle.

18. Is there anything wrong with an athlete eating an energy bar when she misses a meal?

First, keep in mind that use of the term "energy" can be misleading. Numerous products use the word "energy" in their names. This suggests that the product will improve an athlete's stamina or make her more energetic. In truth, calories provide an athlete with energy and three nutrients provide an athlete with calories: carbohydrates, protein and fat. In short, an athlete gets energy from food. Technically, then, a can of soda is an "energy drink," a hot dog is an "energy roll," a pad of butter is an "energy square," a slice of bacon is an "energy strip," a chocolate-chip cookie is an "energy disc" and an ice-cream sandwich is an "energy bar." That being said, there's nothing inherently "wrong" with most of the products that have been dubbed "energy bars." So, an athlete can eat an energy bar — especially when it's more convenient for her because of time constraints. Just don't make a habit of eating energy bars rather than regular foods and meals. The bottom line: there's nothing wrong with energy bars...but there's nothing magical about them, either.

19. Is it safe to use herbs and other nutritional supplements that are natural?

First of all, remember that the Food and Drug Administration doesn't regulate herbs and other nutritional supplements for safety, effectiveness, purity or potency. Due to this lack of federal oversight, an athlete really doesn't know exactly what's in the products. It's not uncommon for independent researchers to find ingredients in the products that weren't listed on the labels. In one study, researchers analyzed 75 different nutritional products and found that seven (9.33%) contained substances that weren't shown on the labels. Moreover, the active ingredient may be higher or lower than the amount listed on the label. Independent testing of 16 dehydroepiandrosterone (DHEA) products found that only eight (50%) contained the exact amount of DHEA that was stated on the labels and the actual levels varied *as much as 150%*. Amazingly, three (18.75%) of the 16 products didn't contain any DHEA whatsoever. And some products may have ingredients that are truly bizarre. In a review of 311 advertisements for nutritional supplements, the researchers noted 235 unique ingredients including ecdysterone which is an insect hormone with no known use in humans. Herbs and other nutritional supplements may also contain contaminants — most likely from the manufacturing process — such as aluminum, lead, mercury and tin.

Many herbs and other nutritional supplements are promoted as "natural." Because a product claims to be "natural" or have "natural" ingredients doesn't mean that it's necessarily safe. Dirt is "natural" but that doesn't mean it's safe to eat. The truth is that many "natural" substances can be quite harmful including high-potency doses of some vitamins, minerals and certain herbs. For instance, large doses of the natural stimulants found in ginseng can cause hypertension, insomnia, depression and skin blemishes. In addition, the medical literature contains numerous reports of severe liver toxicity linked to such widely used herbs as chaparral, comfrey and germander. There are similar safety concerns with high-potency enzymes, inert glandulars and animal extracts. One final point is that it's difficult to predict how some herbs interact with prescription and over-the-counter medications (as well as other nutritional supplements).

Finally, remember that many herbs and other nutritional supplements come with express or implied disease-related claims and are marketed for specific therapeutic purposes for which there may not be valid scientific proof. In one study, researchers reviewed all of the clinical trials that were published in 1966-1992 and compared the pertinent human and/or animal studies to that of the manufacturer's claims. It was found that 8 of the 19 products (42%) had no published scientific evidence to support the promotional claims. Another 6 of the 19 (32%) were judged as being marketed in a misleading manner. The fact of the matter is that the majority of herbs and other nutritional supplements have no recognized role in nutrition.

20. Does the Zone Diet work?

Invented and promoted by Dr. Barry Sears, the Zone Diet calls for a food intake that consists of 40% carbohydrates, 30% protein and 30% fat. There's very little scientific evidence that the Zone Diet is more effective than other diets. In one study, subjects were randomly assigned to one of two diets that provided 1,200 calories per day. One group followed the Zone Diet and the other a "traditional" diet that consisted of 65% carbohydrates, 15% protein and 25% fat. After six weeks, both groups had similar losses of bodyweight and body fat. The fact of the matter is that any weight loss experienced from the Zone Diet — or any other diet, for that matter — is the result of caloric restriction.

With that said, there are a number of concerns with the Zone Diet. For one thing, following the diet doesn't allow for the intake of a variety of foods that are required to meet nutritional needs. Rather, the Zone Diet calls for the consumption of a high amount of protein and fat. To achieve this, an athlete must decrease her intake of carbohydrates. Doing so restricts the intake of healthy foods — such as fruits, vegetables and whole-grain products — which may lead to vitamin and mineral deficiencies. Since fewer carbohydrates are available as a source of energy, she will also fatigue more quickly during physical activities.

More importantly, however, the Zone Diet poses significant health risks. The National Research Council recommends against consuming protein in amounts greater than twice the Recommended Dietary Allowance because high intakes are associated with certain cancers and heart disease. A high intake of fat is also associated with heart disease. Consider this: In the aforementioned study, the group that used the "traditional" diet had a decrease in triglycerides while the group that used the Zone Diet had an increase. (Elevated levels of triglycerides are associated with a greater risk of heart disease.) In addition, a high intake of protein increases the loss of calcium in the urine which may facilitate osteoporosis. A high intake of protein also increases the levels of uric acid which may cause gout in those who are susceptible. Excreting an excessive amount of protein stresses the liver and kidneys. There are additional concerns as well.

REFERENCES

American College of Sports Medicine [ACSM]. 2000. *Guidelines for graded exercise testing and exercise prescription. 6th ed*. Philadelphia, PA: Lippincott Williams & Wilkins.

American Council on Exercise [ACE]. 1991. *Personal trainer manual: the resource for fitness instructors*. San Diego, CA: ACE.

Anderson, O. 2002. You do have a "fat-burning zone," but do you really want to go there to "burn off" fat? *Running Research News* 18 (2): 7-10.

Barron, R. L., and G. J. Vanscoy. 1993. Natural products and the athlete: facts and folklore. *Annals of Pharmacotherapy* 27 (5): 607-615.

Bates, B., M. Wolf and J. Blunk. 1990. *Vanderbilt university strength and conditioning manual*. Nashville, TN: Vanderbilt University.

Blakey, J. B., and D. Southard. 1987. The combined effects of weight training and plyometrics on dynamic leg strength and leg power. *Journal of Applied Sport Science Research* 1 (1): 14-16.

Blattner, S., and L. Noble. 1979. Relative effects of isokinetic and plyometric training on vertical jumping performance. *Research Quarterly* 50 (4): 583-588.

Bobbert, M. F., and A. J. van Soest. 1994. Effects of muscle strengthening on vertical jump height. *Medicine and Science in Sports and Exercise* 26 (8): 1012-1020.

Boocock, M. G., G. Garbutt, K. Linge, T. Reilly and J. D. Troup. 1990. Changes in stature following drop jumping and post-exercise gravity inversion. *Medicine and Science in Sports and Exercise* 22 (3): 385-390.

Bryant, C. X., B. A. Franklin and J. M. Conviser. 2002. *Exercise testing and program design: a fitness professional's handbook*. Monterey, CA: Exercise Science Publishers.

Brzycki, M. M. 1995. *A practical approach to strength training. 3rd ed*. New York, NY: McGraw-Hill/Contemporary.

_____. 1997. *Cross training for fitness*. New York, NY: McGraw-Hill/Contemporary.

_____. 1986. Plyometrics: a giant step backwards. *Athletic Journal* 66 (April): 22-23.

_____. 1993. Strength testing — predicting a one-rep max from reps-to-fatigue. *The Journal of Physical Education, Recreation & Dance* 64 (1): 88-90.

_____. 1999. Free weights and machines. *Fitness Management* 15 (June): 36-37, 40.

_____. 1999. Losing fat: high or low intensity? *Wrestling USA* 35 (2): 14-15.

_____. 2000. Assessing strength. *Fitness Management* 16 (June): 34-37.

Carpinelli, R. N. 1999. Serious strength training. *High Intensity Training Newsletter* 9 (6): 9-10.

Chestnut, J. L., and D. Docherty. 1999. The effects of 4 and 10 repetition maximum *Journal of Strength and Conditioning Research* 13 (4): 353-359.

Cheuvront, S. N. 1999. The Zone Diet and athletic performance. *Sports Medicine* 27 (4): 213-228.

Christenson, D., and S. Melville. 1988. The effects of depth jumps on university football players. *Journal of Applied Sport Science Research* 2 (3): 54.

City of New York Department of Consumer Affairs. 1992. *Magic muscle pills!! Health and fitness quackery in nutrition supplements.* New York, NY: Department of Consumer Affairs.

Clutch, D., M. Wilton, C. McGown and G. R. Bryce. 1983. The effect of depth jumps and weight training on leg strength and vertical jump. *Research Quarterly for Exercise and Sport* 54 (1): 5-10.

Cook, S. D., G. Schultz, M. L. Omey, M. W. Wolfe and M. F. Brunet. 1993. Development of lower leg strength and flexibility with the strength shoe. *The American Journal of Sports Medicine* 21 (3): 445-448.

Costill, D. L., J. Daniels, W. Evans, W. F. Fink, G. S. Krahenbuhl and B. Saltin. 1976. Skeletal muscle enzymes and fiber composition in male and female track athletes. *Journal of Applied Physiology* 40 (2): 149-154.

Desmedt, J. E., and E. Godaux. 1977. Fast motor units are not preferentially activated in rapid voluntary contractions in man. *Nature* 267 (5613): 717-719.

deVries, H. A. 1974. *Physiology of exercise for physical education and athletics. 2nd ed.* Dubuque, IA: William C. Brown.

Dons, B., K. Bollerup, F. Bonde-Petersen and S. Hancke. 1979. The effect of weight-lifting exercise related to muscle fiber composition and muscle cross-sectional area in humans. *European Journal of Applied Physiology* 40 (2): 95-106.

Duda, M. 1988. Plyometrics: a legitimate form of power training? *The Physician and Sportsmedicine* 16 (3): 213-216, 218.

Durak, E. 1987. Physical performance responses to muscle lengthening and weight training exercises in young women. *Journal of Applied Sport Science Research* 1 (3): 60.

Enoka, R. M. 1994. *Neuromechanical basis of kinesiology. 2nd ed.* Champaign, IL: Human Kinetics Publishers, Inc.

_____. 1988. Muscle strength and its development. *Sports Medicine* 6 (3): 146-168.

Ernst,E. 1998. Harmless herbs? A review of the recent literature. *The American Journal of Medicine* 104 (February): 170-178.

Esbjornsson, M., C. Sylven, I. Holm and E. Jansson. 1993. Fast twitch fibres may predict anaerobic performance in both females and males. *International Journal of Sports Medicine* 14 (5): 257-263.

Farley, D. 1993. Dietary supplements: making sure hype doesn't overwhelm science. *FDA Consumer* 27 (November): 8-13.

Fellingham, G. W., E. S. Roundy, A. G. Fisher and G. R. Bryce. 1978. Caloric cost of walking and running. *Medicine and Science in Sports and Exercise* 10 (2): 132-136.

Ford Jr, H. T., J. R. Puckett, J. P. Drummond, K. Sawyer, K. Gantt and C. Fussell. 1983. Effects of three combinations of plyometric and weight training programs on selected physical fitness test items. *Perceptual and Motor Skills* 56 (3): 919-922.

Fowler, N. E., A. Lees and T. Reilly. 1994. Spinal shrinkage in unloaded and loaded drop-jumping. *Ergonomics* 37 (1): 133-139.

Fox, E. L., and D. K. Mathews. 1981. *The physiological basis of physical education and athletics. 3d ed*. Philadelphia, PA: Saunders College Publishing.

Graves, J. E., and M. L. Pollock. 1995. Understanding the physiological basis of muscular fitness. In *The Stairmaster fitness handbook, 2nd ed*, ed. J. A. Peterson and C. X. Bryant, 67-80. St. Louis, MO: Wellness Bookshelf.

Graves, J. E., M. L. Pollock, A. E. Jones, A. B. Colvin and S. H. Leggett. 1989. Specificity of limited range of motion variable resistance training. *Medicine and Science in Sports and Exercise* 21 (1): 84-89.

Hakkinen, K., A. Pakarinen and M. Kallinen. 1992. Neuromuscular adaptations and serum hormones in women during short-term intensive strength training. *European Journal of Applied Physiology* 64 (2): 106-111.

Henneman, E. 1957. Relation between size of neurons and their susceptibility to discharge. *Science* 126: 1345-1347.

Horrigan, J., and D. Shaw. 1990. Plyometrics: the dangers of depth jumps. *High Intensity Training Newsletter* 2 (4): 15-21.

Howley, E. T., and B. D. Franks. 1992. *Health fitness instructor's handbook. 2nd ed*. Champaign, IL: Human Kinetics Publishers, Inc.

Howley, E. T., and M. Glover. 1974. The caloric costs of running and walking one mile for men and women. *Medicine and Science in Sports and Exercise* 6 (4): 235-237.

Humphries, B. J., R. U. Newton and G. J. Wilson. 1995. The effect of a braking device in reducing the ground impact forces inherent in plyometric training. *International Journal of Sports Medicine* 16 (2): 129-133.

Jones, A. 1970. *Nautilus training principles, bulletin #1*. DeLand, FL: Arthur Jones Productions.

_____. 1971. *Nautilus training principles, bulletin #2*. DeLand, FL: Arthur Jones Productions.

_____. 1993. *The lumbar spine, the cervical spine and the knee: testing and rehabilitation*. Ocala, FL: MedX Corporation.

Jones, A., M. L. Pollock, J. E. Graves, M. Fulton, W. Jones, M. MacMillan. D. D. Baldwin and J. Cirulli. 1988. *Safe, specific testing and rehabilitative exercise of the muscles of the lumbar spine*. Santa Barbara, CA: Sequoia Communications.

Jones, N. L., N. McCartney and A. J. McComas, eds. 1986. *Human muscle power*. Champaign, IL: Human Kinetics Publishers, Inc.

Kamber, M., N. Baume, M. Savgy and L. River. 2001. Nutitional supplements as a source for positive doping cases? *International Journal of Sport Nutrition and Exercise Metabolism* 11 (2): 258-263.

Karlsson, J., P. V. Komi and J. H. T. Viitasalo. 1979. Muscle strength and muscle characteristics in monozygous and dizygous twins. *Acta Physiologica Scandinavica* 106 (3): 319-325.

Katch, F. I., P. M. Clarkson, W. A. Kroll and T. McBride. 1984. Effects of sit up exercise training on adipose cell size and adiposity. *Research Quarterly for Exercise and Sport* 55 (3): 242-247

Klissouras, V. 1971. Heritability of adaptive variation. *Journal of Applied Physiology* 31 (3): 338-344.

_____. 1997. Heritability of adaptive variation: an old problem revisited. *The Journal of Sports Medicine and Physical Fitness* 37 (1): 1-6.

Komi, P. V., J. H. T. Viitasalo, M. Havu, A. Thorstensson, B. Sjodin and J. Karlsson. 1977. Skeletal muscle fibers and muscle enzyme activities in monozygous and dizygous twins of both sexes. *Acta Physiologica Scandinavica* 100 (4): 385-392.

Komi, P. V., and J. Karlsson. 1979. Physical performance, skeletal muscle enzyme activities and fiber types in monozygous and dizygous twins of both sexes. *Acta Physiologica Scandinavica* (Supplementum 462): 1-28.

Kramer, J. F., A. Morrow and A. Leger. 1993. Changes in rowing ergometer, weight lifting, vertical jump and isokinetic performance in response to standard and standard plus plyometric training programs. *International Journal of Sports Medicine* 14 (8): 449-454.

Lamb, D. R. 1984. *Physiology of exercise: responses & adaptations. 2nd ed*. New York, NY: MacMillan Publishing Company.

Lambrinides, T. 1990. High intensity training and overtraining. *High Intensity Training Newsletter* 2 (2): 9-10.

_____. 1990. Playing the percentages: is it a good or bad idea? *High Intensity Training Newsletter* 2 (4): 12-13.

Lees, A., and E. Fahmi. 1994. Optimal drop heights for plyometric training. *Ergonomics* 37 (1): 141-148.

Leistner, K. E. 1986. The quality repetition. *The Steel Tip* 2 (June): 6-7.

_____. 1987. More from Ken Leistner. *Powerlifting USA* 10 (April): 17.

_____. 1989. Explosive training: not necessary. *High Intensity Training Newsletter* 1 (2): 3-5.

LeSuer, D. A., and J. H. McCormick. 1993. Prediction of a 1-RM bench press and 1-RM squat from repetitions to fatigue using the Brzycki formula. Abstract presented at the National Strength and Conditioning Association 16th National Conference. Las Vegas, NV.

LeSuer, D. A., J. H. McCormick, J. L. Mayhew, R. L. Wasserstein and M. D. Arnold. 1997. The accuracy of prediction equations for estimating 1-RM performance in the bench press, squat and deadlift. *Journal of Strength and Conditioning Research* 11 (4): 211-213.

Lillegard, W. A., and J. D. Terrio. 1994. Appropriate strength training. *Sports Medicine* 78 (2): 457-477.

Mannie, K. 2001. *Michigan State summer manual.* East Lansing, MI: Michigan State University.

_____. 1988. Key factors in program organization. *High Intensity Training Newsletter* 1 (1): 4-5.

_____. 1990. Strength training follies: the all-P.U.B. team. *High Intensity Training Newsletter* 2 (2): 11-12.

_____. 1993. Lift risks are a weighty matter. *NCAA News* 30 (January 27): 4-5.

_____. 1994. Some thoughts on explosive weight training. *High Intensity Training Newsletter* 5 (1 & 2): 13-18.

Mayhew, J. L., J. L. Prinster, J. S. Ware, D. L. Zimmer, J. R. Arabas, and M. G. Bemben. 1995. Muscular endurance repetitions to predict bench press strength in men of different training levels. *Journal of Sports Medicine and Physical Fitness* 35 (2): 108-113.

McArdle, W. D., F. I. Katch and V. L. Katch. 1986. *Exercise physiology: energy, nutrition and human performance. 2nd ed.* Philadelphia, PA: Lea & Febiger.

Moritani, T., and H. A. deVries. 1979. Neural factors vs hypertrophy in the course of muscle strength gain. *American Journal of Physical Medicine and Rehabilitation* 58 (3): 115-130.

National Collegiate Athletic Association [NCAA]. 1991. No miracles found in many "natural potions." *NCAA News* 28 (July 17): 7.

Parascrampuria, J., K. Schwartz and R. Petesch. 1998. Qality control of dehydroepiandrosterone dietary supplements. *Journal of the American Medical Association* 280 (8): 1565.

Peterson, J. A., ed. 1978. *Total fitness: the Nautilus way*. West Point, NY: Leisure Press.

Peterson, J. A., and C. X. Bryant, eds. 1992. *The Stairmaster fitness handbook*. Indianapolis, IN: Masters Press.

Peterson, J. A., and C. X. Bryant, eds. 1995. *The Stairmaster fitness handbook. 2nd ed*. St. Louis, MO: Wellness Bookshelf.

Pezzullo, D., S. Whitney and J. Irrgang. 1993. A comparison of vertical jump enhancement using plyometrics and strength footwear shoes versus plyometrics alone. *Journal of Orthopaedic and Sports Physical Therapy* 17: 68.

Philen, R. M., D. I. Ortiz, S. B. Auerbach and H. Falk. 1992. Survey of advertising for nutritional supplements in health and bodybuilding magazines. *Journal of the American Medical Association* 268 (8): 1008-1011.

Pipes, T. V. 1979. High intensity, not high speed. *Athletic Journal* 59 (December): 60, 62.

_____. 1994. Strength training & fiber types. *Scholastic Coach* 63 (March): 67-70.

Pitts, E. H. 1992. Pills, powders, potions and persuasions. *Fitness Management* 9 (November): 34-35.

Porcari, J. P. 1994. Fat-burning exercise: fit or farce. *Fitness Management* 10 (July): 40-41.

Riley, D. P. 1982. *Strength training by the experts. 2nd ed*. West Point, NY: Leisure Press.

_____. 1979. Speed of exercise versus speed of movement. *Scholastic Coach* 48 (May/June): 90, 92-93, 97-98.

_____. 1982. Guidelines for strength program. *Scholastic Coach* 51 (May/June): 64-65, 80.

Roberts, D. F. 1984. Genetic determinants of sports performance. In *Sport and human genetics*, ed. R. M. Malina and C. Bouchard, 105-121. Champaign, IL: Human Kinetics Publishers, Inc.

Sale, D. G. 1988. Neural adaptation to resistance training. *Medicine and Science in Sports and Exercise* 20 (5): 135-145.

Sale, D. G., and D. MacDougall. 1981. Specificity in strength training: a review for the coach and athlete. *Canadian Journal of Applied Sport Sciences* 6: 87-92.

Schantz, P., E. Randall-Fox, W. Hutchison, A. Tyden and P.-O. Astrand. 1983. Muscle fiber type distribution, muscle cross-sectional area and maximal voluntary strength in humans. *Acta Physiologica Scandinavica* 117 (2): 219-226.

Scoles, G. 1978. Depth jumping! Does it really work? *Athletic Journal* 58 (January): 48-50, 74-76.

Sharkey, B. J. 1975. *Physiology and physical activity*. New York, NY: Harper & Row.

_____. 1984. *Physiology of fitness*. Champaign, IL: Human Kinetics Publishers, Inc.

Swanger, T., M. Bradley and S. Murray. 1996. *Army strength & conditioning manual*. West Point, NY: United States Military Academy.

Thorstensson, A. 1976. Muscle strength, fiber types and enzyme activities in man. *Acta Physiologica Scandinavica* (Supplementum 443): 1-44.

Thrash, K., and B. Kelly. 1987. Flexibility and strength training. *Journal of Applied Sport Science Research* 1 (4): 74-75.

Vander, A. J., J. H. Sherman and D. S. Luciano. 1975. *Human physiology: the mechanisms of body function. 2nd ed*. New York, NY: McGraw-Hill, Inc.

Verhoshanski, Y. 1966. Perspectives in the improvement of speed and strength preparation of jumpers. *Track and Field* 9: 11-12.

Wateska, M., and M. Bradley. 1998. *Cardinal conditioning*. Palo Alto, CA: Stanford University.

Westcott, W. L. 1983. *Strength fitness: physiological principles and training techniques. Expanded ed*. Boston, MA: Allyn and Bacon, Inc.

_____. 1996. *Building strength and stamina: new Nautilus training for total fitness*. Champaign, IL: Human Kinetics.

_____. 1989. Strength training research: sets and repetitions. *Scholastic Coach* 58 (May/June): 98-100.

Westcott, W. L., R. A. Winett, E. S. Anderson, J. R. Wojcik, R. L. R. Loud, E. Cleggett and S. Glover. 2001. Effects of regular and slow speed resistance training on muscle strength. *The Journal of Sports Medicine and Physical Fitness* 41 (2): 154-158.

Wikgren, S. 1988. The plyometrics debate. *Coaching Women's Basketball* 1 (May/June): 10-13.

Willis, T., and K. A. Beals. 2000. The Zone Diet vs. traditional weight loss diet: effects on weight loss and blood lipid levels. *Journal of the American Dietetic Association* (supplement) 100 (9): A-74.

Wilmore, J. H. 1982. *Training for sport and activity: the physiological basis of the conditioning process. 2nd ed*. Boston, MA: Allyn and Bacon, Inc.

_____. 1974. Alterations in strength, body composition and anthropometric measurements consequent to a 10-week weight training program. *Medicine and Science in Sports* 6 (2): 133-138.

Wilt, F. 1975. Plyometrics: what it is — how it works. *Athletic Journal* 55 (May): 76, 89-90.

Wirhed, R. 1984. *Athletic ability: the anatomy of winning*. New York: Harmony Books.

Wolf, M. D. 1982. Muscles: structure, function and control. In *Strength training by the experts, 2nd ed*, by D. P. Riley, 27-40. West Point, NY: Leisure Press.

Biographies

MICHAEL BRADLEY, M.A., is the Basketball Strength and Conditioning Coach at Florida State University in Tallahassee, Florida. Coach Bradley has served as an assistant strength and conditioning coach at Stanford University (1998-2002), the University of Miami (1995-98), the United States Military Academy (1994-95), the University of South Carolina (1993-94) and Southern Methodist University (1991-93). He earned his Bachelor of Science degree in chemistry from San Diego State University (1989) and his Master of Arts degree in the same discipline from the University of California, Santa Barbara (1990).

MATT BRZYCKI, B.S., is the Coordinator of Recreational Fitness and Wellness Programs at Princeton University in Princeton, New Jersey. He has more than 20 years of experience at the collegiate level as a coach, instructor and administrator. At Princeton University, Mr. Brzycki has also served as the Coordinator of Health Fitness, Strength and Conditioning Programs (1993-2001) and the Health Fitness Coordinator/ Strength and Conditioning Coach (1990-93). Previously, he was an Assistant Strength and Conditioning Coach at Rutgers University (1984-90) and a Health Fitness Supervisor at Princeton University (1983-84). Mr. Brzycki earned his Bachelor of Science degree in health and physical education from Penn State (1983). Prior to entering college, he served in the United States Marine Corps (1975-79). Mr. Brzycki has been a featured speaker at local, regional, state and national conferences and clinics throughout the United States and Canada. He has written more than 225 articles on strength and fitness that have been featured in 39 different publications. Mr. Brzycki has authored, co-authored or edited nine other books. He and his wife, Alicia, have a son, Ryan.

LUKE CARLSON, B.S., is the Strength and Conditioning/Fitness Coordinator at Minnetonka High School in Minnetonka, Minnesota. In this role, he's responsible for designing and implementing strength and conditioning programs for all student-athletes and faculty members. Previously, Coach Carlson served as the Head Strength and Conditioning Coach at Blaine High School (MN), Fitness Specialist at Fitness First Personalized Training Studio (MN) and a member of the strength and conditioning staff of the Minnesota Vikings. In addition to coaching, he's the director of the annual National Strength & Science Seminar. Coach Carlson earned his Bachelor of Science degree in kinesiology from the University of Minnesota where he's currently pursuing a Master of Arts degree in exercise physiology.

CHIP HARRISON, M.S., is the Head Strength and Conditioning Coach (for sports other than football) at Penn State in University Park, Pennsylvania. He earned his Bachelor of Science degree in physical education (exercise science) and his Master of Science degree in physical education (exercise physiology) from Penn State. Coach Harrison has been certified as a Health/Fitness Instructor by the American College of Sports Medicine and a Certified Strength and Conditioning Specialist by the National Strength and Conditioning Association. He and his wife, Sheri, have three sons, Mark, Troy and Stevie.

RACHAEL E. PICONE, M.S., is an Adjunct Instructor of Health Education for the Department of Health, Exercise Science and Dance at the County College of Morris in New Jersey. She earned her Bachelor of Science degree in exercise science from Rutgers University and her Master of Science degree in exercise physiology from The University of Massachusetts. Her graduate work focused on osteoporosis, children's health and strength development and assessment. Ms. Picone is certified as a Group Fitness Instructor by the American Council on Exercise (with specialty recognition in youth fitness) and an Exercise Test Technologist by the American College of Sports Medicine. Ms. Picone has more than 15 years of diverse experience with a professional history encompassing cardiac rehabilitation, health education and promotion, sports and leisure management and personal training. She has benefited from tenures in both educational and corporate positions, most notably Assistant Fitness Director at Princeton University and Assistant Supervisor of corporate fitness centers for AT&T. Ms. Picone has spoken throughout the northeastern United States on a wide variety of health and fitness topics, ranging from the more mainstream (such as strength training and aerobic fitness) to the more esoteric (such as women's health issues, vegetarian nutrition and career planning for the fitness professional). She has authored numerous articles for several trade publications (such as *Fitness Management* and *Club Industry*) and popular web sites. In her spare time, Rachael enjoys hiking, mountain biking, traveling, photography and reading. She also regularly volunteers for charity and fundraising events for established organizations including The American Heart Association, The American Cancer Society, The Visiting Nurse Association and others.

TIM "RED" WAKEHAM, M.S., S.C.C.C., C.S.C.C., is an Assistant Strength and Conditioning Coach at Michigan State University in East Lansing, Michigan. At Michigan State, Coach Wakeham directs the sport-specific strength and conditioning programs for 14 teams and is an adjunct faculty instructor. He has experience working with athletes at the professional (National Football League and National Hockey League) and Olympic levels. Coach Wakeham earned his Bachelor of Science degree from Northern Michigan University and his Master of Science degree from the University of North Dakota. Prior to his current position, he served as the Coordinator of Strength, Conditioning and Fitness at Michigan Technological University. Coach Wakeham is a Certified Strength and Conditioning Specialist and a Certified Strength and Conditioning Coach. He's also an established author and featured speaker at conferences throughout the United States.